IMAGES
of America

PRYOR CREEK

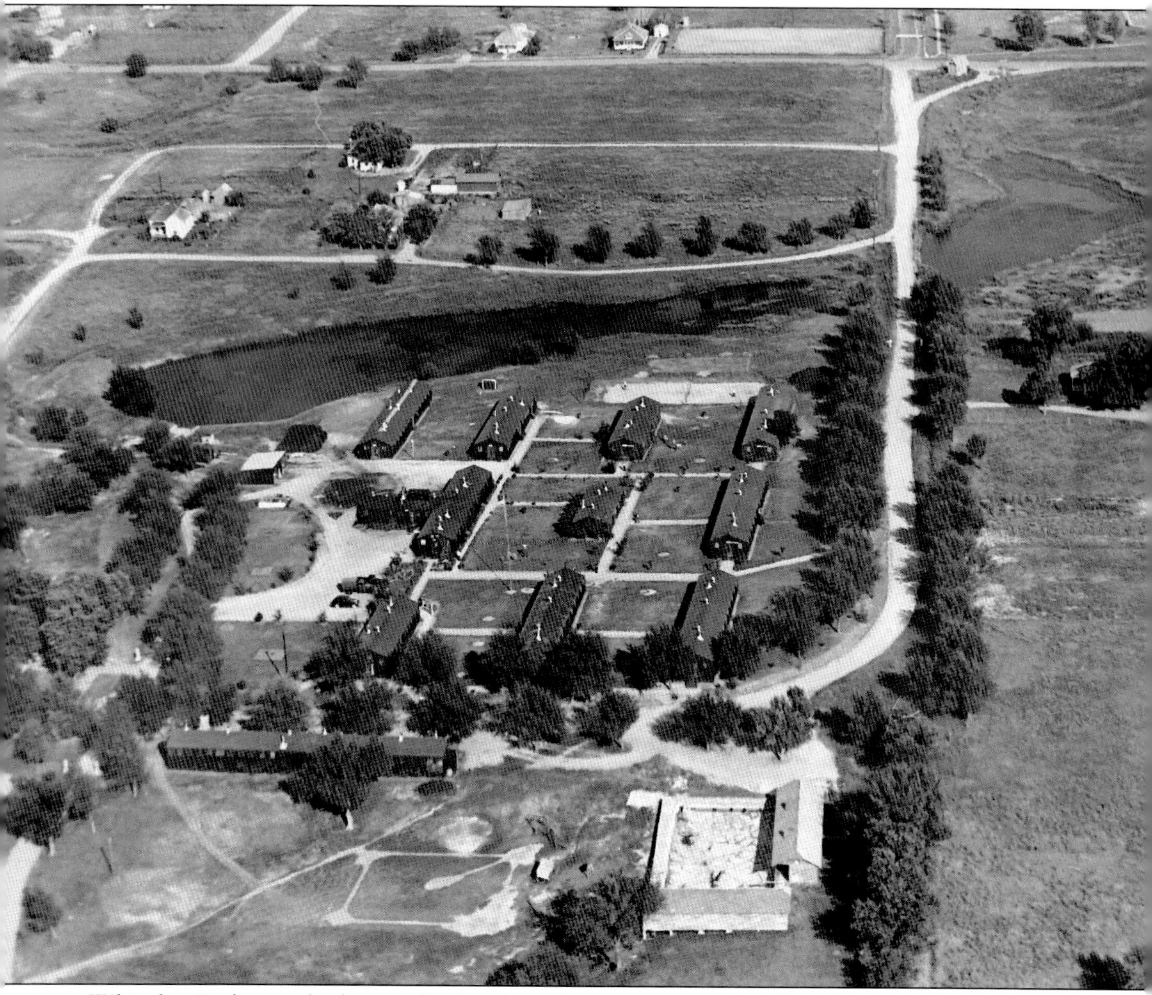

Whitaker Park was the home of a Civilian Conservation Corps (CCC) camp, shown here in September 1940. The CCC camps were established as part of Pres. Franklin Roosevelt's New Deal program to employ citizens in unskilled labor jobs related to conservation and natural resources. (Courtesy of Glen Winters.)

On the Cover: Mayor Thomas J. Harrison was proud to promote his beloved town of Pryor Creek as having the widest Main Street in Oklahoma. And, to prove it, 12 vehicles were lined up across the street in May 1930. The name of Main Street was changed 21 years later to Graham Avenue in honor of the city and county's greatest benefactor, W.A. Graham. (Author's collection.)

IMAGES
of America

PRYOR CREEK

Terry D. Lamar

ARCADIA
PUBLISHING

Copyright © 2016 by Terry D. Lamar
ISBN 978-1-4671-1487-5

Published by Arcadia Publishing
Charleston, South Carolina

Printed in the United States of America

Library of Congress Control Number: 2015939624

For all general information, please contact Arcadia Publishing:
Telephone 843-853-2070
Fax 843-853-0044
E-mail sales@arcadiapublishing.com
For customer service and orders:
Toll-Free 1-888-313-2665

Visit us on the Internet at www.arcadiapublishing.com

This book is dedicated to the following people, who have been very influential in forming my passion and dedication for preserving and recording the written, oral, and photographic history of my community and county: my great-granduncle Ralph Elliott, Aeileen Harrison, George Tilly, Elizabeth Hammer, Cornelia Sifferman, Rose Drew, Clarence Wilson, and Thomas J. Harrison.

Contents

ACKNOWLEDGMENTS

This book would not have been possible without Chris Hardy of the Book Exchange, who was contacted by Arcadia Publishing representatives to do a pictorial history of Pryor Creek and who pointed them in my direction.

Former *Daily Times* publisher Henry Goodman made it possible, almost 25 years ago, for me to possess a portion of the former *Pryor Jeffersonian*'s negative collection—for his foresight, I am humbled and thankful.

Appreciation and thanks are extended to the staff at the Thomas J. Harrison Pryor Public Library for access to the newspaper microfilm collection and other reference materials in its historical archive collection. In particular, current and former staff members Leslie Trogdon, Marie Reist, Susan Newberry, Kim True, and Carolyn Shaver provided a tremendous amount of help over the years with my research.

Vanessa Painter Walker of PhotoRevive in Tulsa is my main photograph scanner. She has spent hundreds of hours scanning over 1,000 photographs for me over the past seven years. She does awesome professional work and was a vital part in the completion of this book.

Terry Aylward at the *Paper* and Cydney Baron at the *Times* have provided access to newspaper libraries at their respective offices, and their assistance is most appreciated.

George Fisher of Priority Printworks as well as Nena West Roberts and Brooks Ledbetter provided positive encouragement throughout the research and writing process.

Sarah Gottlieb, my editor at Arcadia Publishing, showed patience and provided assistance throughout a long and tedious process to complete this publication.

Finally, I am very appreciative to my wife, Paige Lamar, for her unselfish encouragement, sacrifice, and support to make this work possible.

Unless otherwise noted, all images are from the author's collection.

INTRODUCTION

Pryor Creek, Oklahoma, was incorporated as a town under the laws of the Cherokee Nation in 1894 and was officially known as Pryor Creek, Cherokee Nation, Indian Territory. The town is known as Pryor by the US Postal Service. The town was named for Capt. Nathaniel Pryor, a member of the Lewis and Clark expedition, veteran of the War of 1812, trader, frontiersman, and sub-agent to the Osage Indian tribe.

Pryor Creek, or Pryor, is located in northeastern Oklahoma. It was situated along the Texas Road, a major line of transportation for settlers en route to Texas from Kansas and Missouri. Later, the Shawnee Trail skirted the road and was a major trail used by cattlemen driving their herds from Texas to railheads in Sedalia, Missouri. Around 1870, the Missouri-Kansas-Texas Railroad built its line parallel to the Texas Road from Parsons, Kansas, south across Indian Territory to Dennison, Texas. Also important to the town's existence was the Grand River to the east, vital for power, commerce, and recreation.

Pryor Creek is also located along US Highway 69, which is a major north-south route from Missouri and Kansas to Texas. This section of US 69 was also formerly known as the Jefferson Highway, a 2,194-mile stretch connecting Winnipeg, Manitoba to New Orleans.

The first post office, called Pryor Creek, was actually located about seven miles north of the present town. That post office existed from 1878 to 1884. A post office was established from 1882 to 1887 on the site of the present town and was called Coo-Y-Yah, Indian Territory. Coo-Y-Yah is the Cherokee term for huckleberry. From 1887 to 1909, the post office name reverted back to Pryor Creek; in 1909, the name was again changed to Pryor.

Until 1902, students attended subscription schools or Indian schools. The present-day public school system was established in the fall of that year, and the high school was fully accredited in 1910. Also in 1902, a federal courthouse was established; it existed until Oklahoma statehood in 1907. The Whitaker Orphans Home, established in 1897, became a state institution in 1908. The facility closed in 1983 and became an Oklahoma Army National Guard base.

In the early part of the 20th century, Pryor had about five grain elevators and cotton gins, which were vital contributors to the county's agricultural economy.

Three major-league baseball players have lived, worked, and are buried in Pryor. Chad Kimsey, a 1925 graduate of Pryor High School, was a pitcher for the St. Louis Browns, Chicago White Sox, and Detroit Tigers. While a pitcher with the White Sox in 1933, he gave up Babe Ruth's 680th home run. Kimsey was killed in a dump-truck accident in 1942 and is buried in Fairview Cemetery. Hank Wyse, a pitcher for the Chicago Cubs, was the last Cubs pitcher to appear in a World Series, in 1945. After retiring from baseball he moved to Pryor, where he worked as an industrial electrician. He died in 2000 and is also buried in Fairview Cemetery. Cliff Mapes played for the New York Yankees and Detroit Tigers. After retiring from baseball, he moved to Pryor and worked at the John Deere fertilizer plant. His wife's grandfather, James L. Taylor, was the first city clerk. He died in 1996 and is buried in Graham Memorial Cemetery.

One of Pryor's most famous visitors was child actor Carl Switzer, best known as Alfalfa in *The Little Rascals* and *Our Gang* series. In September 1937, he and his family stopped in downtown Pryor for a meal at Ma Mitchell's coffee shop while traveling from back east to California. Another movie star, Western character actor Chill Wills, came to Pryor in 1952 to greet fans at the Allred Theater.

Pryor is also the hometown of the late Shaun Burchett, former world champion steer roper in 1987 and 1988 and a 2008 inductee to the ProRodeo Hall of Fame. Burchett was killed in a traffic accident near Whitesboro, Texas, on January 26, 1992. Burchett, a 1982 graduate of Pryor High School, is buried in Fairview Cemetery.

In August 1941, Pryor was selected as the site for a smokeless powder plant, to be operated by the DuPont Company. The facility would make gunpowder for a world war that the United States had not entered. The plant would be the largest construction project undertaken in the region, costing more than $84,000,000 and employing over 11,000 people. The plant closed in 1945, at the completion of the war. The DuPont Powder Plant site and its 15,000 acres would become Oklahoma's largest industrial park, Mid-America Industrial Park. Gene Redden, brought in to oversee the conversion of the facility to a peacetime industrial complex, remained the administrator until his death in 1990. He was succeeded by Sanders Mitchell and David Stewert.

Downtown Pryor was destroyed by the fifth-deadliest tornado in Oklahoma history on April 27, 1942. The storm caused the deaths of 52 people and injuries to more than 400 residents.

Twice in the 1950s, *Life* magazine featured Pryor citizens in its pages. W.A. Graham appeared in the June 4, 1951, issue in the article "The World's Oldest Millionaire Becomes a Centurion." Norvelle Green was featured in the July 12, 1954, issue in the story "*Life* Goes to a Colossal Cake Party in Pryor, Oklahoma."

Two sitting US presidents, Theodore Roosevelt in 1905 and Lyndon Johnson in 1966, have visited Pryor.

In 1962, a city charter election was held for changing the official city name from Pryor Creek to Pryor. It failed by a vote of 583-297. A few months later, postal patrons were asked to vote in a survey to change the post office's name from Pryor to Pryor Creek. That measure failed. Currently, there is again a discussion by community leaders and townspeople about getting the US Postal Service to change the post office name to Pryor Creek.

One

Around Town

The landscape of what was to become the community of Pryor Creek started with dirt streets and just a couple of stores. The first merchants are believed to have been Tip Mayes, W.T. Whitaker, and John L. Price. There were no schools or churches until Whitaker built one of each about 1890. In 1892, John C. Hogan established his mercantile store on the corner of what are now Graham Avenue and South Mill Street, in the present location of Kentucky Fried Chicken.

The oldest building in downtown, built about 1896, was the Parker drugstore, located next to Margaret Edwards' NAPA auto parts store. In 1900, John Hogan and W.A. Graham built a modern brick-and-mortar mercantile store on the southeast corner of Graham Avenue and Mill Street. Other permanent buildings went up along Main Street, including a modern three-story hotel owned by Joe Mayor in 1910.

Also during this time, three independent newspapers operated along Main Street: *Pryor Creek Clipper*, *Mayes County Democrat*, and *Mayes County Republican*. Currently, two papers are supported by the community, the *Paper* and *Pryor Daily Times*.

By the 1930s, Pryor was a bustling community with a very active downtown business district. The town of almost 2,000 people supported two banks, First National and American National. In 1933, two privately owned hospitals were built, Herrington and Whitaker. In 1954, a county-owned hospital, Grand Valley, was opened.

During the height of agricultural production, Pryor supported three grain elevators and a few cotton gins, as well as two milk plants, Creamline Dairy and Meadow Gold, and a cheese plant operated by Norman Yordi.

The community has supported up to three funeral homes operating at a time. Currently, Stephens-Key and Shipman funeral homes are in operation.

Pryor has also been home to many churches, including First Baptist, First United Methodist, First Church of God, First Christian, St. Mark Catholic Church, and St. Martin's Episcopal, all in the downtown business district. They were later joined by First Presbyterian, St. John's Lutheran, North Elliot Church of God, Immanuel Baptist, Seventh-Day Adventist, Assembly of God, Freewill Baptist, the Church of Jesus Christ of Latter-day Saints, and others.

Today, Pryor Creek is centrally located at the junction of US Highway 69 and Oklahoma 20 in northeastern Oklahoma. Rail service for freight transportation is provided by the Union Pacific Railroad. Pryor Creek is the county seat of Mayes County, named for the late Samuel Houston Mayes, former chief of the Cherokee Nation. Located just south of the city is Mid-America Industrial Park, the largest state-owned industrial park in Oklahoma.

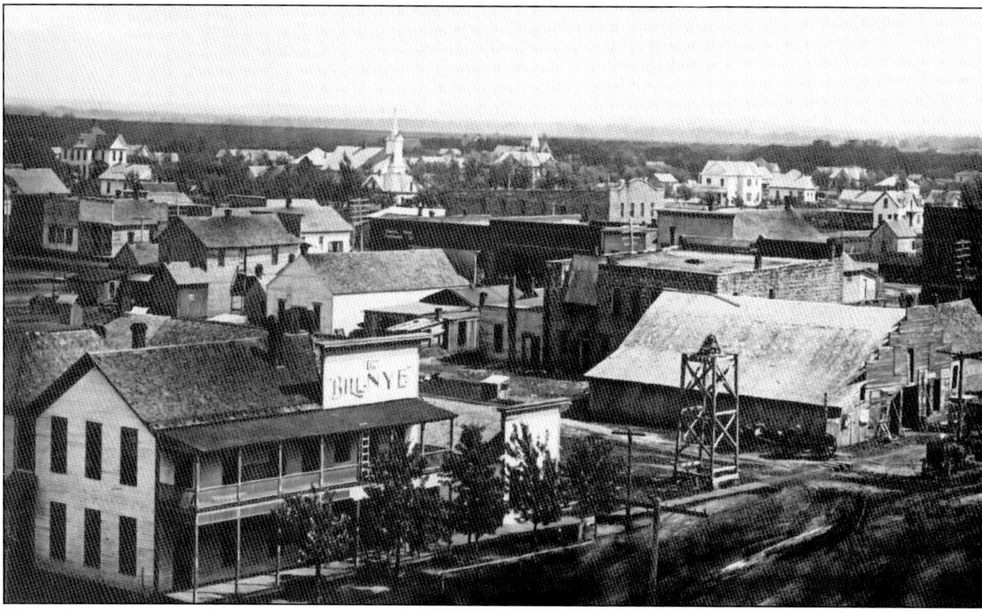

This photograph of downtown Pryor Creek was taken about 1907 along the east side of North Mill Street. Alongside the dirt street is the Bill-Nye Hotel (lower left). To the right of the hotel and bell tower is the "north" alley and the north side of what is now the NAPA auto parts building.

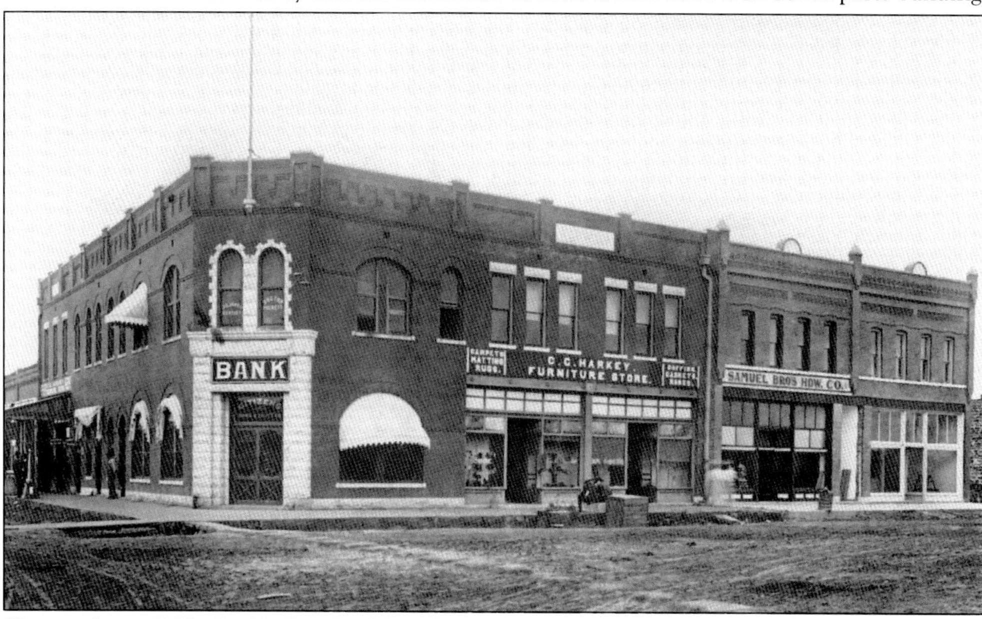

Shown about 1905, the Harkey Building, located at Graham Avenue and Adair Street, was an early mercantile company that also housed the Citizens Bank and Thomas J. Harrison's Post Office Bookstore. Later, the building was sold to O.L. Hardy, who ran an insurance agency. The structure became known as the Historic Hardy Building. It was destroyed in the 1942 tornado. Later, two of Pryor's favorite stores, Pearl Cole's Merle Norman Cosmetics and Don Stover Shoes, were located in what was the Harkey storefront, as shown here. The adjacent building at right, known as the Samuel & Poffenback Building, was home to Samuel Brothers Hardware. It was destroyed by fire in 1909 and then rebuilt.

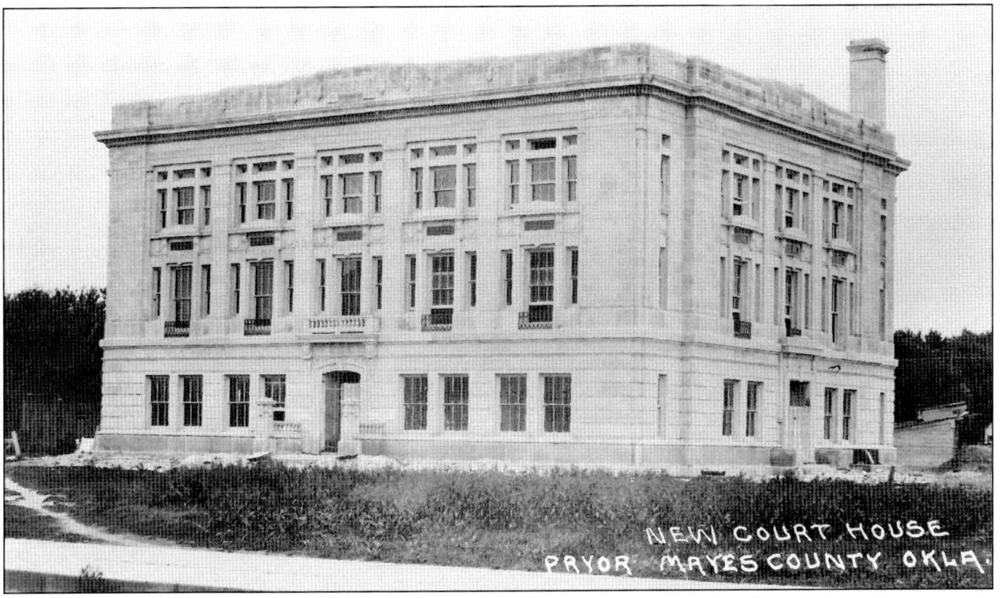

The second Mayes County Courthouse, constructed in 1921–1922, was located on the grounds of the first building, which had been erected in 1902. The building, constructed of Bedford stone shipped by rail from Indiana, cost about $168,000, including furniture. The courthouse was reportedly the only Oklahoma courthouse built without bond indebtedness. Instead, it was funded with millage level taxation and from the collection of back taxes and penalties.

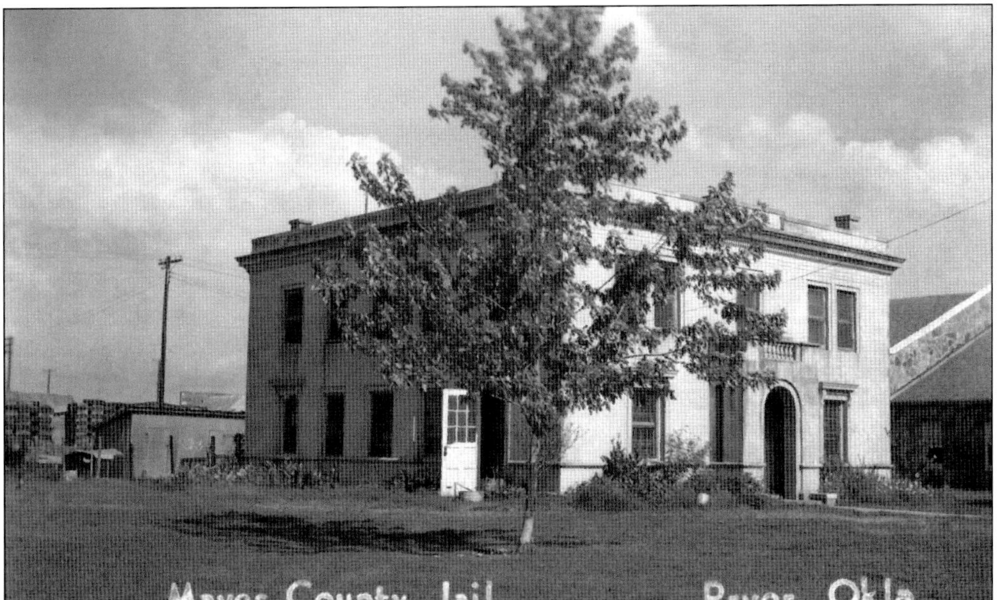

The Mayes County Jail was constructed in 1922–1923 as part of the courthouse project. The jail included accommodations for both white and black prisoners, as well as women. The $18,000 building was paid for by local banker and civic leader W.A. Graham The facility was remodeled in 1959 and used until May 2000, when a modern county lockup opened adjacent to the old facility. (Courtesy of Leslie Sandusky.)

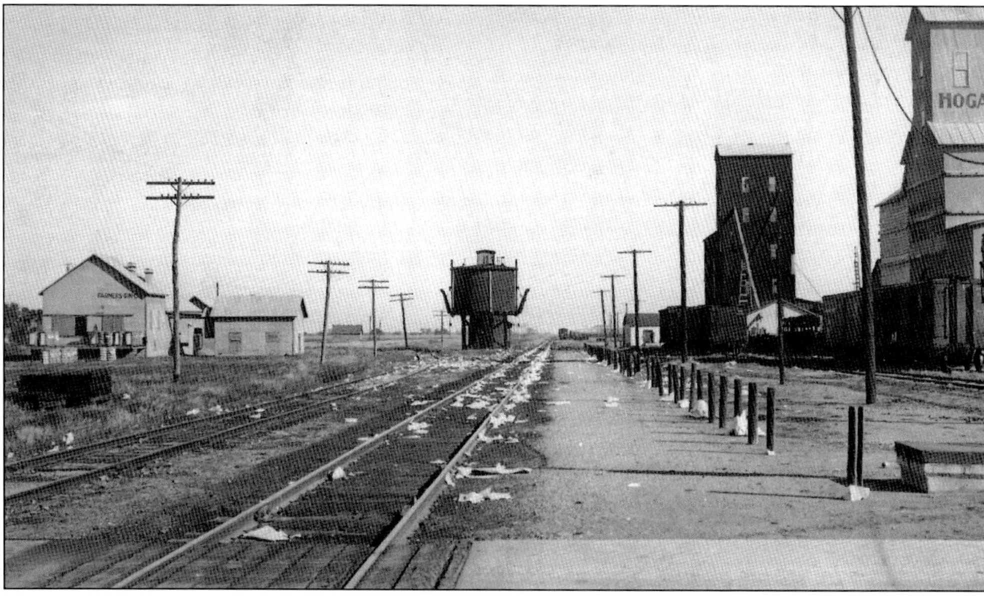

This c. 1915 photograph faces north from the main rail crossing. Visible are the Missouri-Kansas-Texas (Katy) Railroad water tank (center), Hogan-Hayden elevator (right), and Farmer's cotton gin (left). In 1913, the city came up with a proposal to the railroad to build the water tank; the city would sell water to the railroad, which would be a win for both.

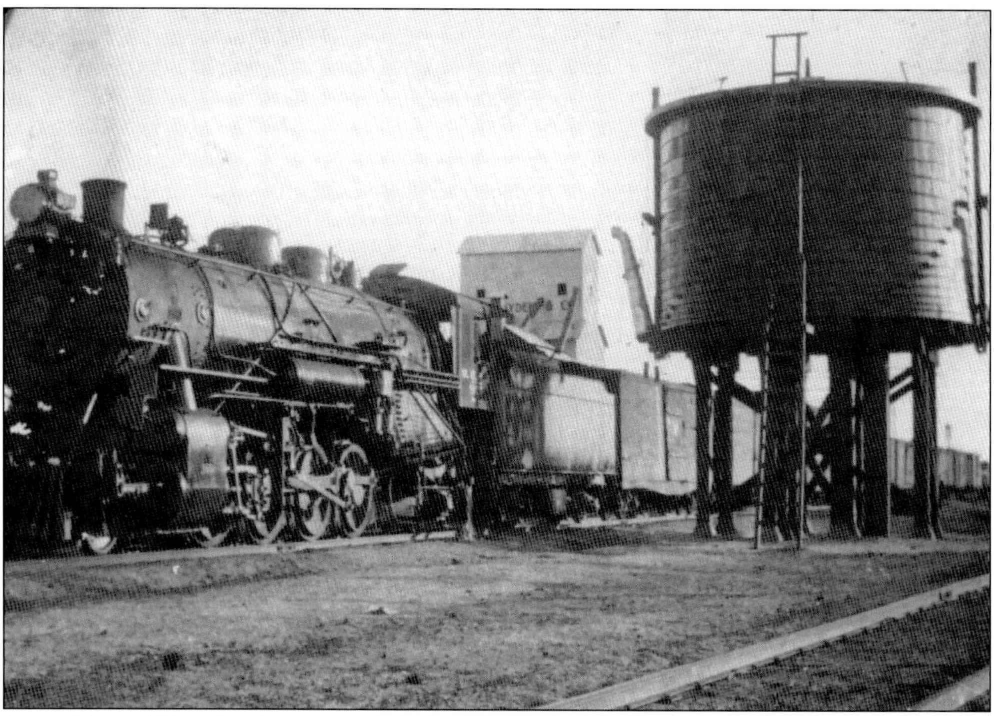

A northbound Katy freight train is parked at the water tank around 1915. The Missouri-Kansas-Texas Railroad built its line from Kansas through Indian Territory (now Oklahoma) to Texas between 1870 and 1872. Passenger train service was discontinued at the local depot in June 1965. The Katy Railroad merged with Union Pacific Railroad 33 years later.

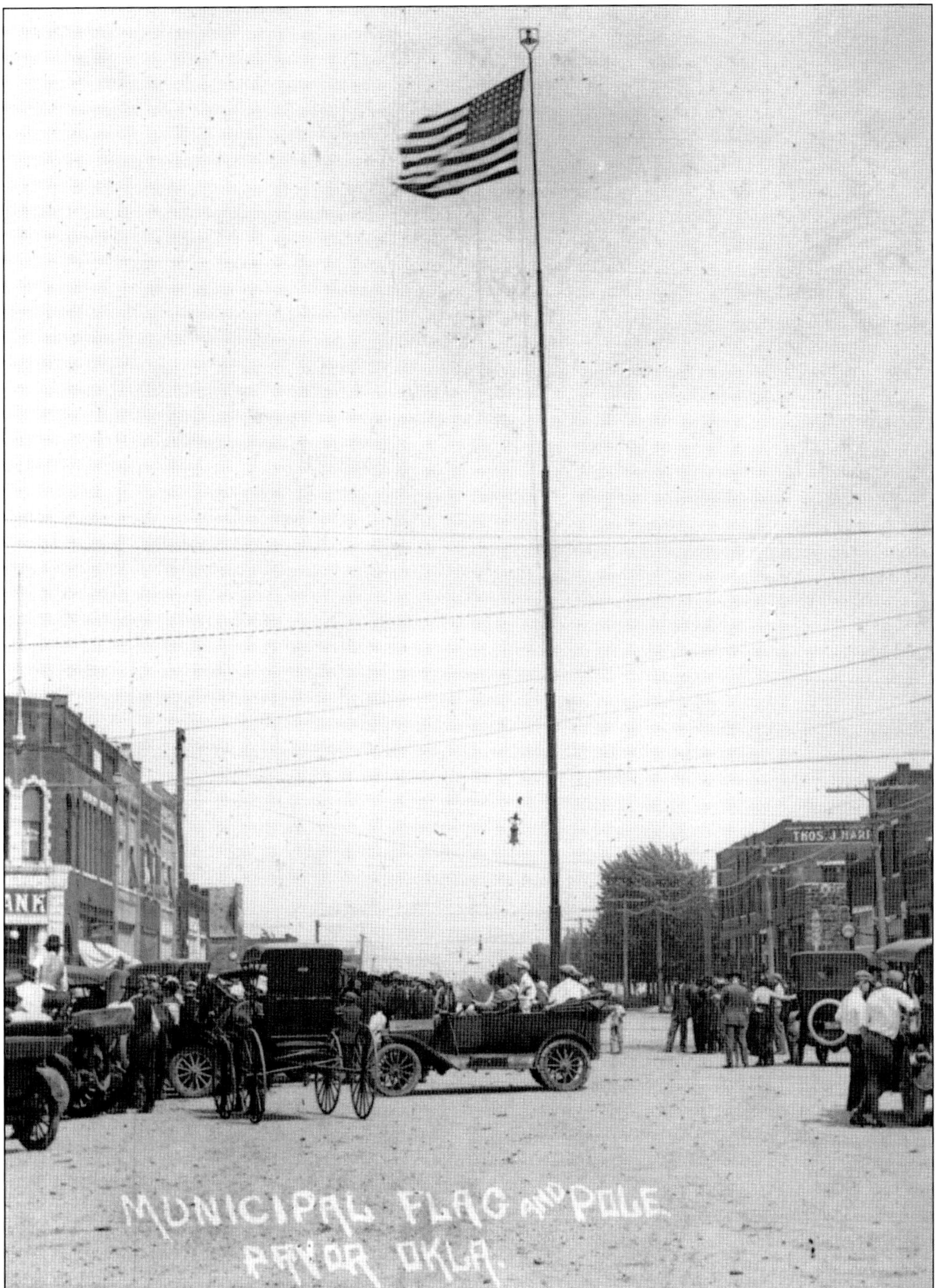

Pryor Creek's flagpole was a landmark in the community from World War I to May 1939. Erected in 1917, the flagpole was the brainchild of Rev. R.M. Phillips of the First Christian Church, who convinced the community of the need for a symbol of patriotism to show support for servicemen going to war in Europe. Over the years, the flagpole became a symbol of American pride and was the orientation point for visitors trying to find the location of homes and other sites. The pole was removed from the middle of Main Street in 1939 due to an increase in automobile traffic—the pole was deemed unsafe to the motoring public.

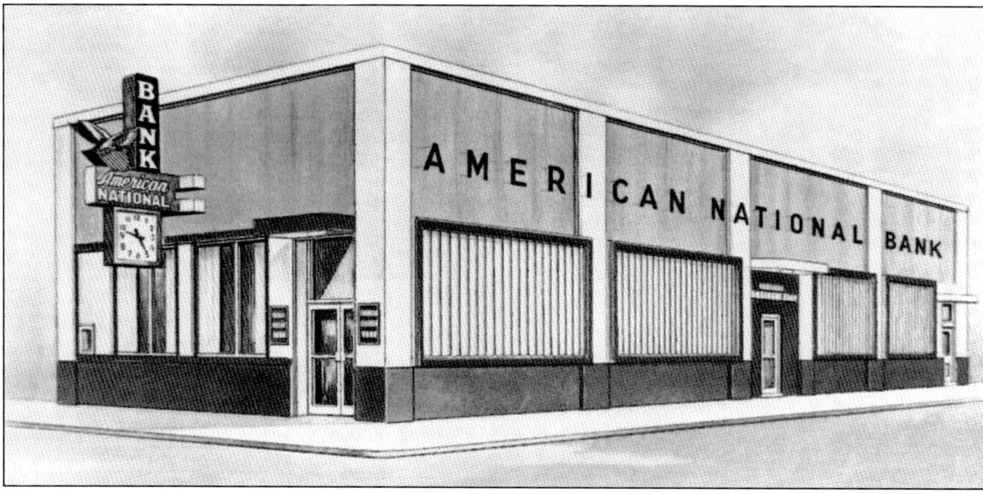

The American National Bank, located on the southeast corner of Adair Street and Graham Avenue, was established after the failure of the First State Bank in 1912. It had a long run until being sold to the Bank of Oklahoma and then, eventually, to RCB Bank.

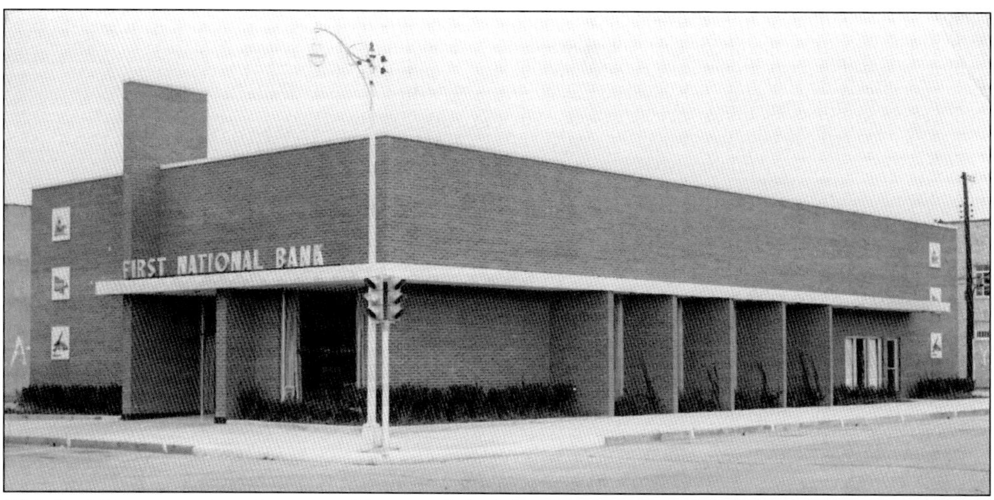

This building served as the second home of the First National Bank from 1958 until 1981. Now known as First Priority Bank, it was established in 1900 by W.A. Graham, who owned the bank until his death in 1951. Nolen Jacobs purchased the bank from the Graham estate's trustees in 1957 and immediately began plans to construct a new facility. In the fall of 1980, Jacobs broke ground for construction of a third home for the bank a block east. The bank moved into that facility the next year. Nolen Jacobs died in 1994, and his son J. Michael Jacobs assumed the helm. Thus, the bank saw only three owners in 115 years.

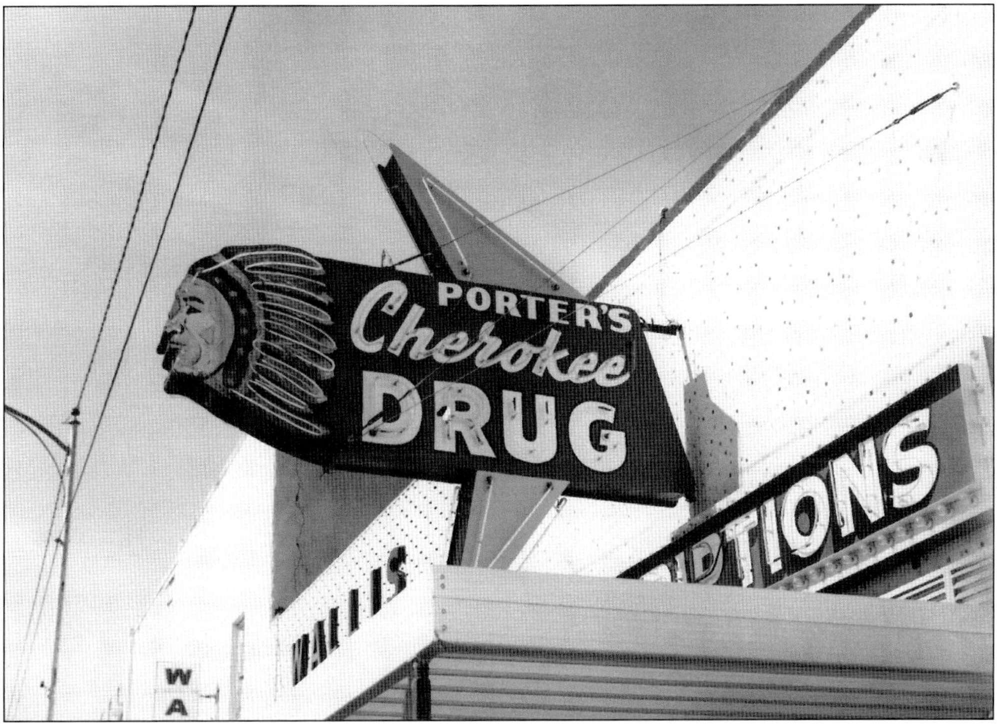

One of the community's favorite spots was the lunch counter at Cherokee Drug, located at 221 East Graham. Doyle "Hokie" Foreman had purchased the Fowler Drug Store in 1949. About 10 years later, Elmer Haddan Jr. merged his drugstore on North Vann with Foreman's business. The store was then sold to John Porter. Sue Haddan Arnold acquired the store about 1978 and closed it around 1985.

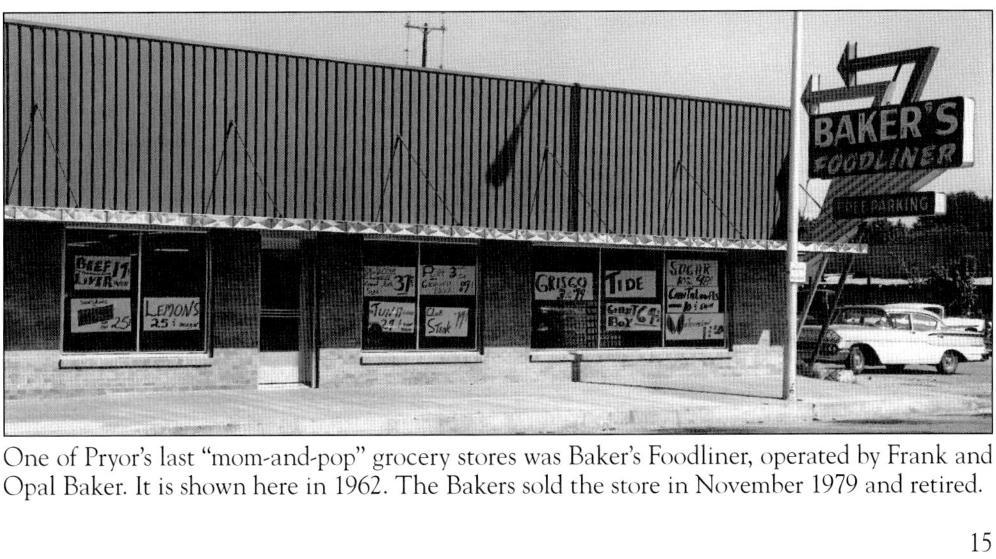

One of Pryor's last "mom-and-pop" grocery stores was Baker's Foodliner, operated by Frank and Opal Baker. It is shown here in 1962. The Bakers sold the store in November 1979 and retired.

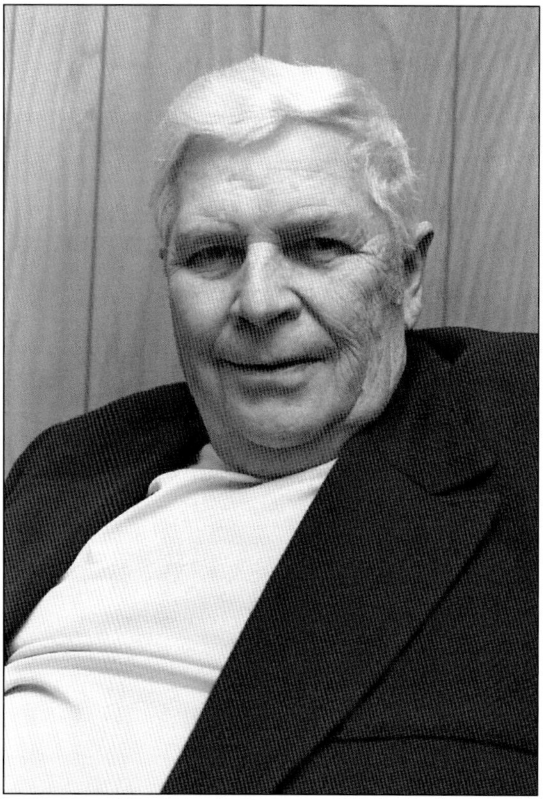

Dr. Ed Werling came to Pryor in 1936 to join the staff at Whitaker Hospital. He then became a partner in ownership of the facility. Seeing the need for a modern county medical facility, he and Dr. Paul Cameron were instrumental in the establishment of Grand Valley Hospital (GVH). They closed their facility upon opening GVH in December 1954. Werling (1906–1979) continued to practice until shortly before his death.

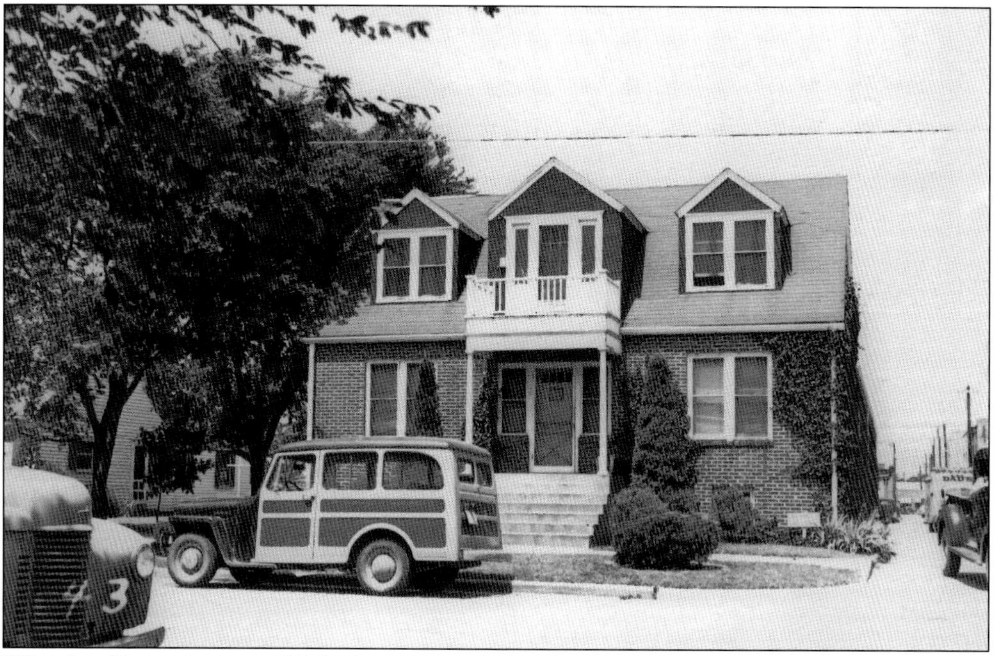

Whitaker Hospital was established in 1933 and closed in 1954, when a modern county hospital opened. The facility was operated by Dr. W.J. Whitaker and Dr. Ed Werling. After the retirement of Whitaker, Dr. Paul Cameron became a partner with Werling in about 1941.

Dr. G.E. Moots came to Pryor in 1947 after graduating from medical school in Missouri. A longtime community leader, Moots (1922–1992) served on the city council and as civil defense director.

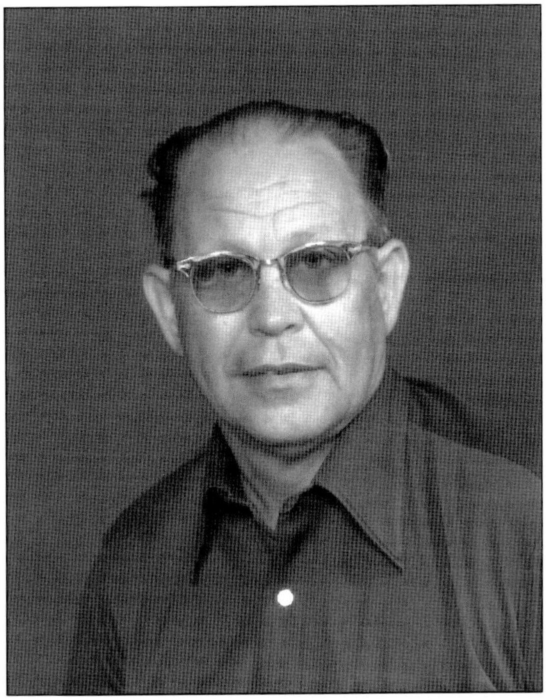

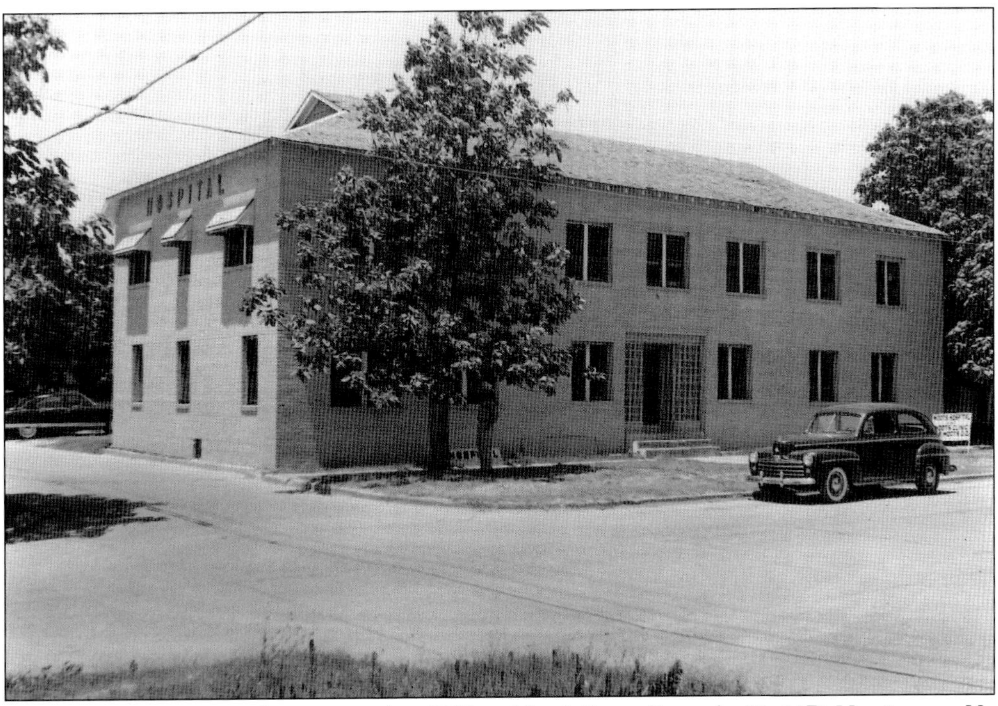

The Herrington Hospital was opened in 1933 on North Rowe Street by Dr. V.D. Herrington. He then sold the facility in 1947 to Dr. G.E. Moots, who changed the name to Moots. Dr. Moots operated the facility until closing it in 1989. The idle building was destroyed by fire in 1994. The original facility was a single-story structure. It was rebuilt to look as it does here following the 1942 tornado.

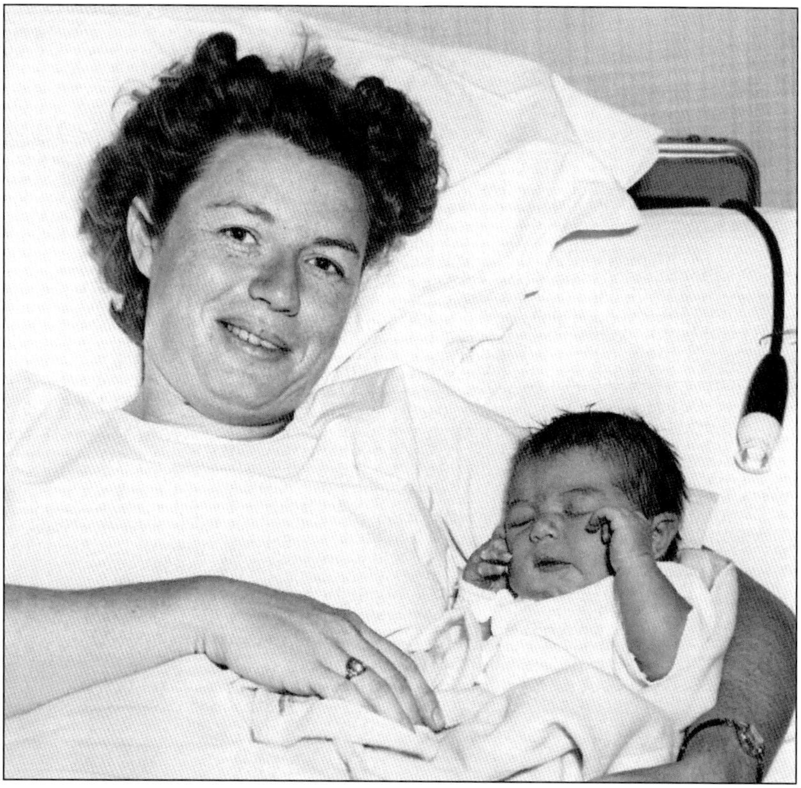

Brenda Katen, shown here with her mother, was the first baby born at Grand Valley Hospital. She is the daughter of Mr. and Mrs. Robert Katen.

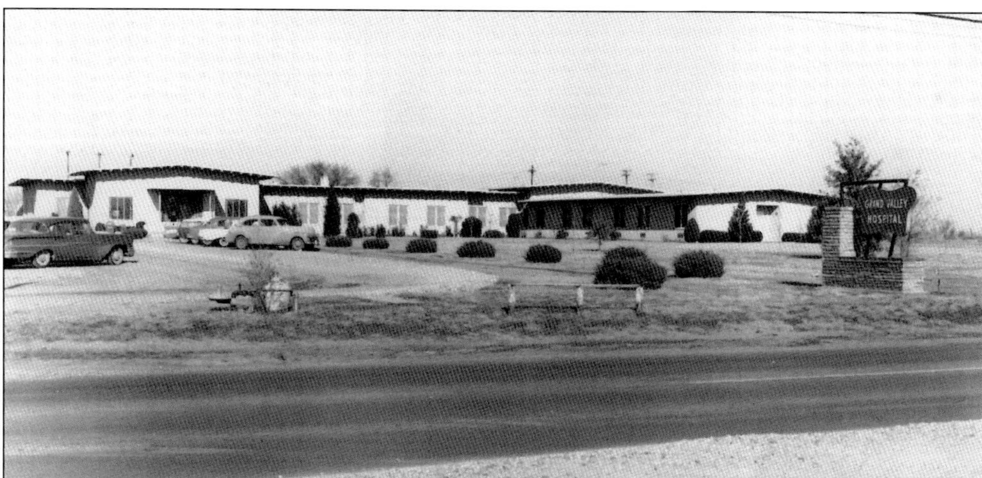

Grand Valley Hospital was opened in December 1954 on the eastern edge of Pryor. The county-owned hospital was constructed with a $250,000 bond issue, which was supplemented by $200,000 in federal grant money. The county then leased the facility to the Oklahoma Baptist Association, which operated the facility. The first chief of staff was Dr. Paul Cameron. Doctors on staff, in addition to Cameron, were E.H. Werling, Bill Bynum, Warren Gwartney, and C.B. Pinkerton. Rates were $12 for private rooms and $9 for semiprivate rooms. The first day of operation saw 13 patients: 10 transfers from Whitaker Hospital and 3 new admissions. On that first day, two babies were born: Brenda Katen and Laura Stott.

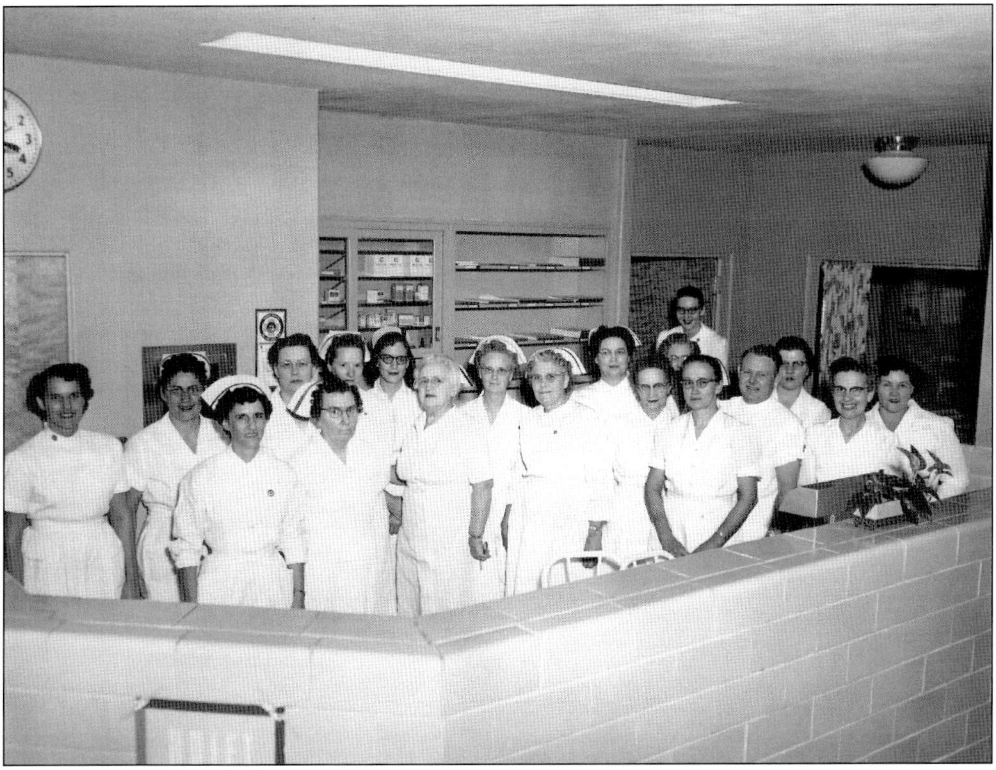

The nursing and aide staff at Grand Valley Hospital, seen in December 1955, included Alice Toner, Sina Vanover, Mary Hughes, Odelia Jackson, Mattie Swartzendruber, Delia Mayes, Anna Gibson, Edna Jones, Elva Nicodemus, Jeanette Kent, Lucille Nelson, Maude Cunningham, Sadie Mosier, Loretta Sigle, Goldie Duncan, Vera Motter, Emma Boyer, Patsy Moore, Billie Payne, and Waunell Haley.

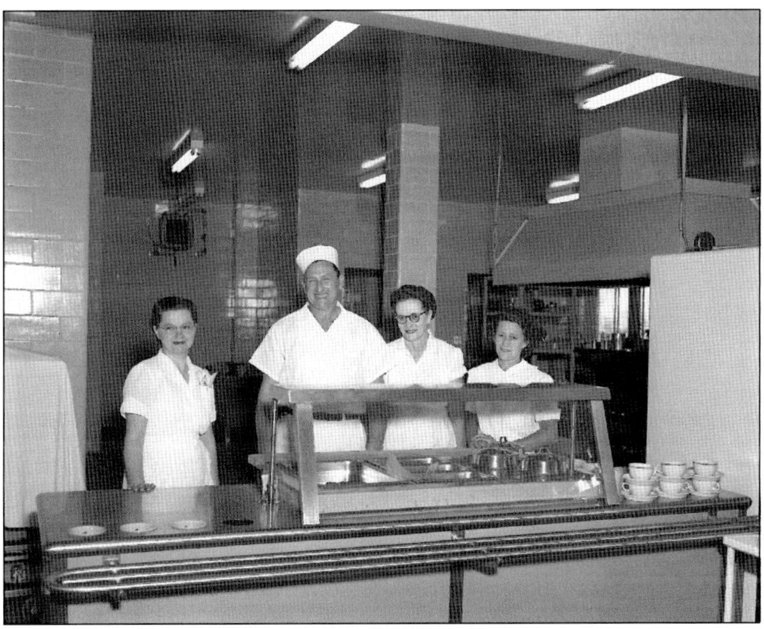

The Grand Valley Hospital food service staff poses in December 1955. They are Paul Dennis, Nancy Fields, Zelma Hamer, and Ruth Kirby.

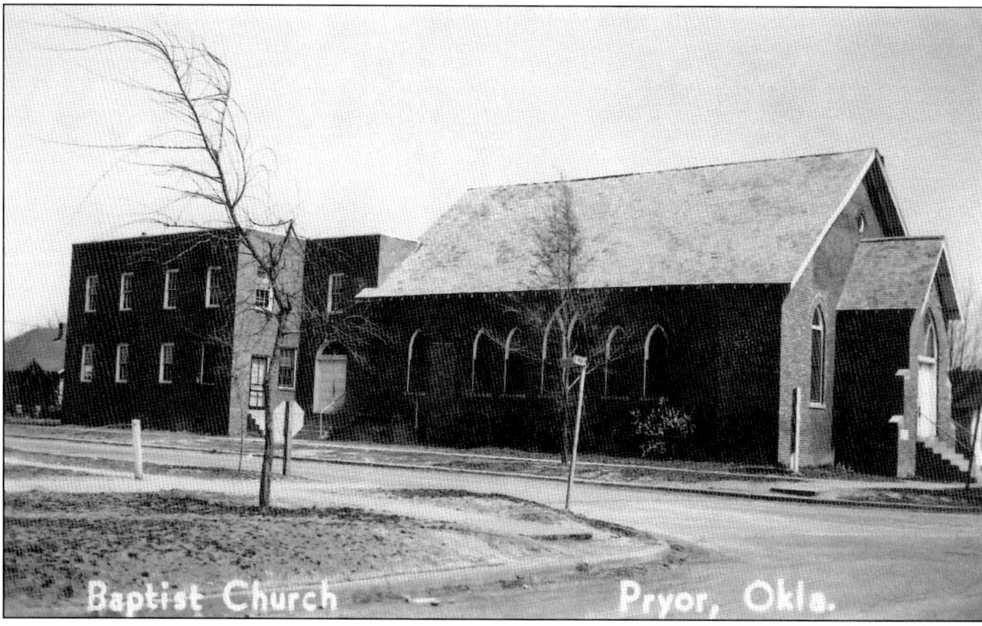

The First Baptist Church building, shown here around 1940, was destroyed in the 1942 tornado. The church's congregation was organized in January 1899 with five charter members. (Courtesy of Leslie Sandusky.)

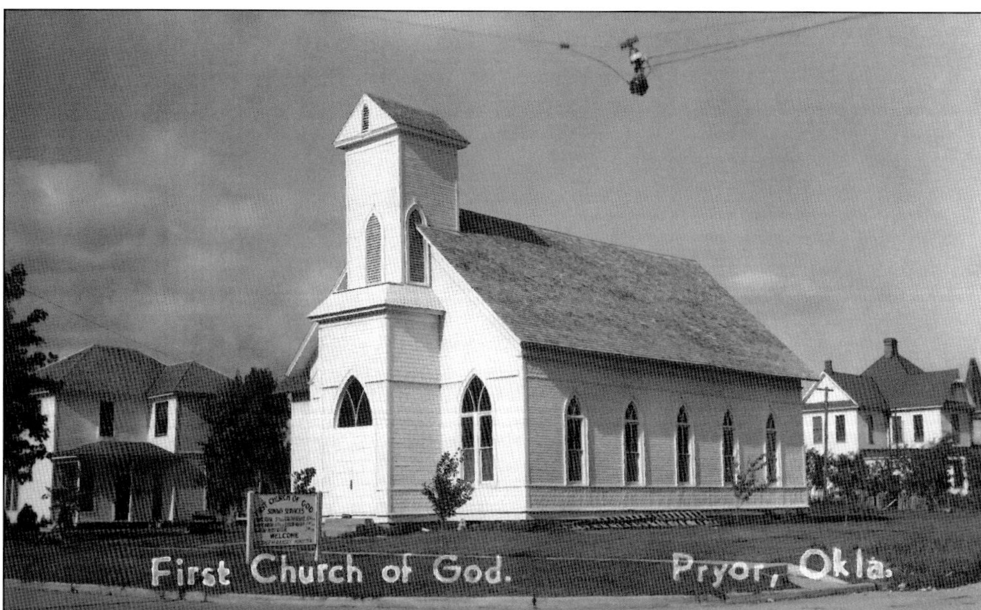

The First Church of God, shown here about 1941, was originally established as the Cumberland Presbyterian Church. The local Church of God congregation purchased the property around 1920 for about $1,500. (Courtesy of Leslie Sandusky.)

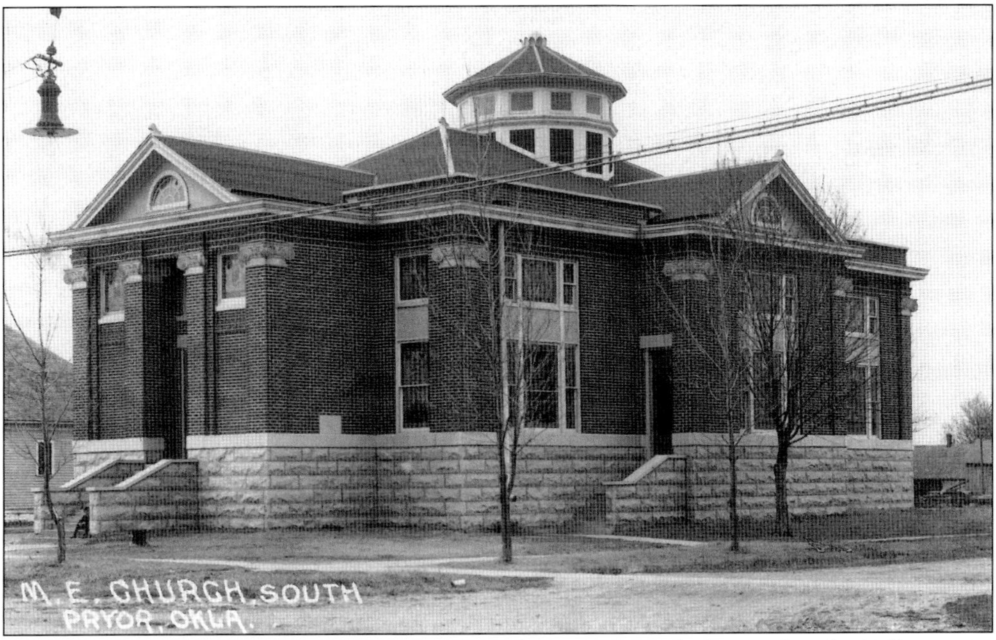

The First United Methodist Church was constructed in 1916. Severely damaged in the 1942 tornado, it was rebuilt and served the congregation until the current sanctuary was opened in 1963.

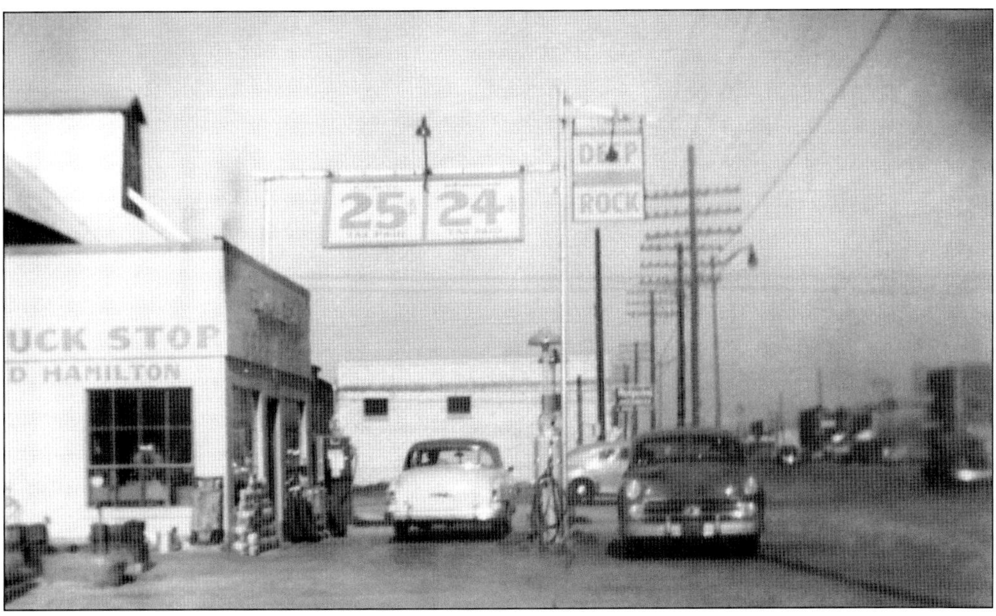

The Ed Hamilton service station at 102 South Mill Street was the scene of a tragic explosion and fire on November 14, 1951. The blaze killed four and injured two. Those killed were William Dempsey Odle, Denver Griffin, Cecil Strop, and William Ellingsworth. Ed Hamilton and Henry Falling were injured. Pryor fire chief Neil Sansing said that the explosion was caused by either static electricity igniting gas fumes or spilled gasoline on an exhaust pipe.

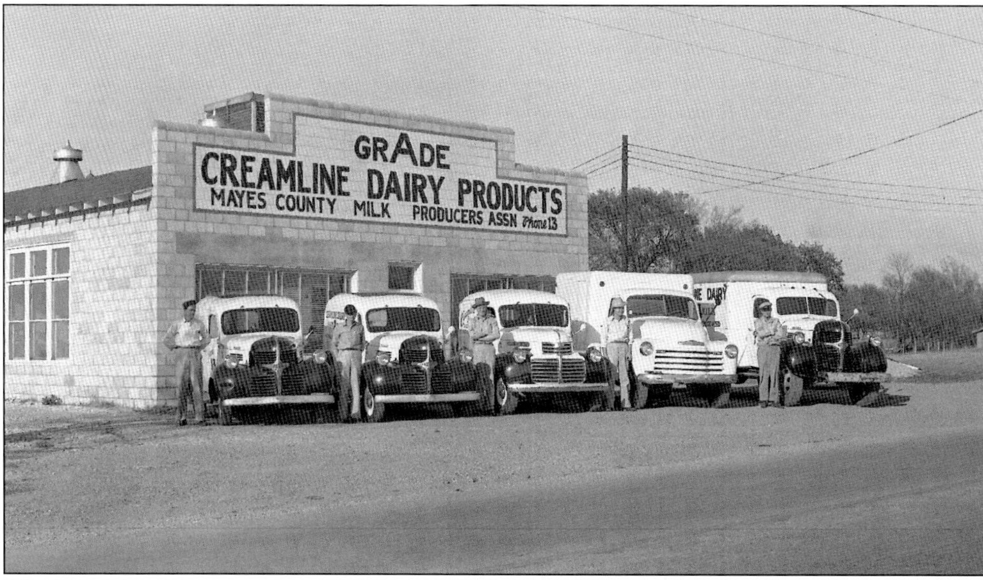

The Creamline Dairy was opened in May 1947 by local dairy farmers and businessmen who formed a producers' association and built a modern processing plant. Those men were Fred Qualls, Al Watkins, O.J. Miller, W.T. Gooldy, Stanley Huggans, D.C. Fryer, Wallace Watkins, and Dick Fuller. The delivery drivers pictured here are unidentified.

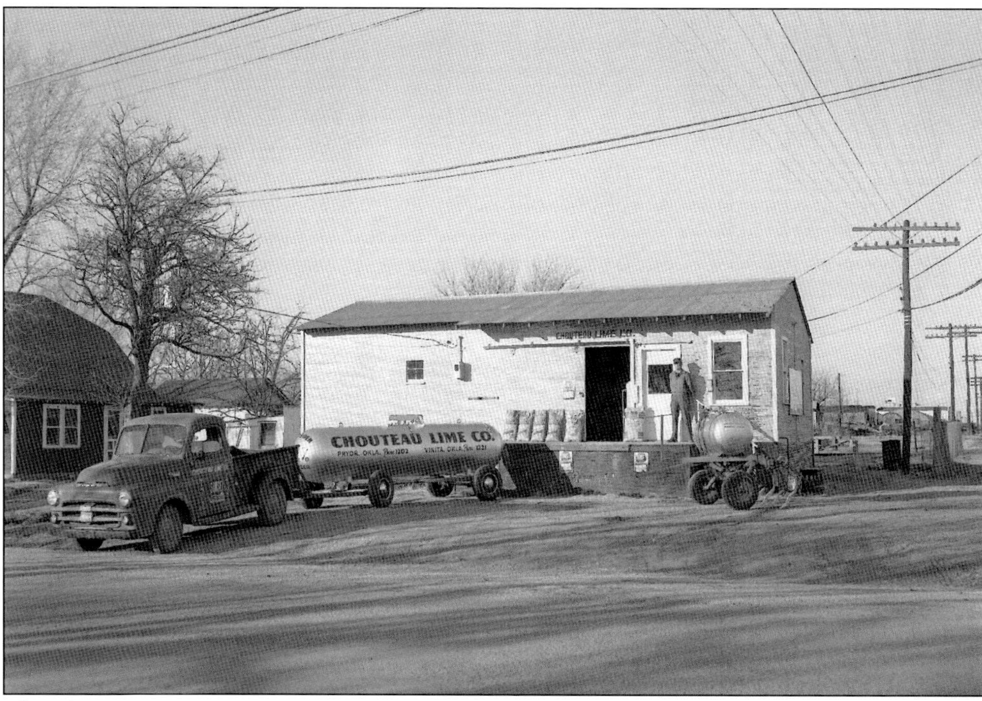

The Chouteau Lime Company was established by Quentin Ogden in the 1940s as an agriculture supply store for Mayes County farmers. This original location, in a small warehouse along the railroad right-of-way, was home to the firm for about 30 years. The business then expanded to the south and the west, with several lots housing the company's main store and warehouses. The business is now owned by the Head family.

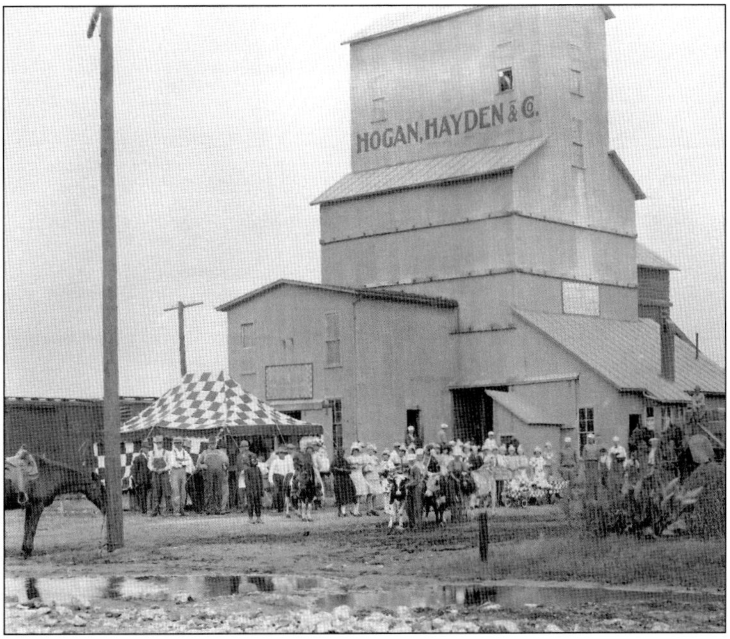

The Hogan-Hayden elevator is shown here in October 1926 hosting a Purina Feeds promotions exhibit and youth farm-animal parade. Hogan-Hayden started in the grain business in 1910 and eventually branched out to locations in Chouteau, Locust Grove, Adair, Chelsea, and Muskogee. It then merged to become the Bouldin-Thornton Grain Company. The elevator was destroyed by fire in April 1931.

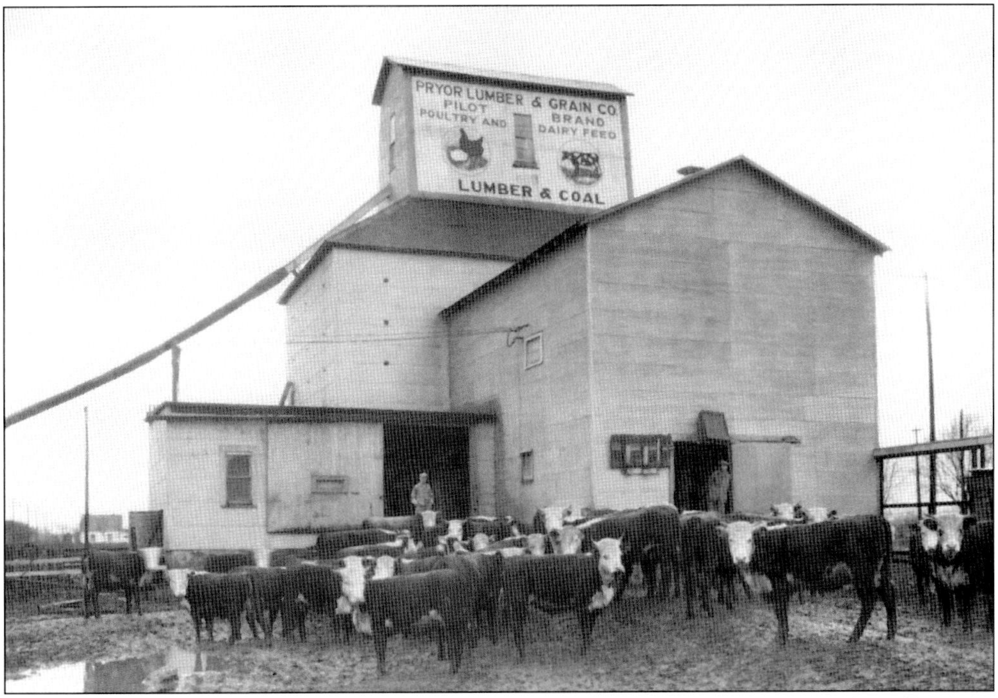

The original Pryor Lumber & Grain Company building was located at 46 South Mill Street. Owned by W.A. Graham, it was a dealer in farm supplies, feed, coal, lumber, seed, and paint. The company was managed by O.J. Borum, who eventually purchased the firm from Graham. In 1914, the city's three grain elevators paid out over $524,308 for wheat, hay, oats, and corn sold by area farmers. This was the last remaining elevator in Pryor until it was torn down in 1968. At that time, the firm was operated by O.J. Borum's son Wallace. The site is now the home of Charlie's Chicken restaurant. (Courtesy of Becky Hawkins.)

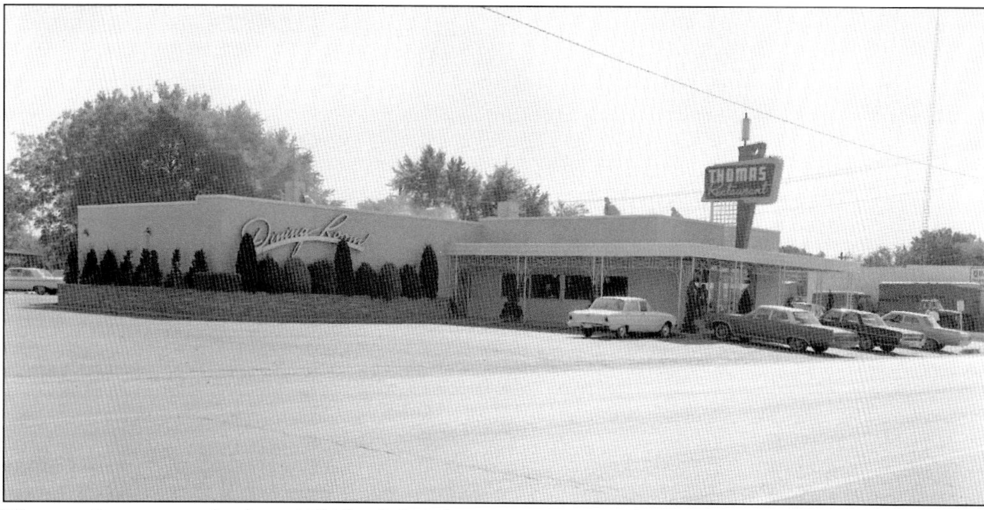

Thomas Restaurant, built in 1954 by C.B. Thomas, was a popular eating establishment frequented by travelers from many states. Known for steaks, homemade pies, and breakfast, the business was later run by Darrell Anderson. He had gone to work for Thomas as a dishwasher while still in school and worked his way up to management. Upon his retirement, Thomas gave the business to Anderson. The restaurant was destroyed by a devastating fire in May 2006.

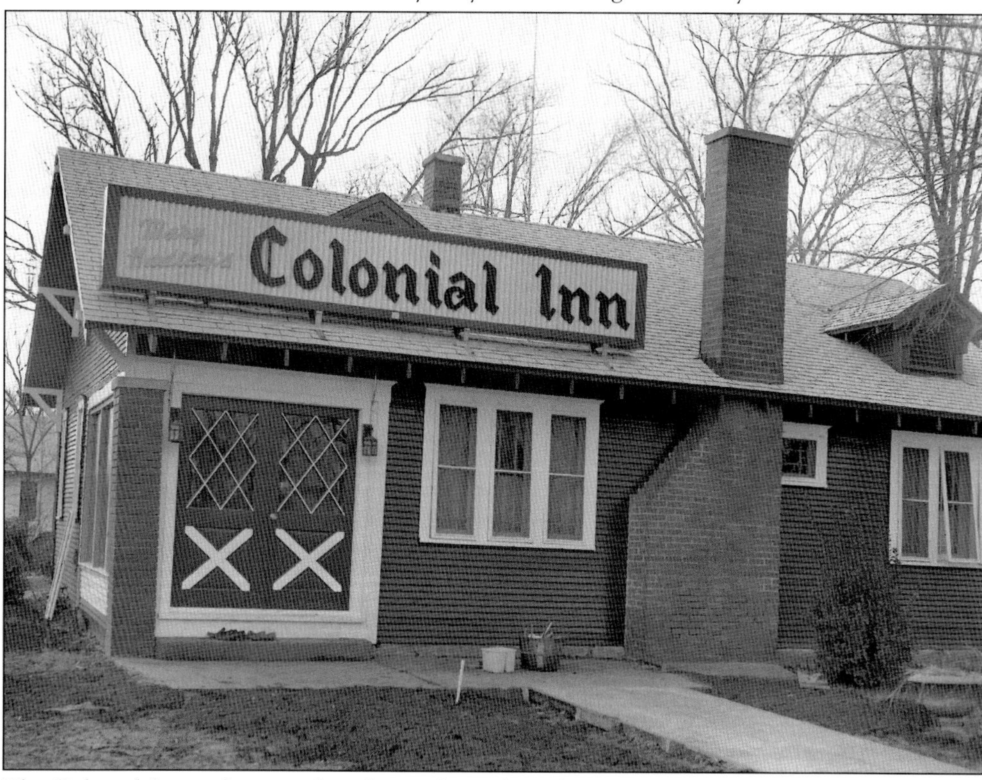

The Colonial Inn, a favorite place for steaks and spaghetti, was established in 1967 by Jim and Mary Hadley. With a Colonial American theme, the restaurant was located in the home of former mayor and laundryman Warren Hadley. The Hadleys sold the business to Joe and Joanna Littlefield in 1970.

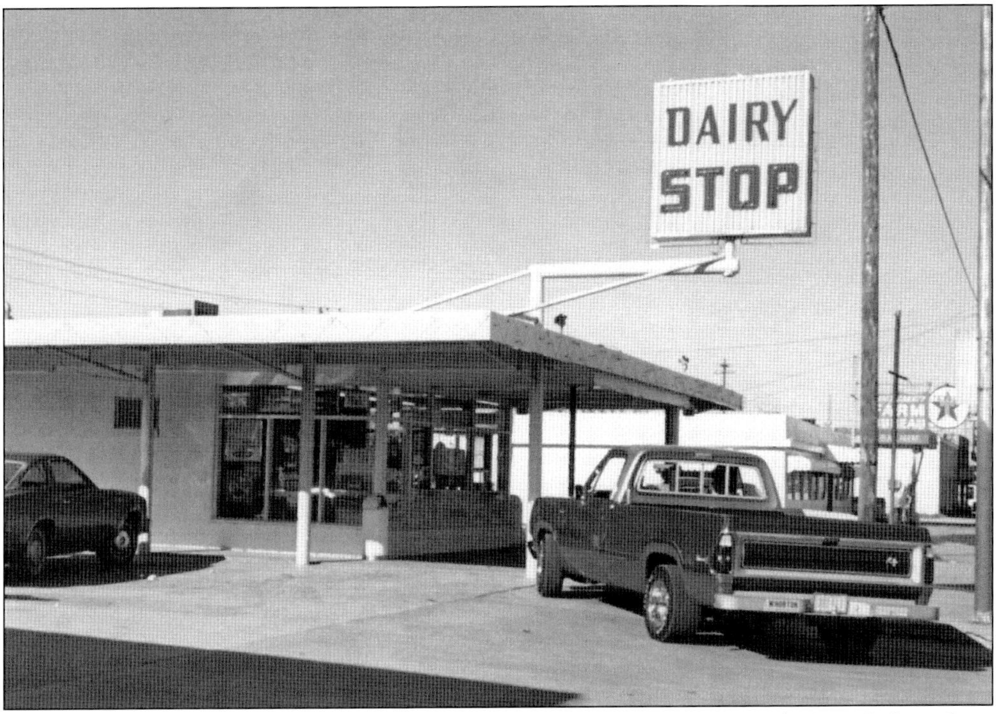

The Dairy Stop was a popular drive-in located on South Mill Street. It was the Dari-Delite when, on August 26, 1966, Pres. Lyndon Johnson stopped in for an ice-cream cone on his way to give a speech at an industrial park south of town. The cones were made by Jeannie Driskell and served by Julie Kelly and Terry Davis. Dairy Stop owners included Manse and Betty Holland, Larry and Kay Nusz, and Dot Coulston.

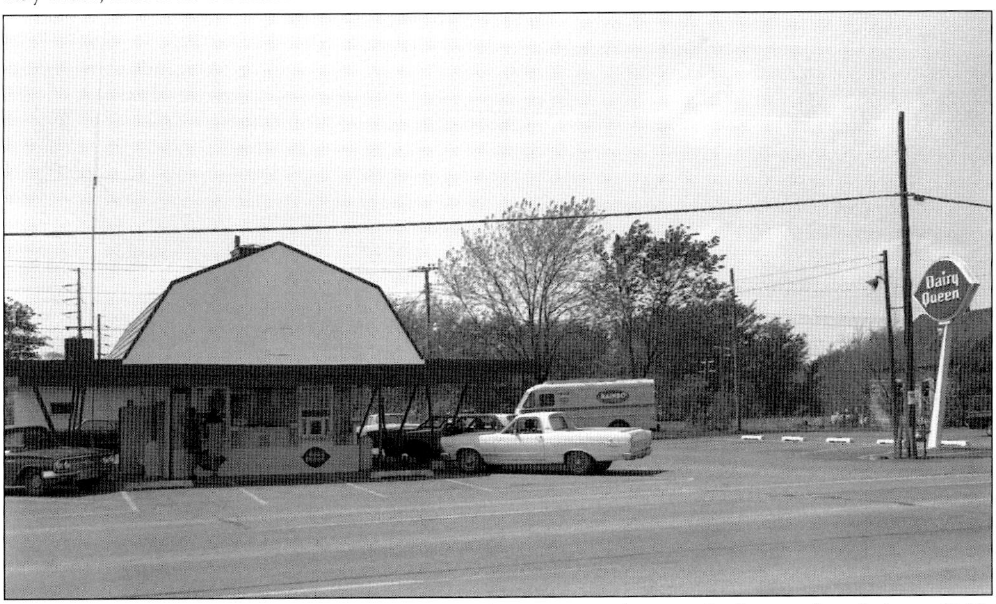

The Dairy Queen on South Mill Street was always a popular spot before it closed about 1989. During its existence, operators included Lyle H. McAlmond, Leroy and Oma Lee Stephens, Manse and Betty Holland, Jerry and Margaret Shearer, and, finally, Bob and Barbara Wallace.

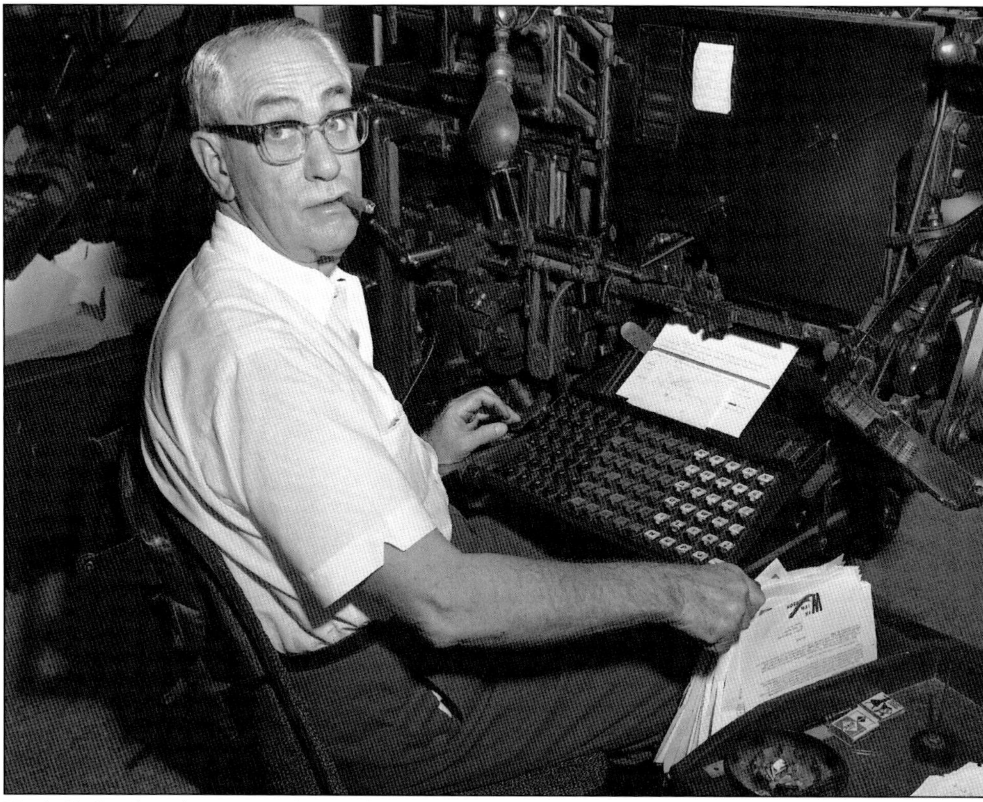

Haskell Gaither (1908–1992) was the owner and publisher of the *Pryor Jeffersonian* (the "Jeff") for over 40 years. Starting as a "printer's devil" for local newspaperman Milt Butler at age 12, Gaither later attended Oklahoma Baptist University, where he obtained a journalism degree in 1931. Gaither became associated with ownership of the newspaper during World War II.

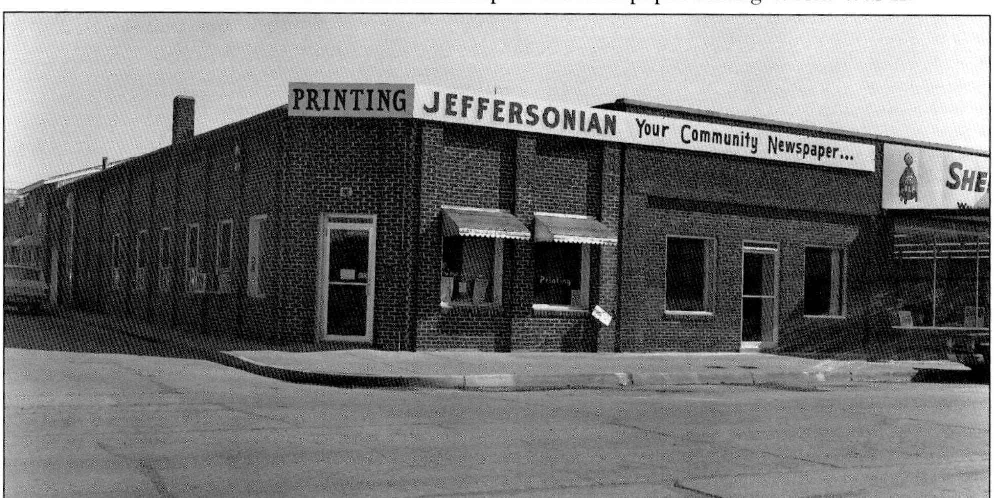

The *Pryor Jeffersonian* was the favorite hometown weekly newspaper from 1935 until 1986. The paper was established by Joe and Jack Butler, who later sold the paper to Haskell Gaither. He was later joined by his son Haskell Lee Gaither. The Gaithers sold the paper to their daily competitor, who eventually ceased operation in 1987.

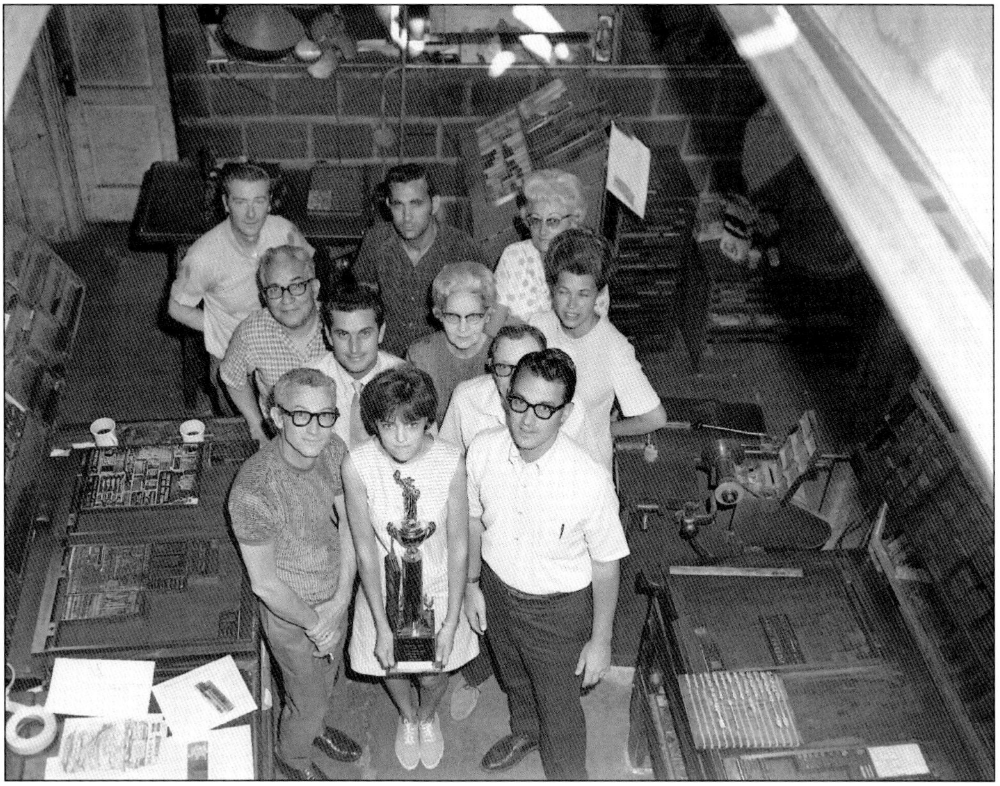

The *Daily Times* staff poses with a Tulsa State Fair sweepstakes trophy awarded to the paper in September 1969. Shown here are, from left to right, (first row) Charles Cooper, Kathy Willyard, Bud Ballard (partially obscured), and Jack Hardy; (second row) Cleon Seabolt, Jim Hartman, Helen Rush, and Barbara Hanson; (third row) George Mack, Frankie Littlefield, and Estelle Stewert. Virgil Wilson is not pictured.

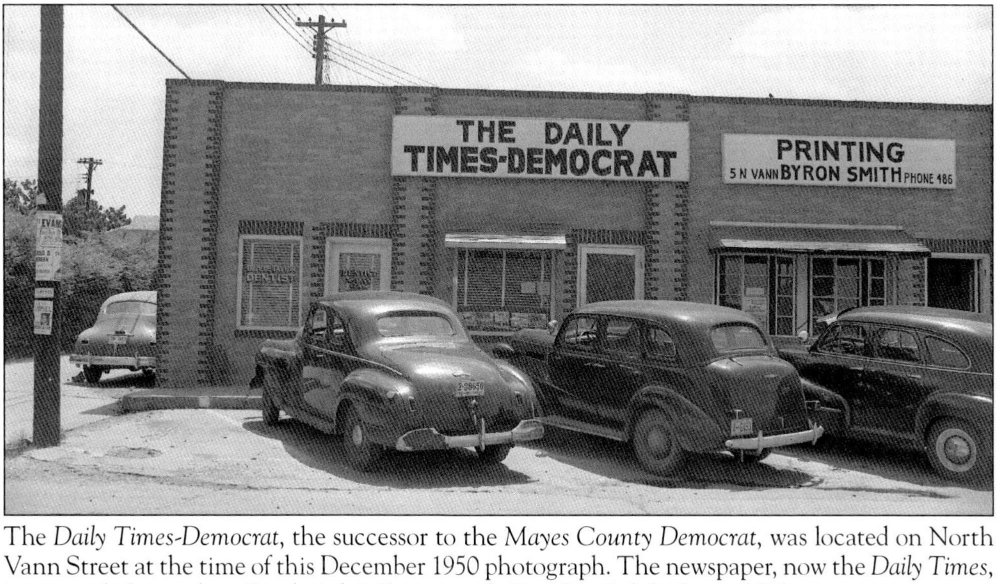

The *Daily Times-Democrat*, the successor to the *Mayes County Democrat*, was located on North Vann Street at the time of this December 1950 photograph. The newspaper, now the *Daily Times*, is currently located on South Adair Street, with Carolyn Ashford as publisher.

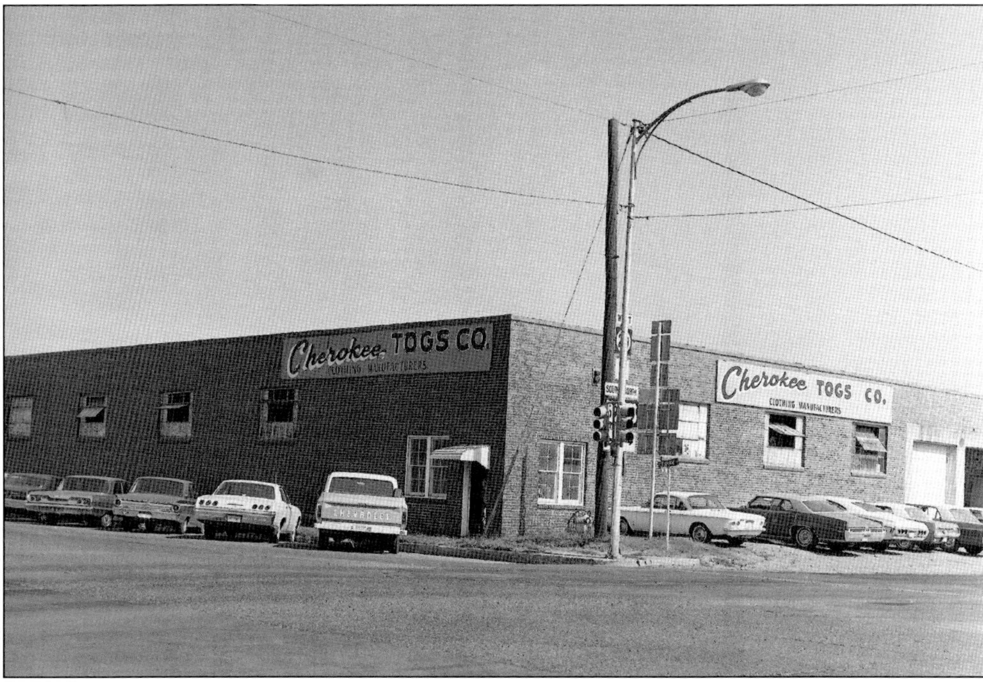

The clothier Cherokee Togs Company specialized in Western goods. The plant shown here was the former Griffin Grocery warehouse, located on the northwest corner of Graham Avenue and Mill Street. The plant started in 1948, hiring 100 women to sew and assemble clothing. In 1951, the company was awarded a defense contract to make fatigue caps for the US Army. The building was demolished in 1988.

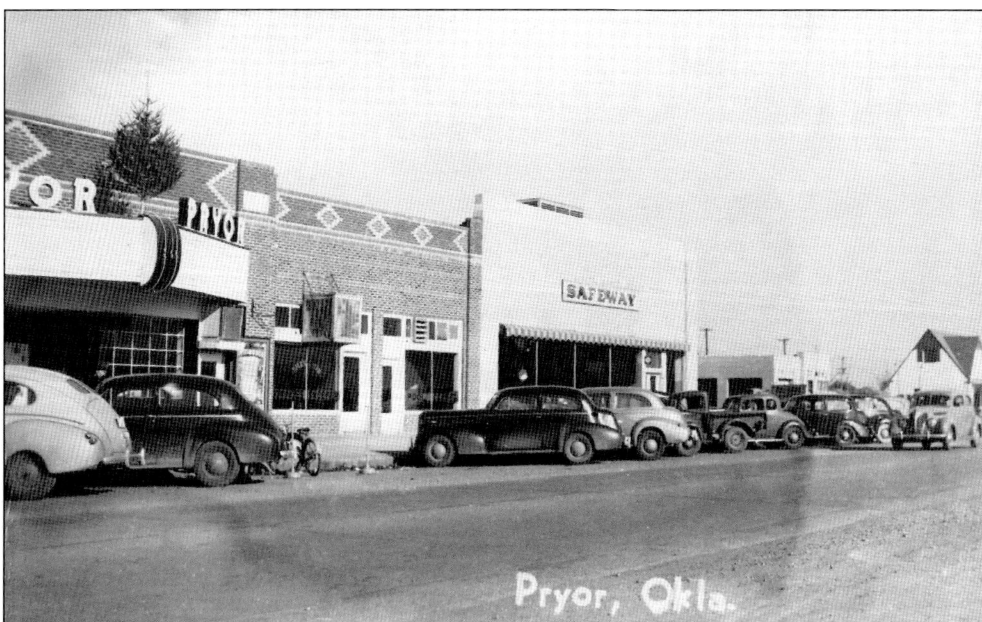

The Gooldy Building, constructed after the 1942 tornado, housed the New Pryor Theater, Bill's Club, and Safeway.

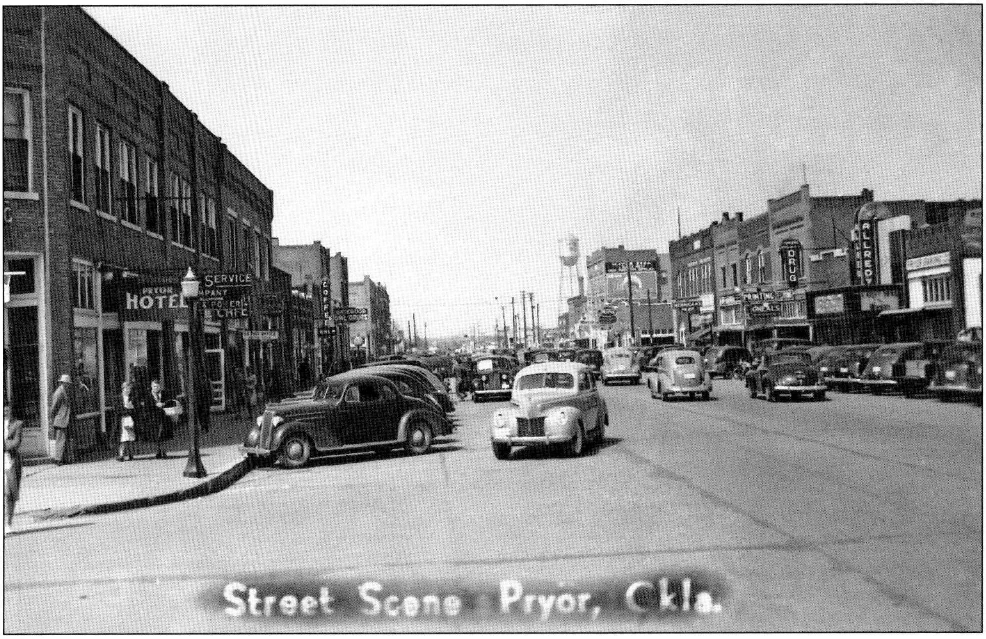

This c. 1940 photograph looks west on Main Street from Vann Street. Businesses seen on the right include Pryor Baking Company, Allred Theater, Fowler Drug, and Hennigan's Men's Shop. On the left are the Pryor Hotel, Public Service Company, and the US Post Office. Farther down the street are Ma Mitchell's Coffee Shop and Gatewood Owl Drug. The 1942 tornado would drastically change the landscape of downtown.

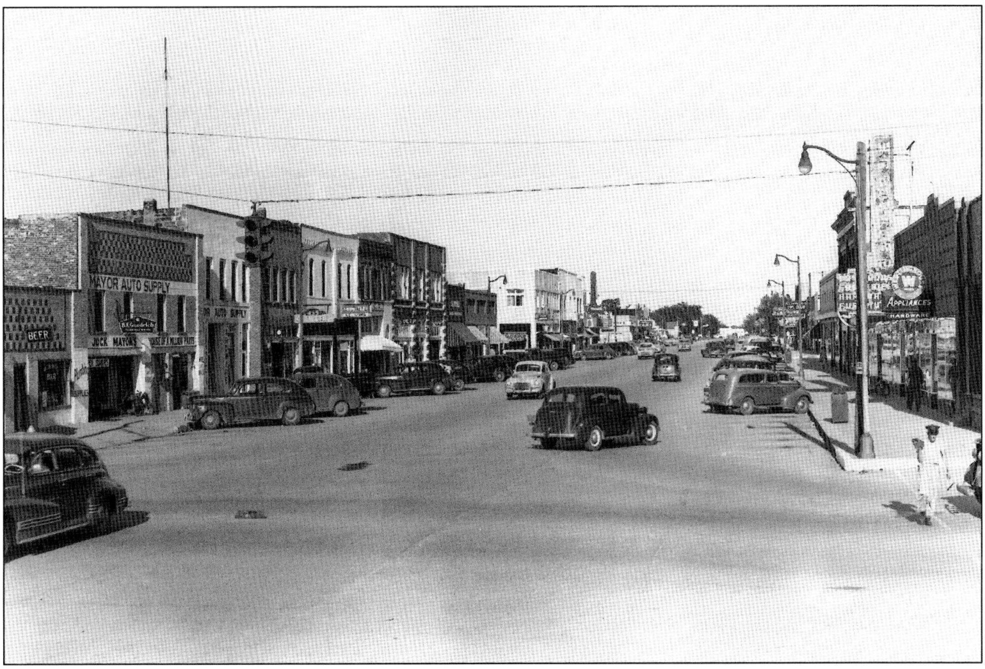

Looking east on Main Street from Mill Street (US 69), this photograph was taken about 1949. On the right is Graham Dry Goods and Hardware. On the left are Jock Mayor's Auto Supply (the "House of a Million Parts"), City Cab, Nelson's Furniture, the Hardy Building, and Fowler Drug.

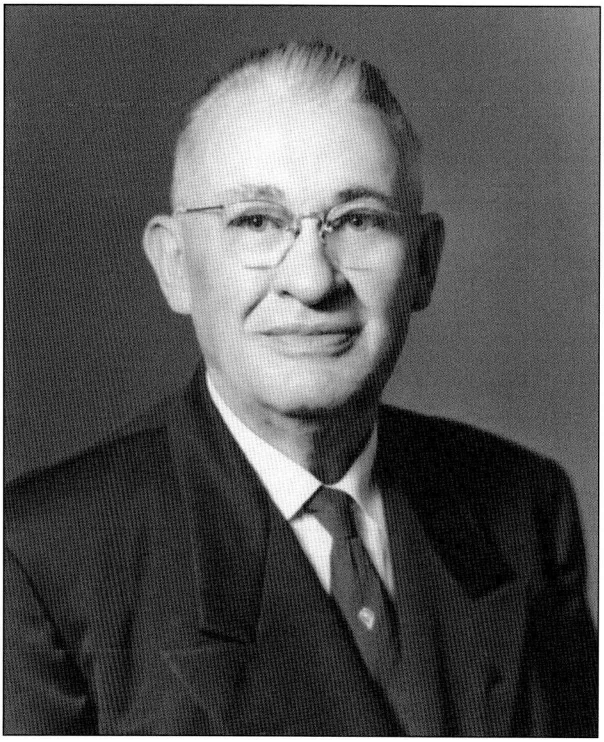

Norvelle Green (1892–1954) was the founder of Green Funeral home in 1935 and operated it until his death. He was a longtime rodeo promoter and charter member of the Rotary Club. At the time of his death, Green was campaigning as the Republican nominee for state senate. He was also a former mayor of Picher, Oklahoma.

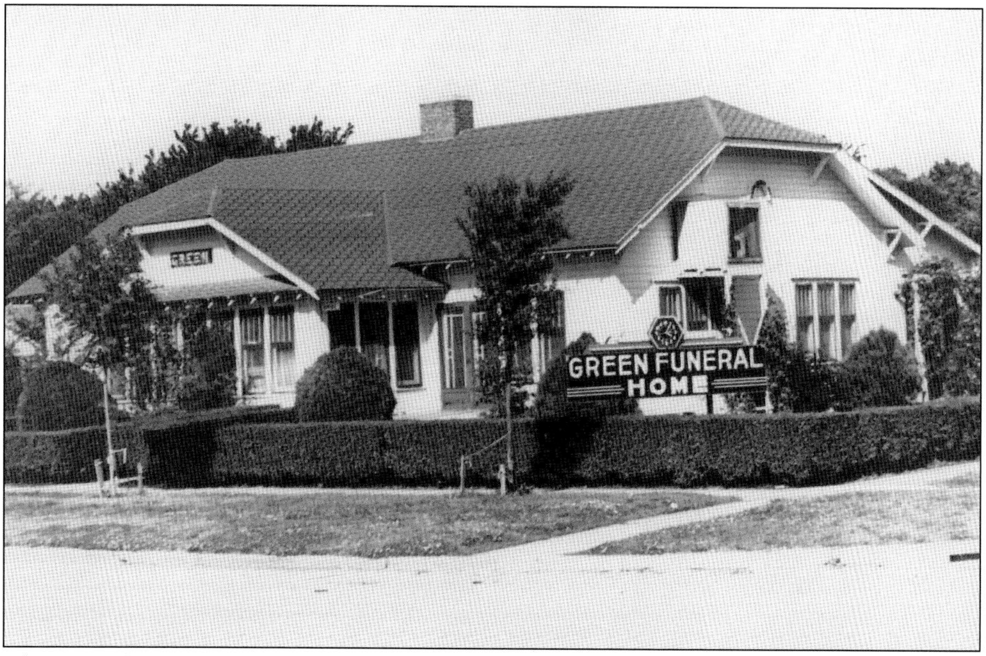

The original Norvelle Green Funeral Home, located at 101 North Rowe Street, was established in 1935. Following the death of Green, the funeral home was run by his son George. Around 1973, George Green sold the business to J. Clair Wilson and Floyd Cunningham. The business closed in the 1990s after being sold numerous times following the retirement of Wilson and death of Cunningham.

R.L Terry (1865–1938) came to Pryor Creek, Indian Territory, in about 1897 and went to work for the Hogan Mercantile Company, selling furniture and caskets. The firm was sold to W.A. Graham, who saw the need for a town undertaker. Terry was sent to mortuary school by Graham. In 1908, he established the Terry Funeral Home, operating it until his death. For several years, he donated a community Christmas tree for the City of Pryor Creek and sponsored large Christmas festivities for town and county residents.

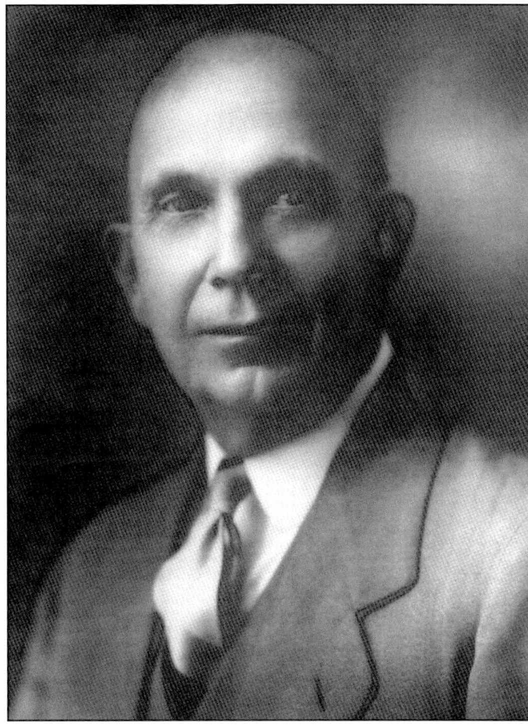

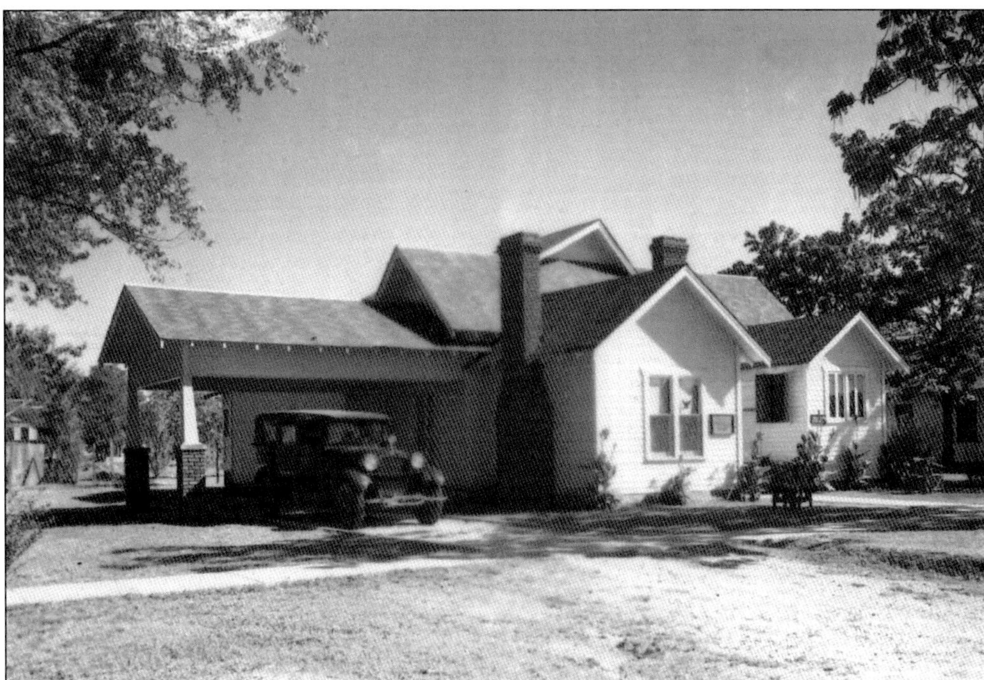

Established in 1908, the Terry Funeral Home was located in the unit block of North Vann Street and owned by R.L Terry until his death in 1938. His wife then sold the firm to Norvelle Green seven months later. From 1941 to 1945, the Terry property was the second site of the Harris Funeral Home.

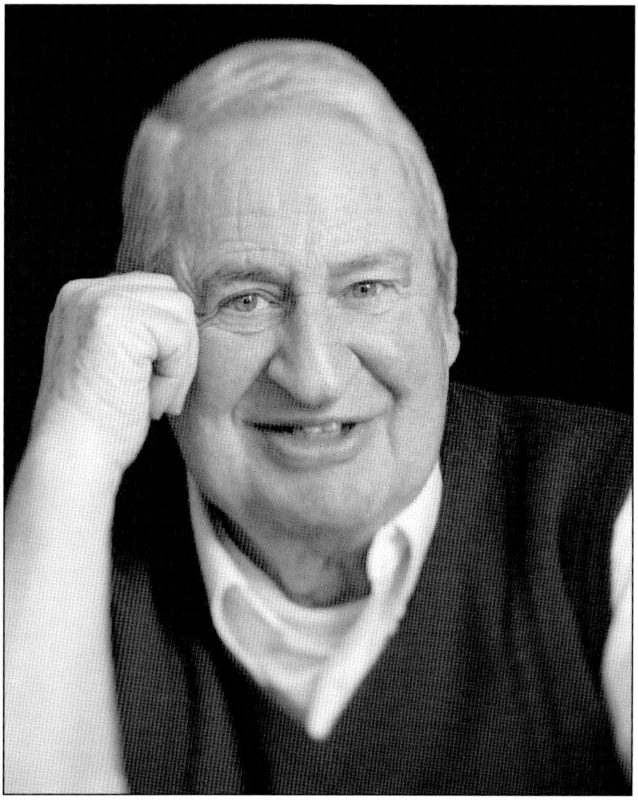

Jim Green (1927–2006) owned the Jim Green Funeral Home from 1958 to about 1997. A native of Picher, Oklahoma, he was the son of Pryor funeral director Norvelle Green and brother of funeral director George Green. (Courtesy of Tim Bonet.)

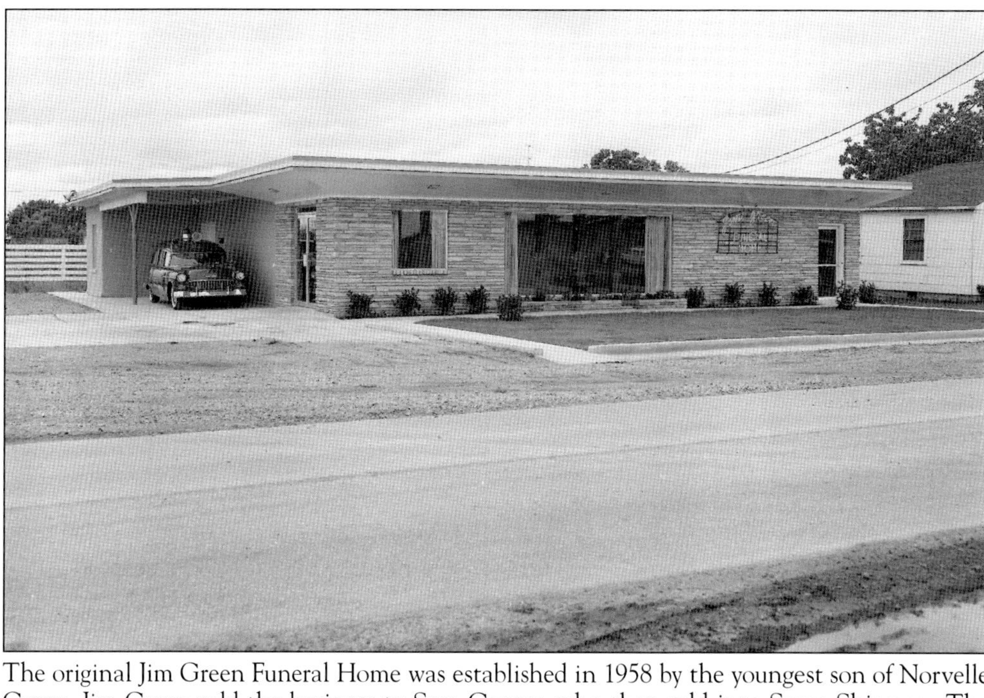

The original Jim Green Funeral Home was established in 1958 by the youngest son of Norvelle Green. Jim Green sold the business to Sam Garner, who then sold it to Steve Shipman. The home is operated today under Shipman's name.

Raymond Harris (1912–1971) was a 1934 graduate of the Williams Institute of Embalming. He was a very active member of the Pryor Round-Up Club, a charter member of the Lions Club, and a former city councilman.

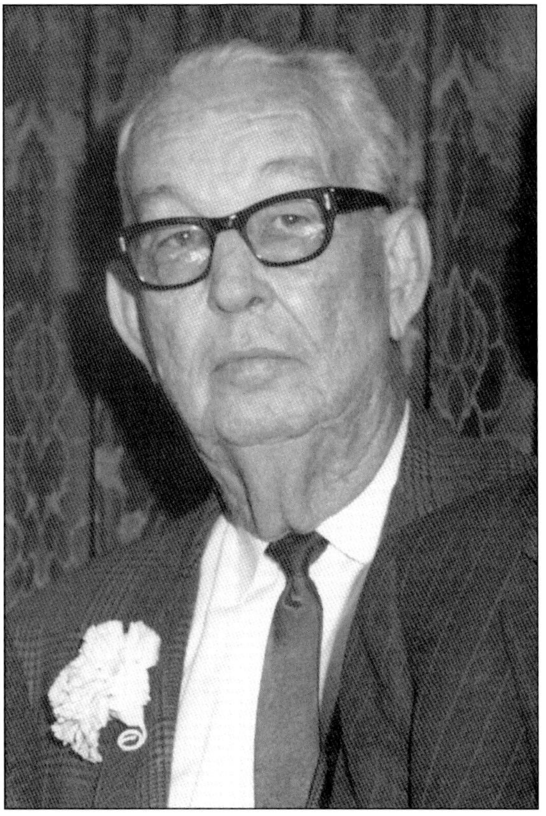

The Harris Funeral Home, shown here in 1968, was established in 1940 by Raymond and Kay Harris. In 1945, they purchased the W.A. Graham Home and moved their business and residence to that location. Following the death of Raymond Harris in 1971, the business was run by Kay, who partnered with Jack Luginbuel and, later, Al Trolinger, before selling all interest to J. Clair Wilson and Floyd Cunningham about 1979. The beautiful three-story home was built about 1904 by T.R. Crookshank, who sold it to Graham.

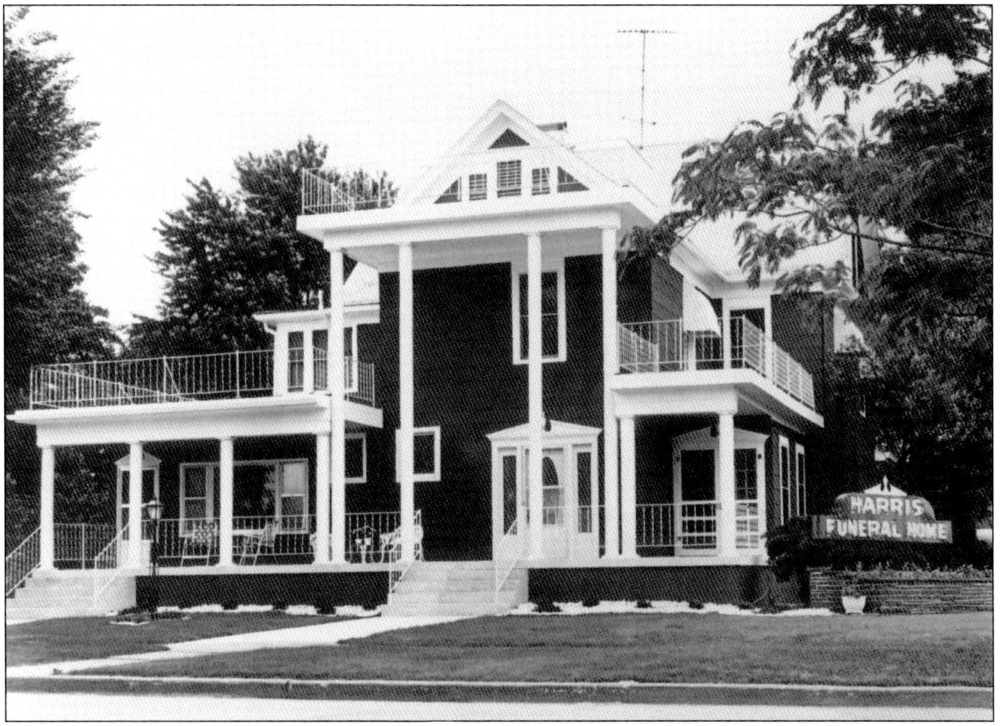

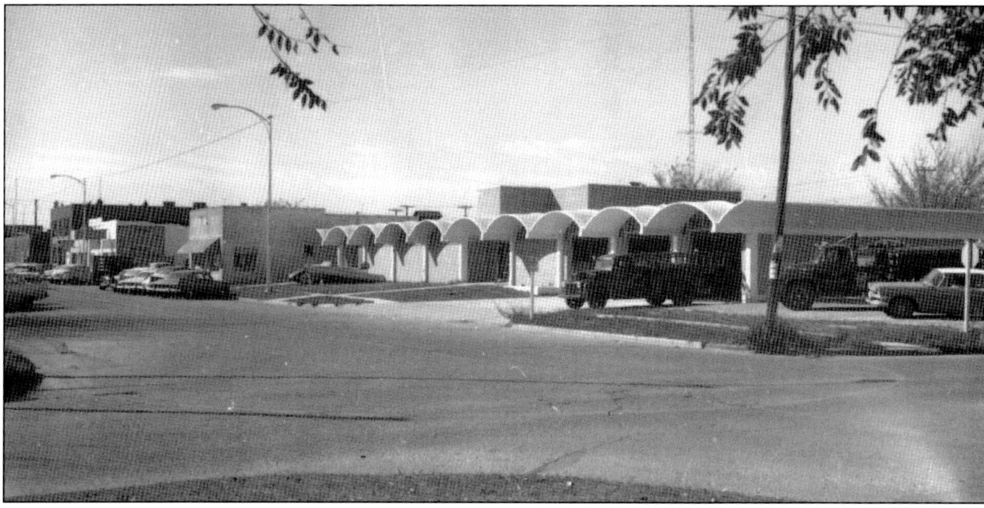

The City-County Building was erected in 1959 by the W.A. Graham estate at a cost of $141,000. The new public safety facility housed the police and fire departments, the city-county jail, the office of the county sheriff, a vault, and a municipal courtroom. To the left of the complex is the Sunshine Hatchery, the Glencliff Ice-Cream store, and the Pete Clark Dodge dealership.

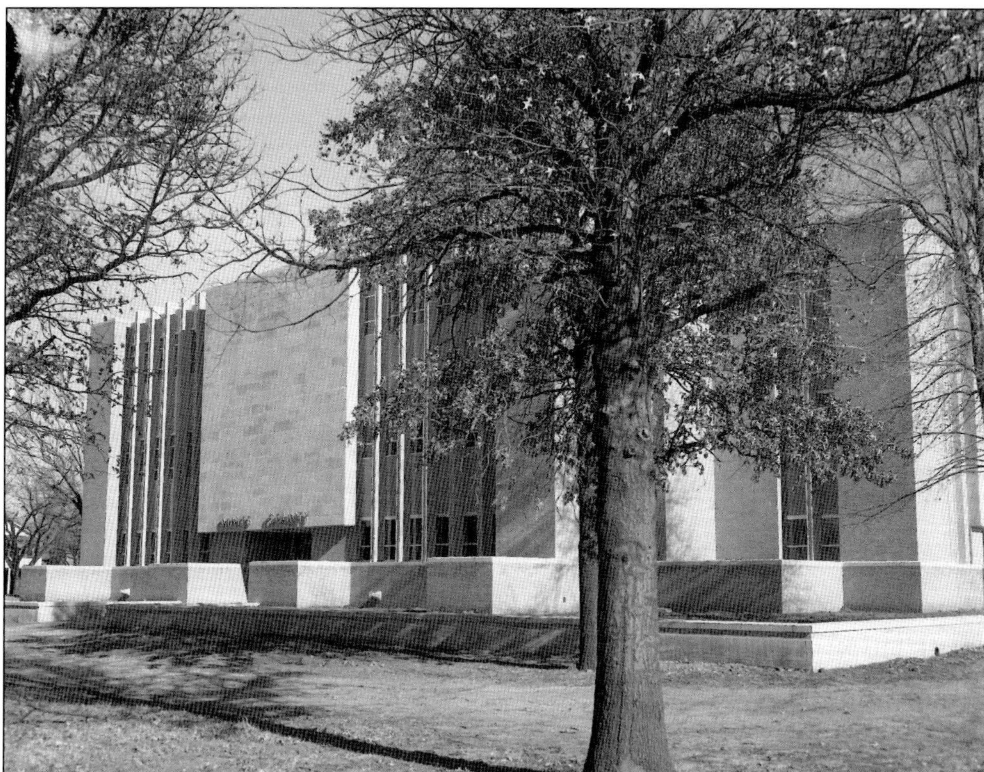

The 1921 Mayes County Courthouse was remodeled in 1959 at a cost of $373,000. The building housed the county commissioners, election board, the courts, the welfare office, and offices of the assessor, clerk, treasurer, district attorney, and the welfare department. In April 2006, it was demolished after the construction and opening of a new courthouse.

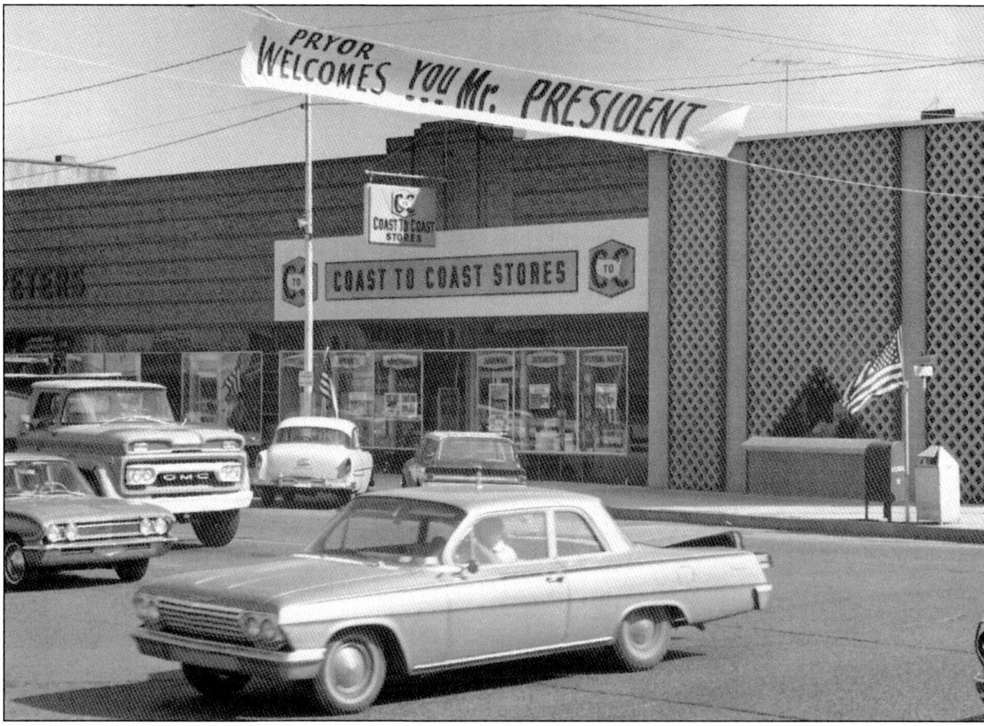

This banner welcomed Pres. Lyndon Johnson to Pryor Creek on August 26, 1966. Johnson came to town to give a dedication speech at the Mid-America Industrial Park, located south of town.

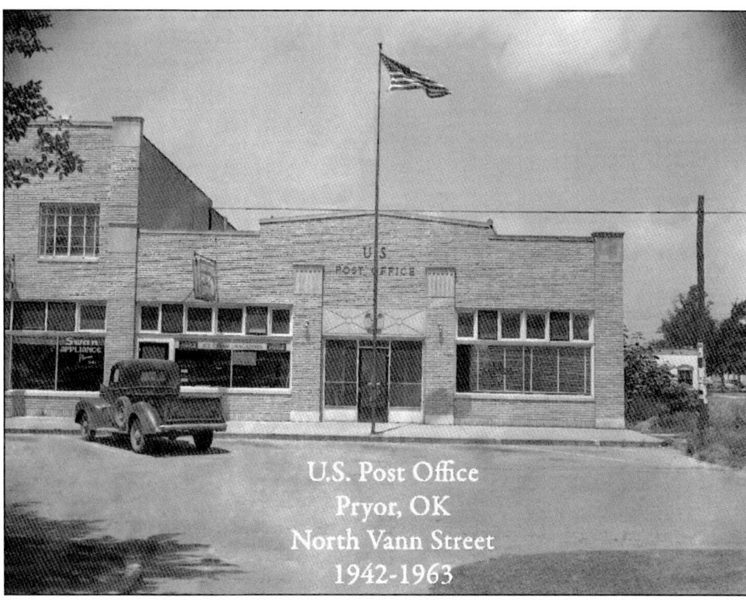

The north end of the Mitchell Building, on North Vann Street, was home to the US Post Office from 1942 to 1963. Jack Butler was postmaster during this period. The building, owned by C.D. Mitchell, was under construction at the time of the tornado. It escaped the storm's wrath with very little damage.

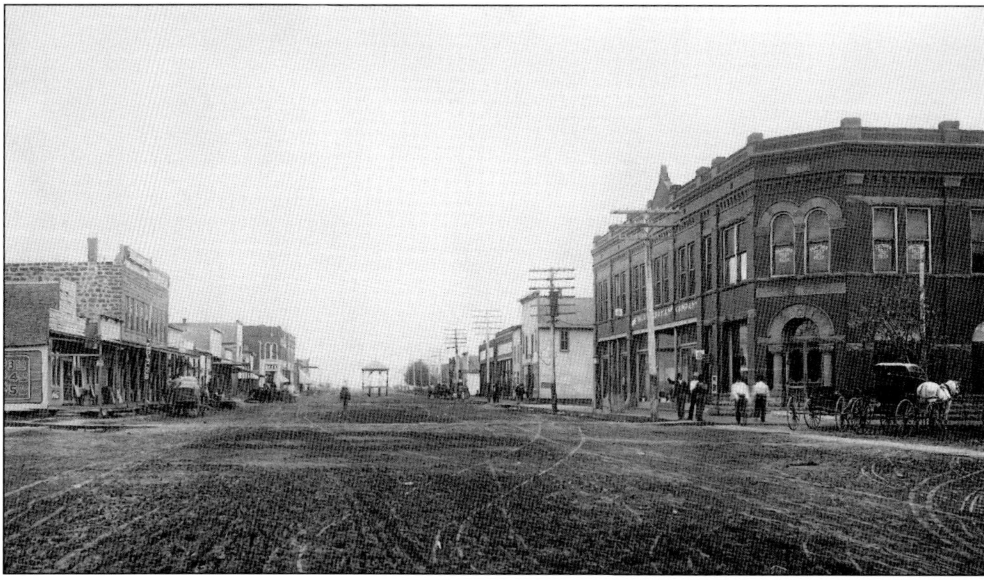

This impressive photograph, taken around 1905, shows the W.A. Graham Company and First National Bank on the right. Note the telephone lines on the south (right) side of the street, with the main trunk of the phone line entering a second-floor window of the building. The main telephone office and operator were located inside that window. Note the gazebo in the middle of the dirt street. Adjacent to the gazebo is the Citizens National Bank. On the left are the C.E. Herald store and a café, along with Parker's Drug Store.

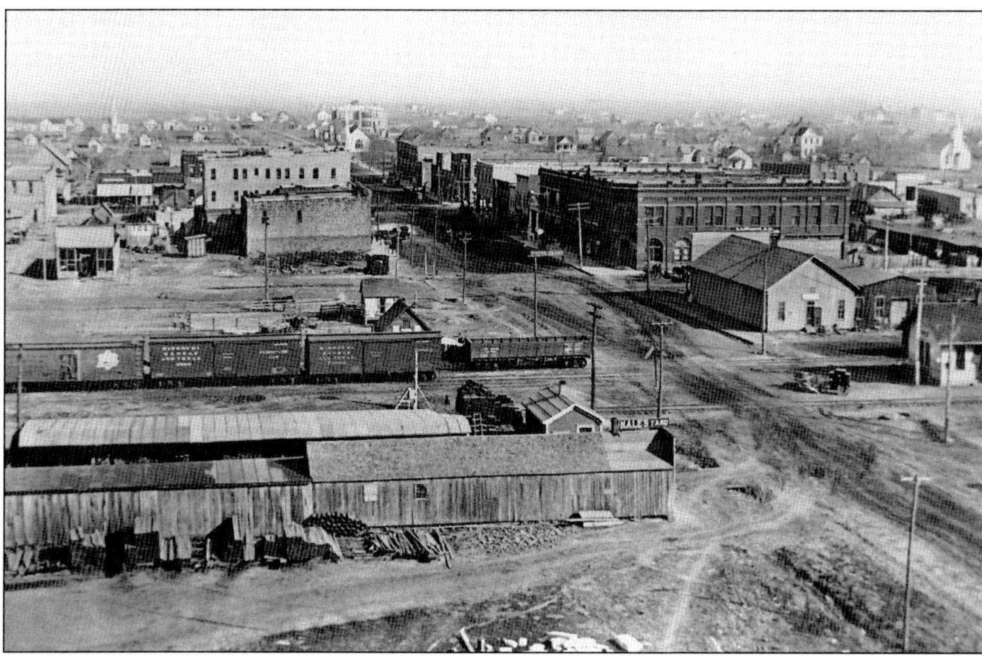

This bird's-eye view of the Pryor Creek skyline faces east from the Katy tracks about 1911. On the right is Hale's Lumber yard, now the Municipal Utility Board warehouse. On the right is the Katy depot, now the location of a Kentucky Fried Chicken restaurant.

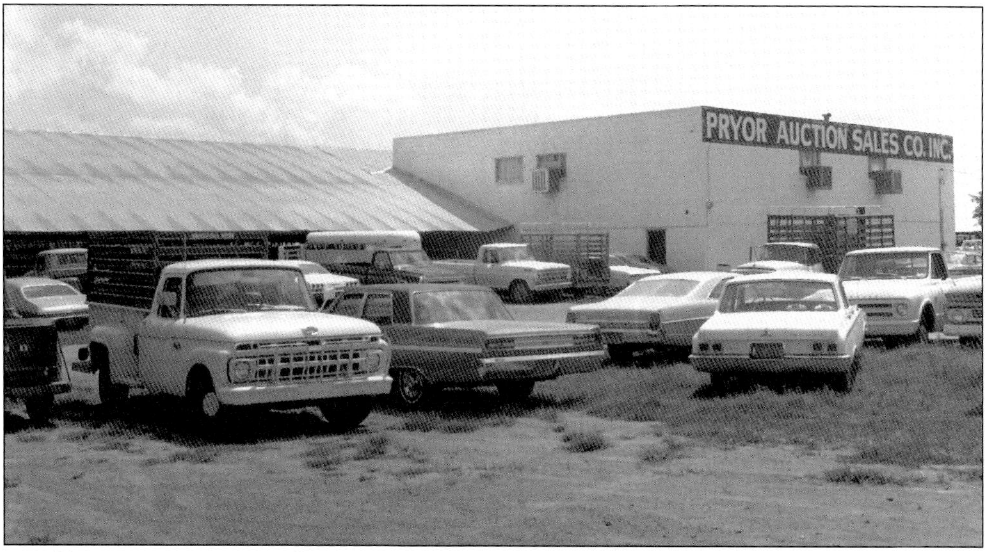

Local businessmen R.A. Wilkerson, Frank Baker, Bo West, Ellsworth Hammer, Ralph Jackson, Nolen Jacobs, Bill Chupp, and Jay Martin organized a corporation to build modern stockyards in 1959. The first sale held at the Pryor Stockmen's Auction sale barn took place in July 1960. By 1966, the sale was a $6 million operation, receiving and selling cattle in a six-state area. Within two years and under management of the Couch brothers, the sale barn employed 54 people with an $80,000 payroll. In later years, the auction was operated by Wayne Chidester. It held its last sale and closed in December 2002.

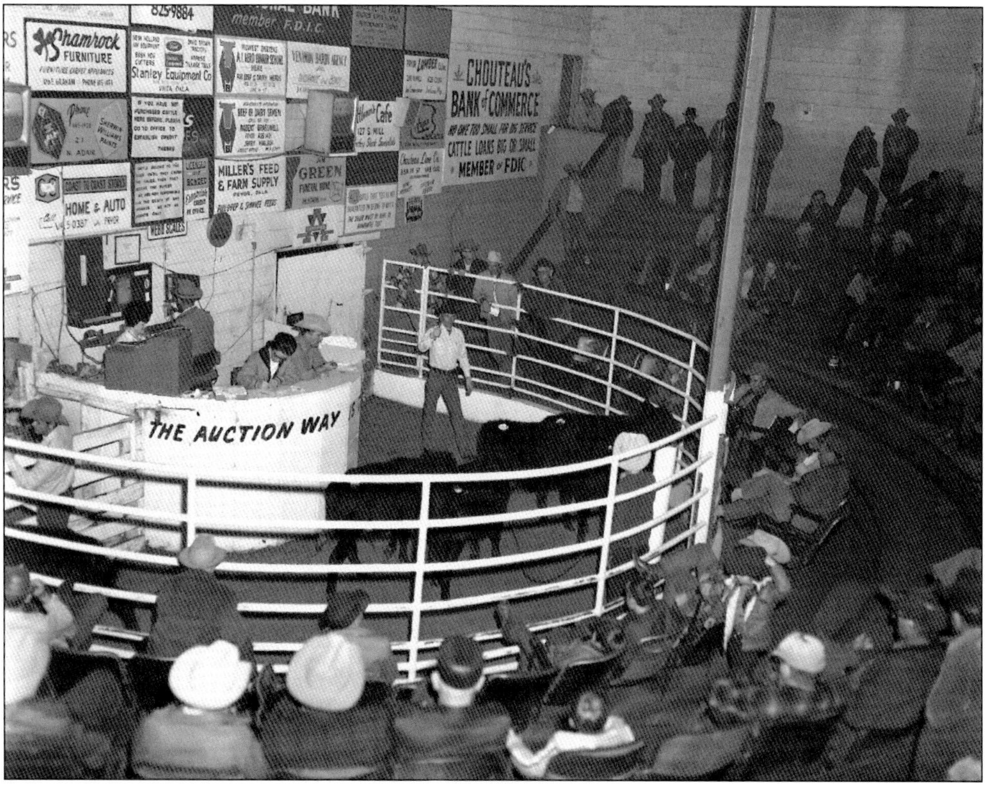

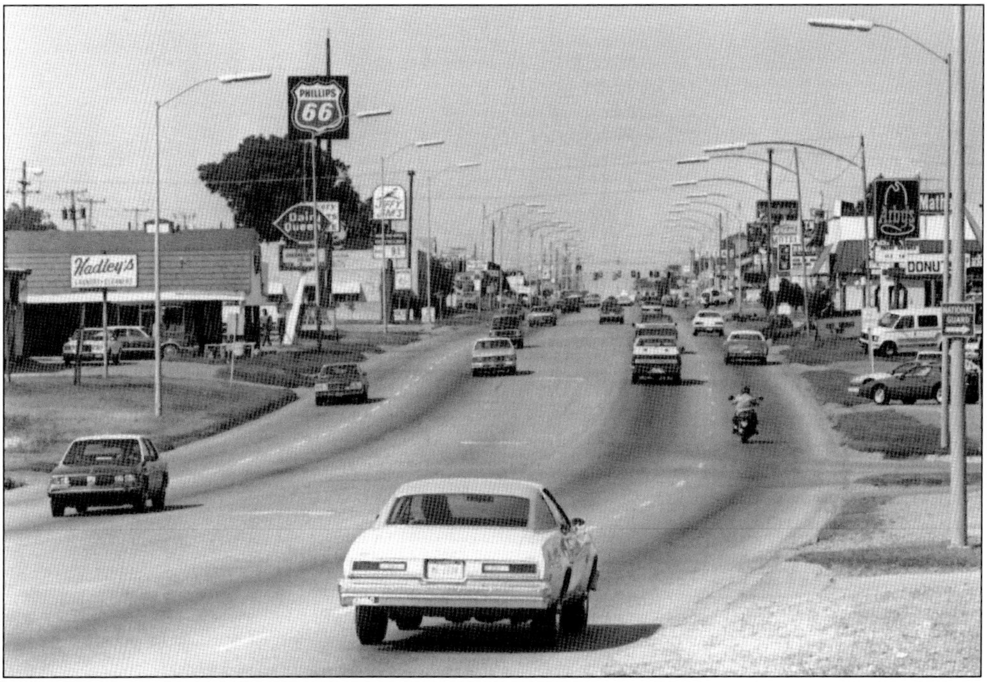

This photograph faces north on Mill Street at Park Avenue about 1985. At left are Dairy Queen, Jiffy Jim's (note that gasoline was 91¢), and the police station. On the right are Jerry's Donuts, Arby's, Bob & Jo Realty, Braum's, the Grand Motel, and Hardee's.

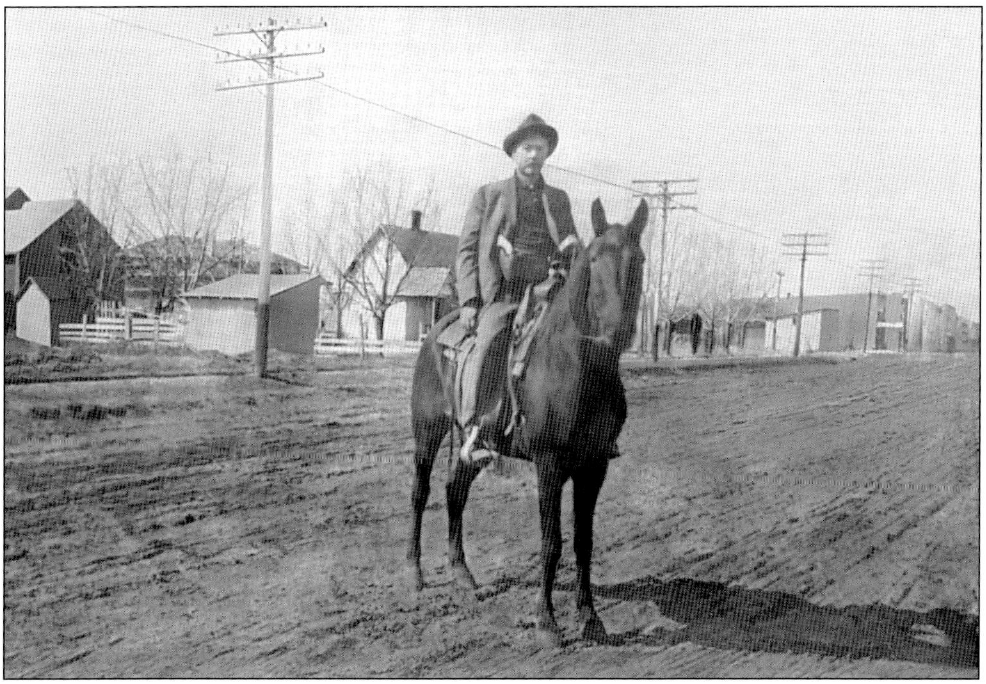
Perd Taylor (1872–1932) sits on his horse in what is now the intersection of Graham Avenue and Coo-Y-Yah Street. Taylor was a lawman, serving as a deputy sheriff, deputy US Marshal, and a prison guard. (Courtesy of Niecca Taylor Pruitt.)

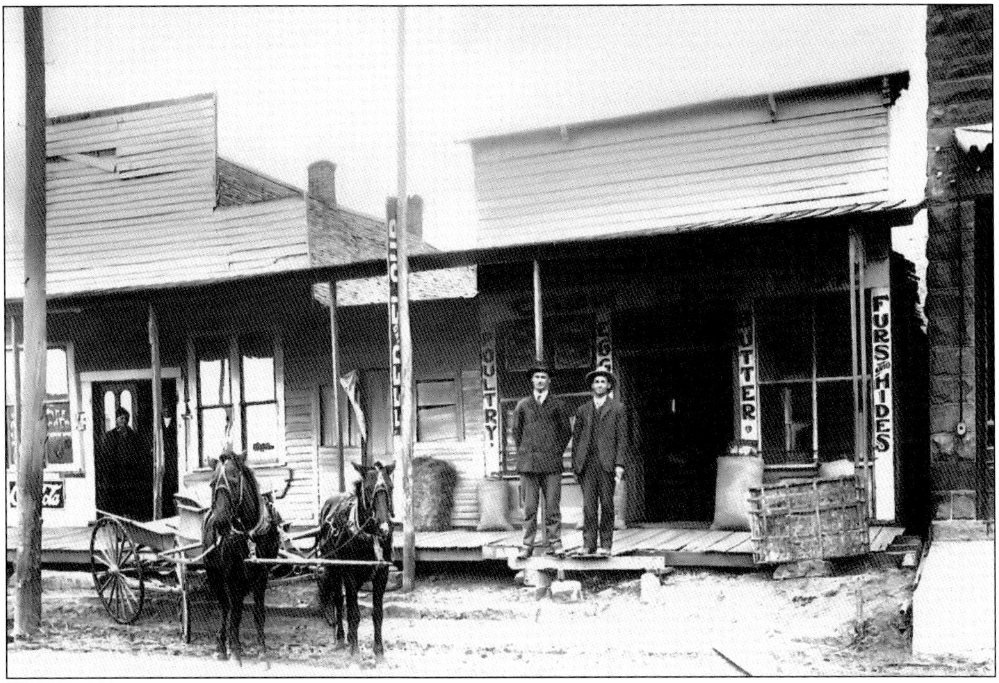

This 1902 photograph shows the C.E. Herald store and restaurant, located at what is now 103 East Graham Avenue. Herald was a dealer in feed, produce, and hides, and later established the first movie theater in town. (Courtesy of Bob Herald.)

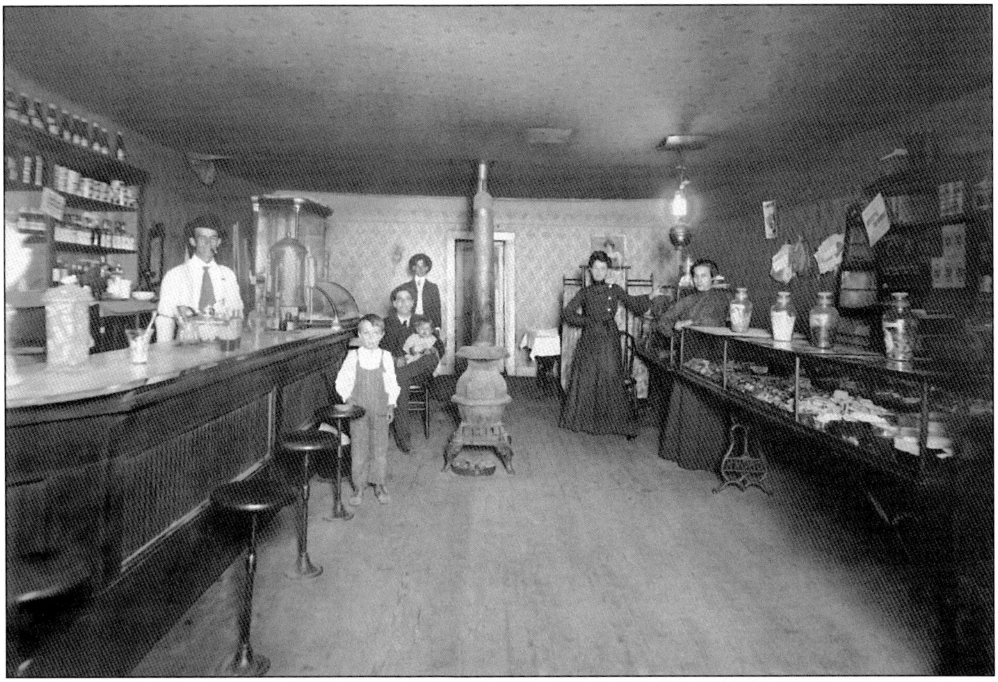

Pictured in the interior of C.E. Herald's store are Mr. Herald (far left), his young sons Howard (in overalls) and Everett (sitting on man's lap), and his wife, Maude (far right). (Courtesy of Bob Herald.)

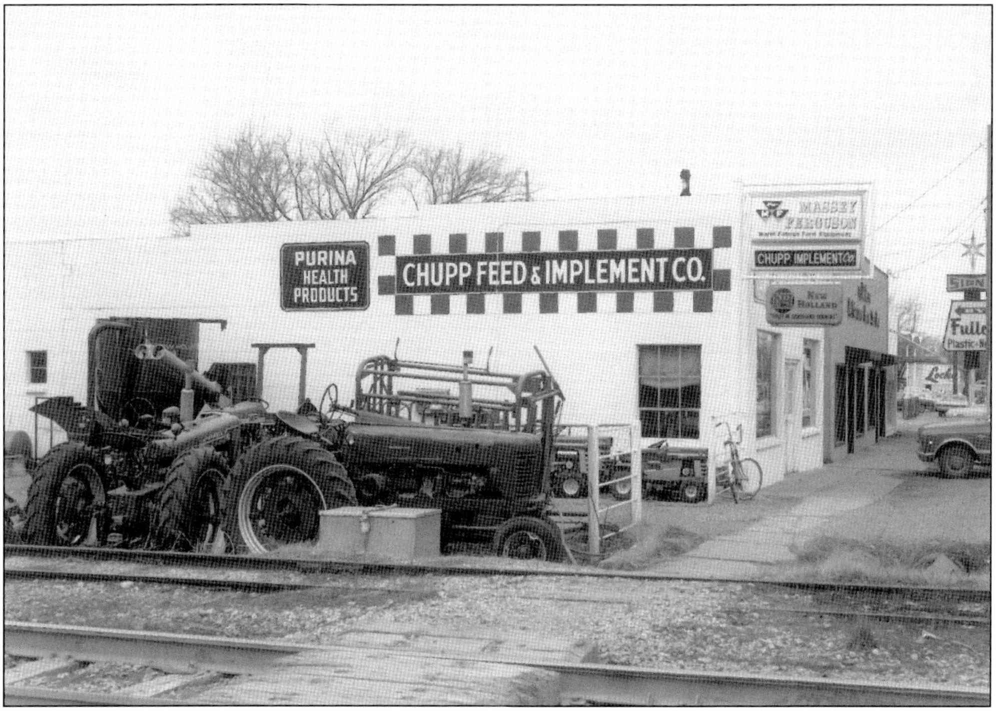

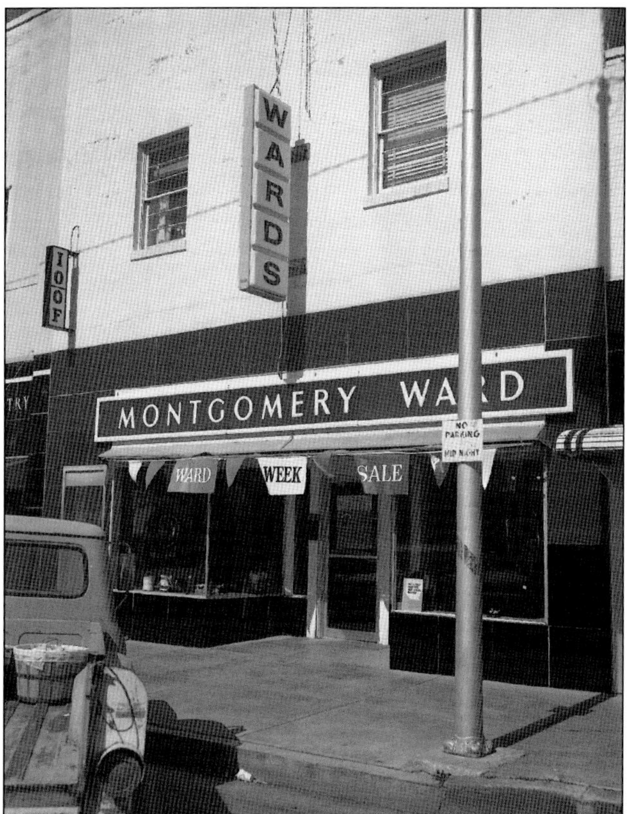

Shown here about 1978, Chupp Feed & Implement store on West Graham Avenue was established by Bill Chupp. It has long been a supplier to the county's vast agriculture industry. Now selling only farm machinery in a modern location on highway frontage south of town, the firm is one of the leading tractor dealerships in the region.

The Montgomery Ward store is shown here in October 1963. In the late 1970s, the store moved to a larger location on South Elliot Street and added an automotive service department. The store was managed by Margie Ogilvie.

Two

Whitaker State Home

The Whitaker State Home was founded by W.T. Whitaker in 1897 as a place for orphaned white children in the Cherokee Nation, Indian Territory. Even though the Cherokee Nation maintained schools and orphan asylums of its own, no such institution existed for orphaned white children.

W.T. Whitaker, a Cherokee citizen himself, recognized that need and, in 1897, established the Whitaker Orphan's Home, located on the southeast edge of Pryor Creek. W.T., his wife, and 11 of their own children received those children in need into their home. The orphanage was supported by donations and a working farm.

Following a disastrous fire in November 1903 that destroyed the Cherokee Orphans Asylum at Salina, Whitaker offered to take in the residents of that facility until the Cherokee government could make other arrangements. Many of the children remained at Whitaker until they could be adopted.

Oklahoma attained statehood on November 17, 1907. During the first session of the Oklahoma legislature, a bill establishing the Whitaker State Orphan's Home as a state institution was passed into law by Gov. Charles N. Haskell. W.T. Whitaker was named the first superintendent of the home at an annual salary of $1,000. He oversaw about 69 children. A $39,300 budget was approved to hire staff, and a plan was made for improvements to buildings and infrastructure.

By 1911, the main campus consisted of 40 acres and a 320-acre farm with 14 buildings housing 287 children and 25 staff and teachers. By 1943, the number of children approached 350. Then, two years later, the campus school was put under the control of Pryor Public Schools.

By 1950, a $43,000 dairy barn was constructed to maintain a modern milking facility, accommodating over 120 Holstein dairy cows. In addition, a $50,000 swimming pool was constructed in 1954.

For over 30 years, Whitaker State Children's Home produced outstanding boxing and basketball programs as well as top-producing livestock programs. In 1962, the state altered the main mission, from care of orphaned and neglected children to that of juvenile-delinquent supervision. The Whitaker campus was integrated in 1969 and closed in 1983. Then, a year later, it was transferred to the Oklahoma Military Department. The campus is now an Oklahoma Army National Guard Base, with the Thunderbird Youth Academy as the main tenant.

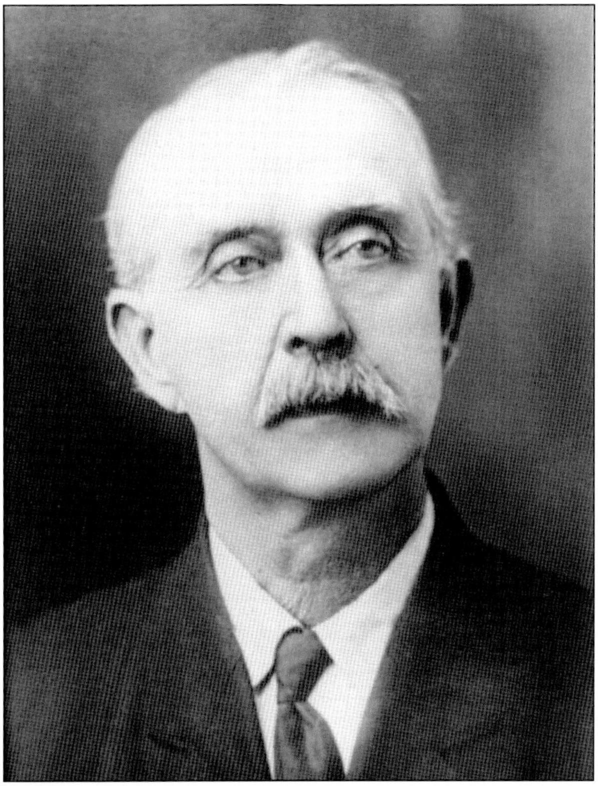

W.T. Whitaker (1854–1922) was the founder of Whitaker Orphan's Home, established in 1897 for orphaned white children in the Indian Territory. A native Cherokee from North Carolina, he settled at Chouteau and ran a mercantile store. In 1887, he moved his family to Pryor Creek, where he built the first school and church. Shortly after Oklahoma attained statehood, Whitaker's orphanage was made a state institution, with Whitaker remaining as superintendent until 1909, when he retired from the home. In 1909 he established Whitaker Park, which is now the main city park in Pryor Creek. With one of his sons, he developed and built residential divisions in the southeast part of town. Whitaker died in 1922 and is buried in Fairview Cemetery.

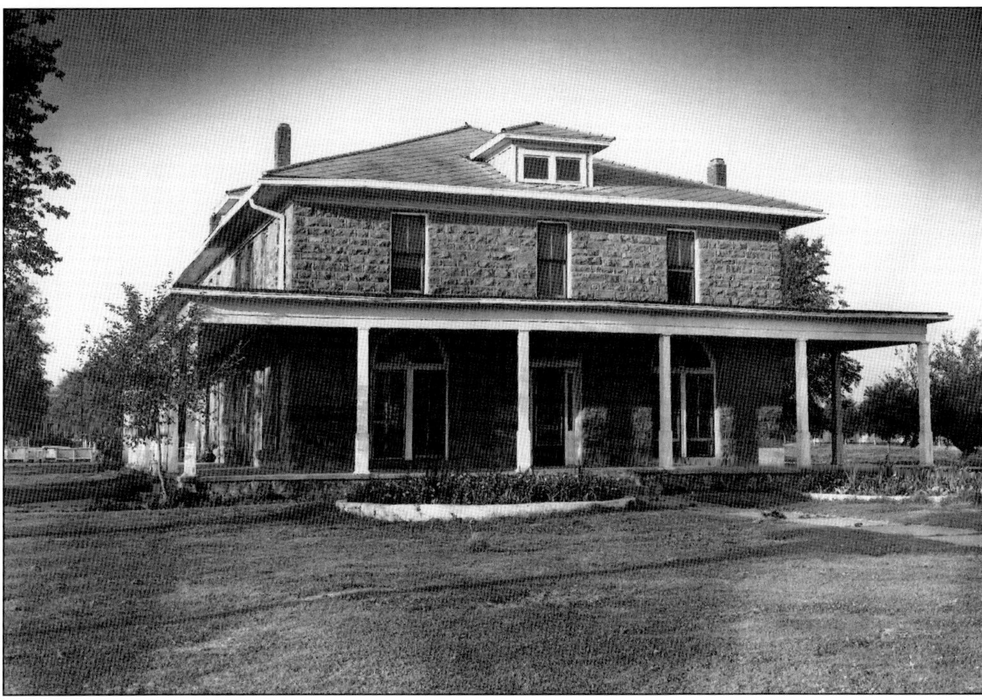

Whitaker Hall is one of the few remaining original structures of the orphanage. It is now the headquarters building for the Oklahoma National Guard base that calls the campus home.

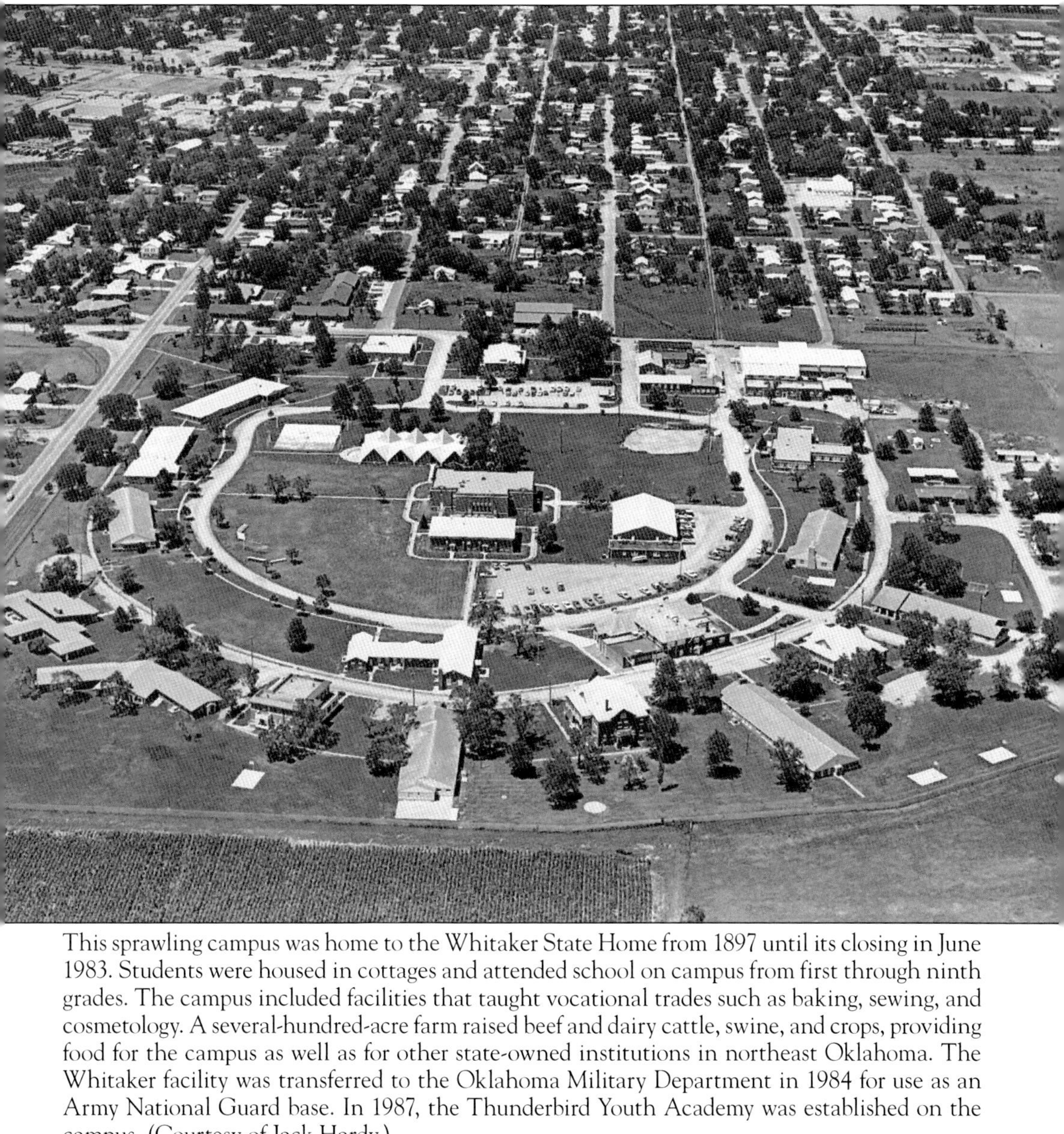

This sprawling campus was home to the Whitaker State Home from 1897 until its closing in June 1983. Students were housed in cottages and attended school on campus from first through ninth grades. The campus included facilities that taught vocational trades such as baking, sewing, and cosmetology. A several-hundred-acre farm raised beef and dairy cattle, swine, and crops, providing food for the campus as well as for other state-owned institutions in northeast Oklahoma. The Whitaker facility was transferred to the Oklahoma Military Department in 1984 for use as an Army National Guard base. In 1987, the Thunderbird Youth Academy was established on the campus. (Courtesy of Jack Hardy.)

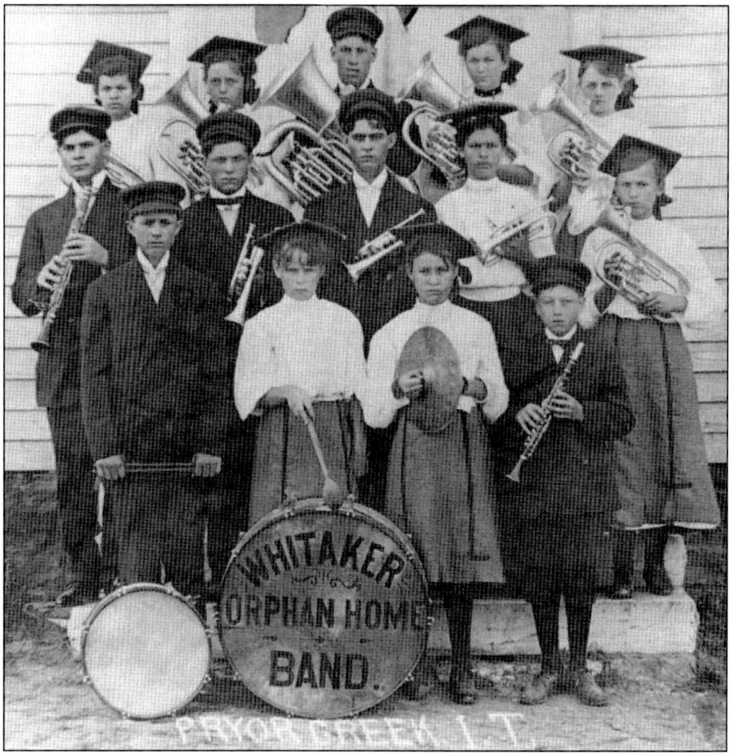

The Whitaker Orphan Home Band is shown here in July 1907. The members are, from left to right, (first row) Walter Hill, Palvina Heath, Irena Heath, and Claude Whitaker; (second row) Bennie Karr, Burton Osborn, Denton Miller, Martha Goins, and Annie Lukasavage; (third row) Stella Goins, Maybelle Greenwood, Mike Proctor, Bessie Locke, and Minnie Hill.

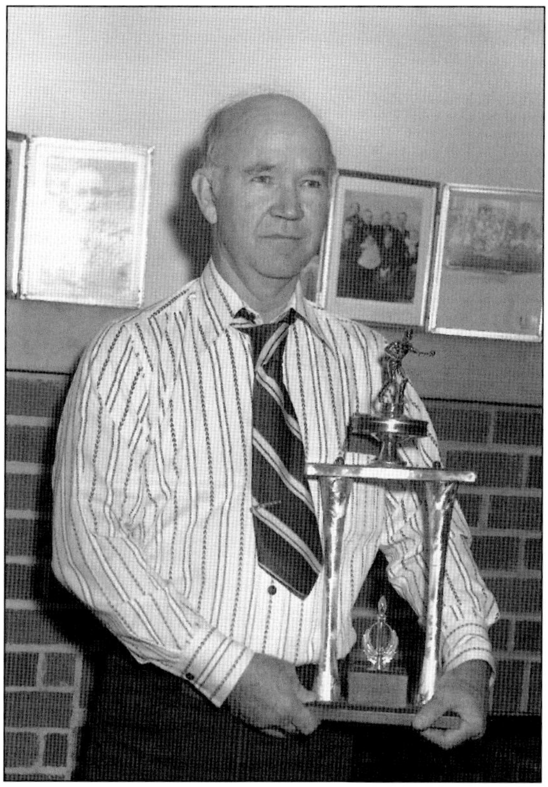

Melvin "Pop" Wilson (1915–2008) was the assistant administrative superintendent at Whitaker State Home. In addition, he was the boxing coach, mentoring many young men both in and out of the ring.

The Whitaker School, completed in 1921, was put under the control of the Pryor Public School system around 1945. The school accommodated children from kindergarten through ninth grade. Students entering high school attended Pryor High School. For the last 20 years of the school, principals included Wilber Monson, Nelson Devers, and Jerry Haynes.

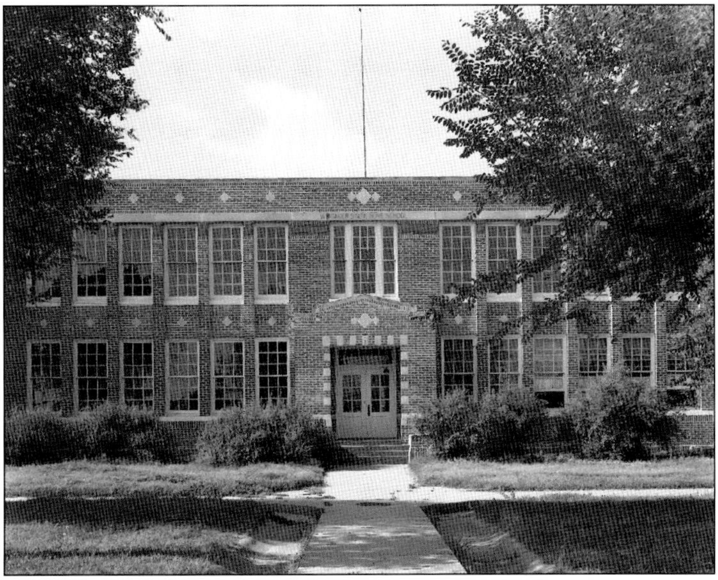

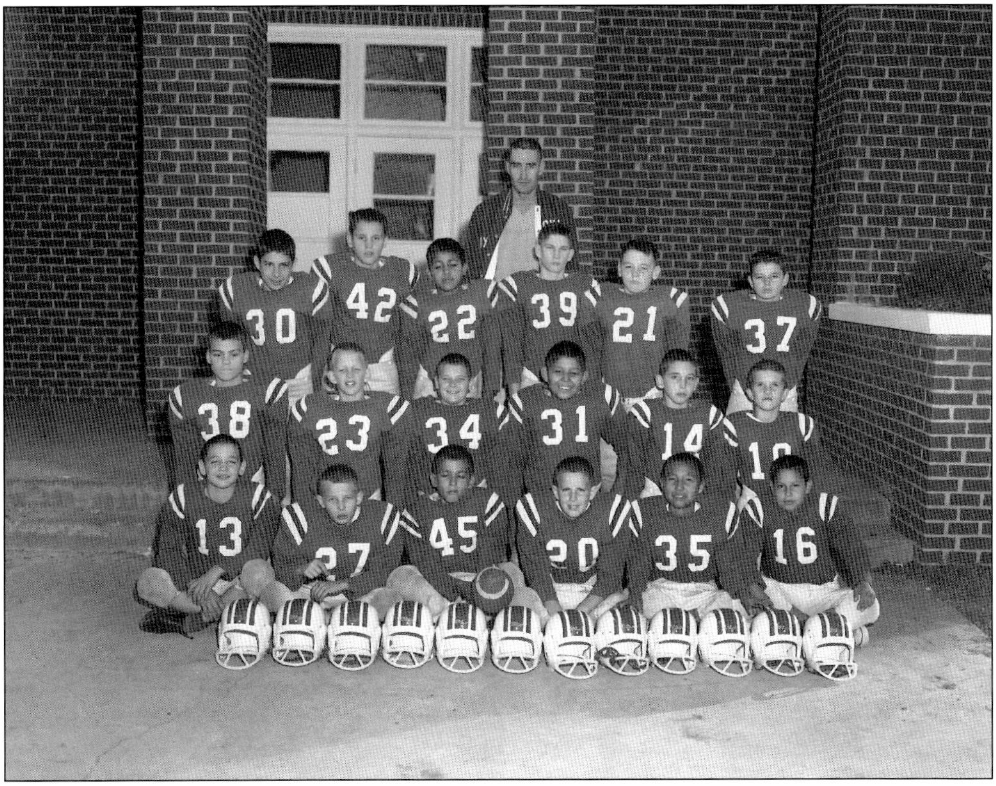

The Whitaker State Home peewee football team won the 1963 city championship after defeating Washington Elementary 44-6. The players shown here are, from left to right, (first row) Larry McDonald, Don Saffell, Herbert Smith, Jimmy Scott, Joe Beaver, and William Patton; (second row) Donald Dunigan, Jimmie James, Arthur Saffell, Amos Beaver, Jimmy Neal, and Leo Miller; (third row) Billy White, Ronnie Roche, Francis Longhat, Roy Clark, Albert McDonald, and Roy Dunigan. Standing in back is coach Bob Sellards.

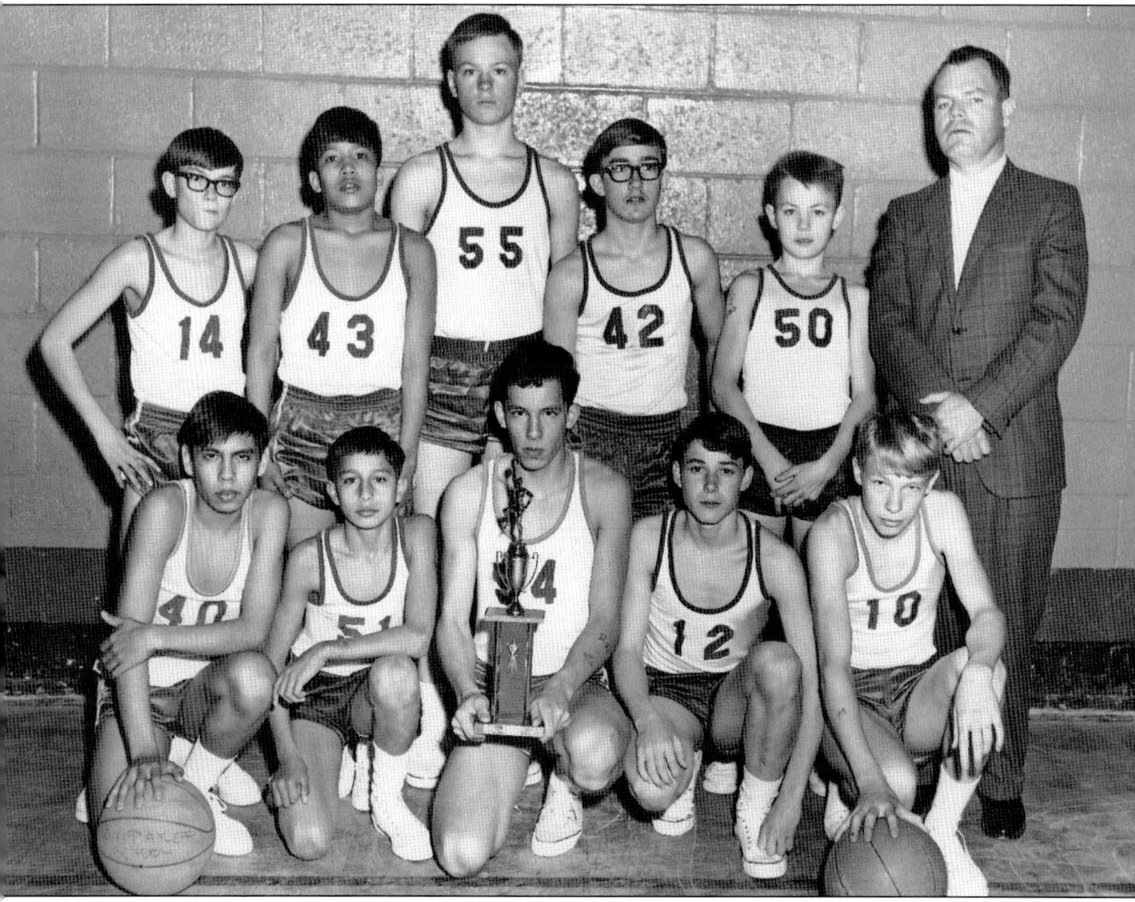

In the late 1960s and early 1970s, Whitaker Junior High School produced championship basketball teams under the leadership of Bob Lancaster and Nelson Devers. This photograph, taken in March 1969, shows a team that had just completed the season in second place in the Seneca Indian School tournament. The team members are, from left to right, (first row) Gary Pohleman, Ronny Rodriguez, Robert Deere, Hal O'Connor, and Oran Cook; (second row) Don Owens, Al Kionute, Coy Brown, David Dale, and Cletus Berry. Standing at right is coach Nelson Devers. Robert Deere, now of the Okmulgee, Oklahoma, area, was probably one of the best junior high basketball players ever coached by Devers. Devers, who also served as principal of the Whitaker School, was a great mentor and role model to hundreds of Whitaker students and residents. He made such a tremendous impact on so many that he is still held in high esteem by those whose lives he touched.

Three

Schools

The modern Pryor Public School system was organized on August 7, 1902, with the first term starting in October for the 1902–1903 school year. A modern high school building opened in the spring of 1909, following the passage of a $25,000 bond issue.

The high school was officially accredited in May 1910; the first high school graduate was Mamie Hatcher, in 1912. In 1915, a new high school building was erected, and the original structure became the grade school. A new high school building was constructed in 1921 on Graham Avenue between Coo-Yah and Hogan Street. This school would last 21 years, until it was heavily damaged in the 1942 tornado. A new high school built on South Hogan Street was destroyed by fire on January 12, 1969. The present high school was opened in 1971. In 1937, a new Central Grade School was constructed across the street from the high school. This school existed until 1962, when it was converted to the junior high school. It served in that capacity until the middle of the 1976–1977 school year, when it was replaced with a new junior high building.

In the early 1950s, voters passed bond issues by very large margins to construct Washington, Roosevelt, and Jefferson Elementary Schools. Lincoln Elementary School opened in 1968. Washington Elementary was closed in May 2011.

Pryor school athletic teams have won state championships in boys' and girls' cross-country, softball, girls' soccer, basketball, and track, as well as boys' golf. School teams have been state runners-up in baseball, football, girls' and boys' basketball, girls' track, and cross-country.

The first exchange student to attend Pryor High School was Giorgio Zucchi, of Regio Emilia, Italy, during the 1961–1962 school year.

Dr. Larry G. Burdick, superintendent of schools from 1968 to 2008, was responsible for much of the success of the school district in terms of growth, infrastructure, and fiscal responsibility. He was followed by Don Raleigh, who, in his seven-year tenure, has been responsible for millions of dollars in construction of new facilities, improvements, and additional growth.

Current school board members include Fred Sordahl, Paul Melchior, Wes Miller, Dean Robertson, and Raymond Greninger.

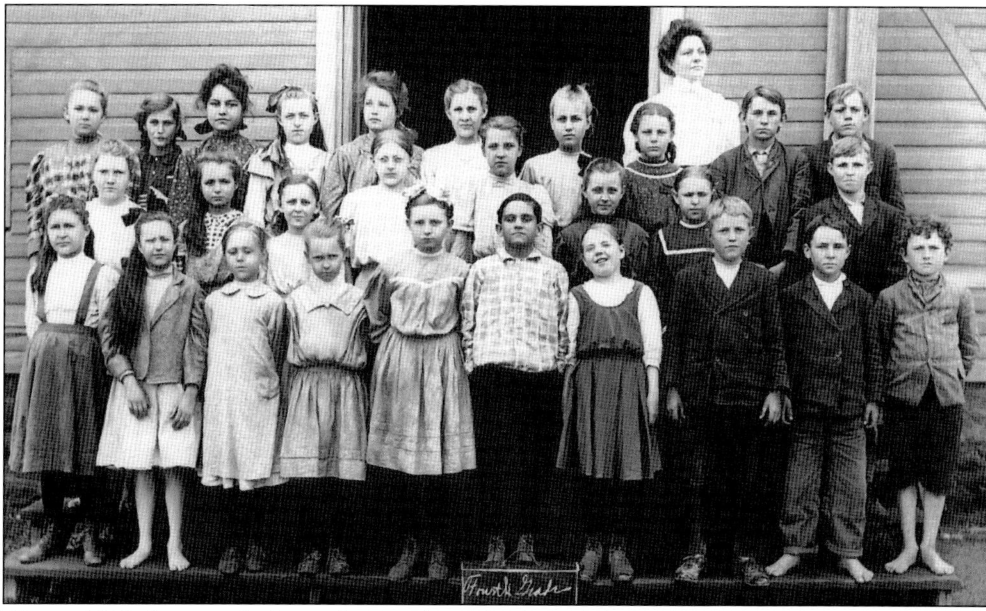

This c. 1908 photograph shows the fourth-grade class of the Pryor Creek Public School. Welch Harrison is in the first row, second from right. The present public school district was organized on August 7, 1902; classes started two months later. Serving on the first school board were J. Howard Langley, P.W. Samuel, Dr. W.T. Tilly, L.C. Harrison, John B. Choate, and W.B. Chapman. (Courtesy of Robbie Taylor.)

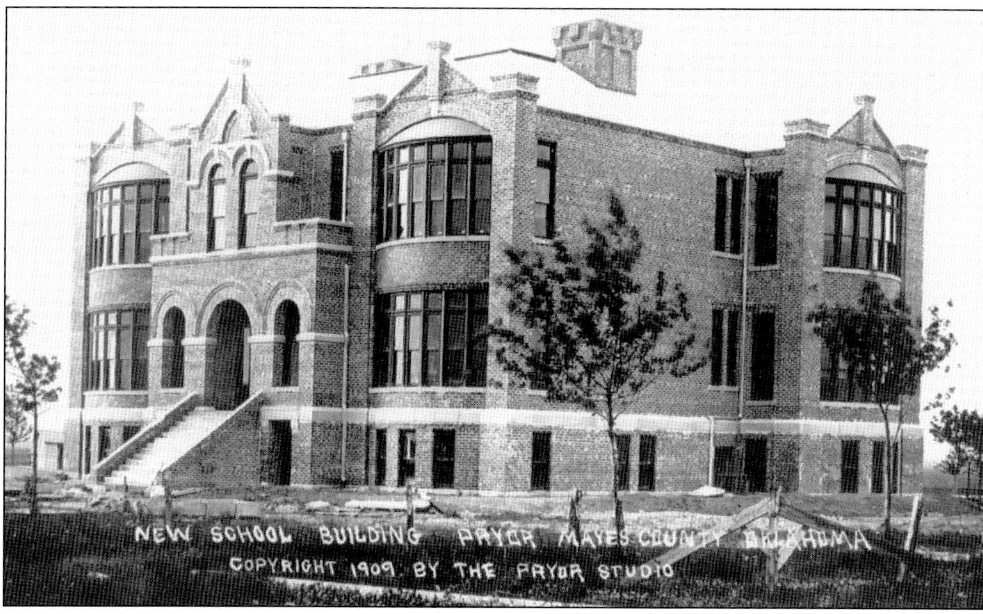

This beautiful school building was constructed with funds from a $25,000 bond election passed in August 1908. The contracted lowest bidder erected the building for $20,498, and it opened in the spring of 1909. Pryor High School was officially established and accredited in 1910. This meant that future graduates could be accepted to state institutions of higher learning. The first high school graduating class was in 1912, and it comprised one student, Mamie Hatcher. After the construction of a new high school building in 1915, this became the grade-school facility.

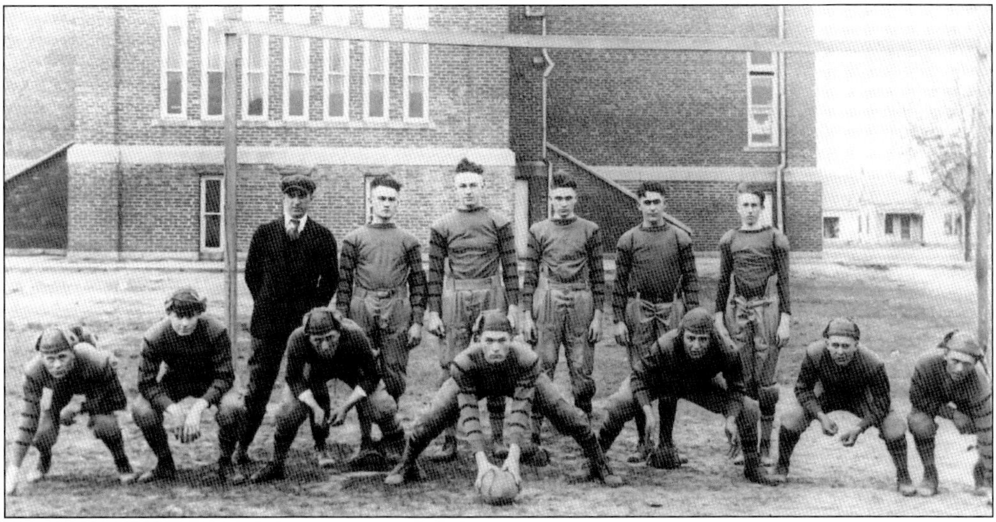

Members of the first Pryor High School football team, in 1917, pose for a photograph. From left to right are (first row) Leon Lary, Hugh Stites, John Duffield, Joe Miller, O.D. Mayor, Dewey Moore, and Jess Mayes; (second row) coach Harry Faulkner, John Hogan, Gordon Bristow, Carr Gatewood, Chick Livingston, and Ross Humphrey. Team members not pictured are Karl Hogan, Ross Young, Carl Langley, and Everett Miller. The 1917 Tigers went 3-2 under Coach Faulkner.

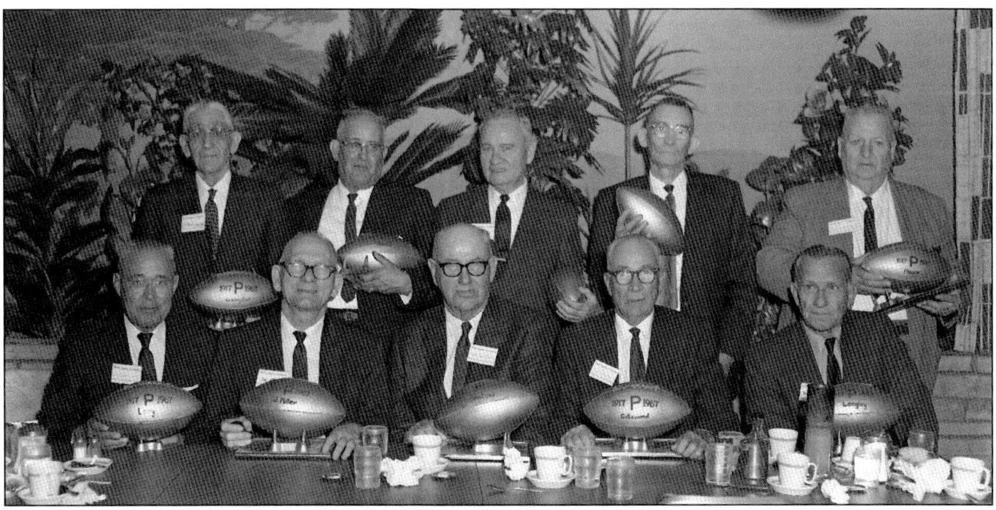

In October 1967, ten members of Pryor's first football team attended a 50th reunion, held in conjunction with the homecoming game at Tiger Stadium. Before the game, a reception sponsored by the Quarterback Booster Club was held at the Park Lodge Motel, followed by a steak dinner at Thomas Restaurant, where each honoree was presented with a golden football. At the ball game, Gordon Bristow, captain of the 1917 team, walked onto the field with current team co-captains for the coin toss. Pictured here are, from left to right, (seated) Leon Lary, Joe Miller, Gordon Bristow, Carr Gatewood, and Carl Langley; (standing) Chick Livingston, Dewy Moore, John Hogan, Everett Miller, and O.D. Mayor.

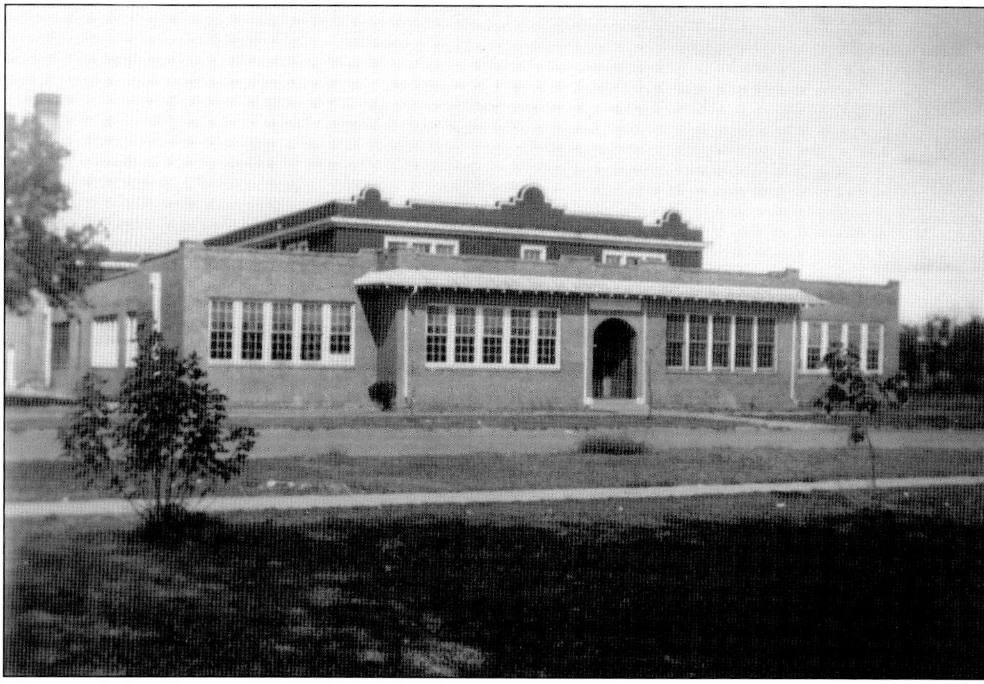

This stately building was Pryor High School from 1921 to 1942. It was erected by V.O. McCormick Construction Company. The design was controversial, as many people thought the one-story building would not be as "impressive" as a two- or three-story school. The school consisted of 14 classrooms, an auditorium, music room, superintendent's office, library, and gymnasium.

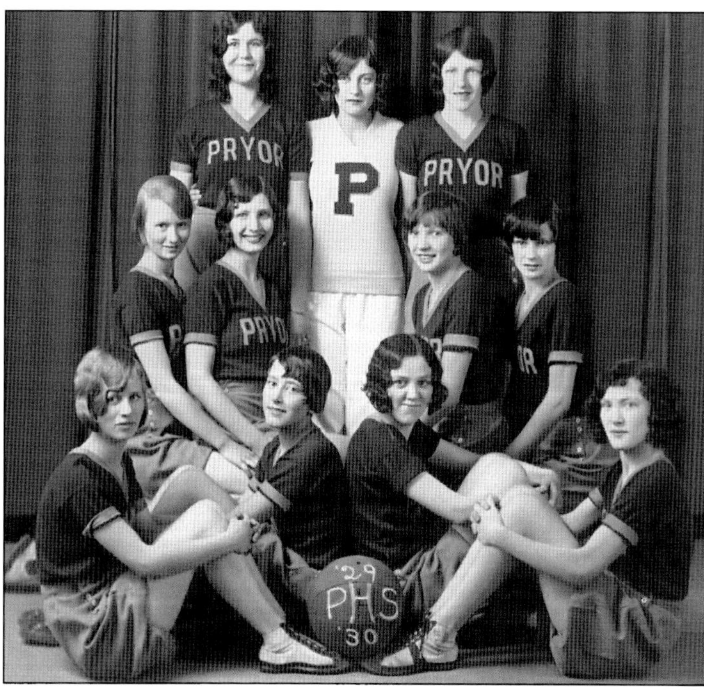

The 1930 Pryor High School girls' basketball team poses for a photograph. From left to right are (first row) Ruth Robbins, Beuna Harris, Edith Crabtree, and Mavis Crabtree; (second row) Opal Robbins, Toka Lee Fields, Beula Schultz, and Ina Morgan; (third row) Mabel Webb, coach Ruby Conklin, and Clara Whisnant. The team was unbeaten that year, won two tournaments, and defeated Chouteau 24-19 for the district title. (Courtesy of Jean Davis.)

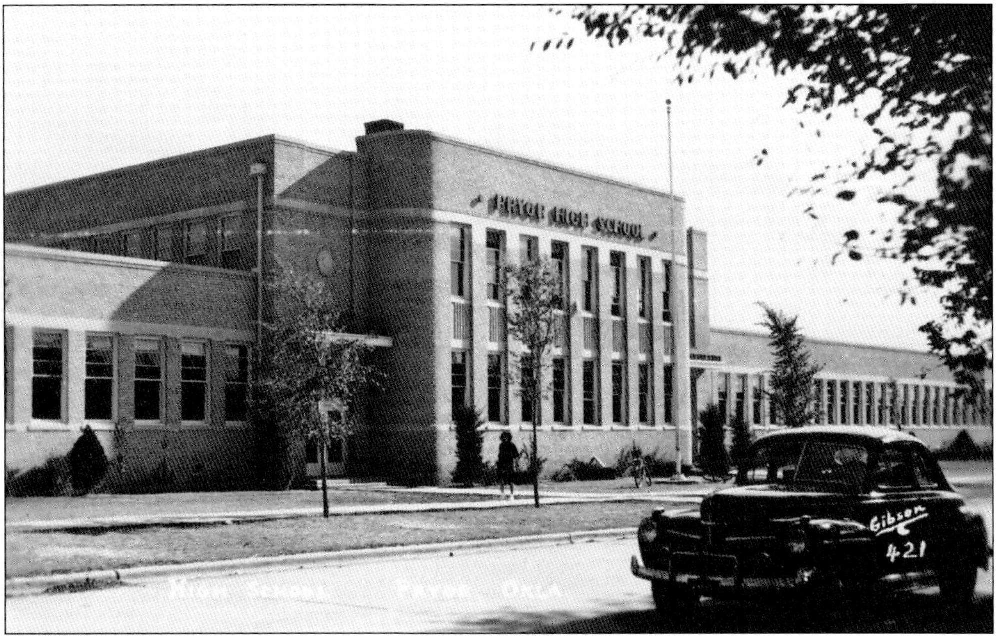

This high school building was completed in 1943, after the 1921 school was heavily damaged in the 1942 tornado. The $176,000, 24-room structure was built by Southwest Builders of Austin, Texas, and accommodated the senior high and junior high students. The building was destroyed by fire on January 12, 1969.

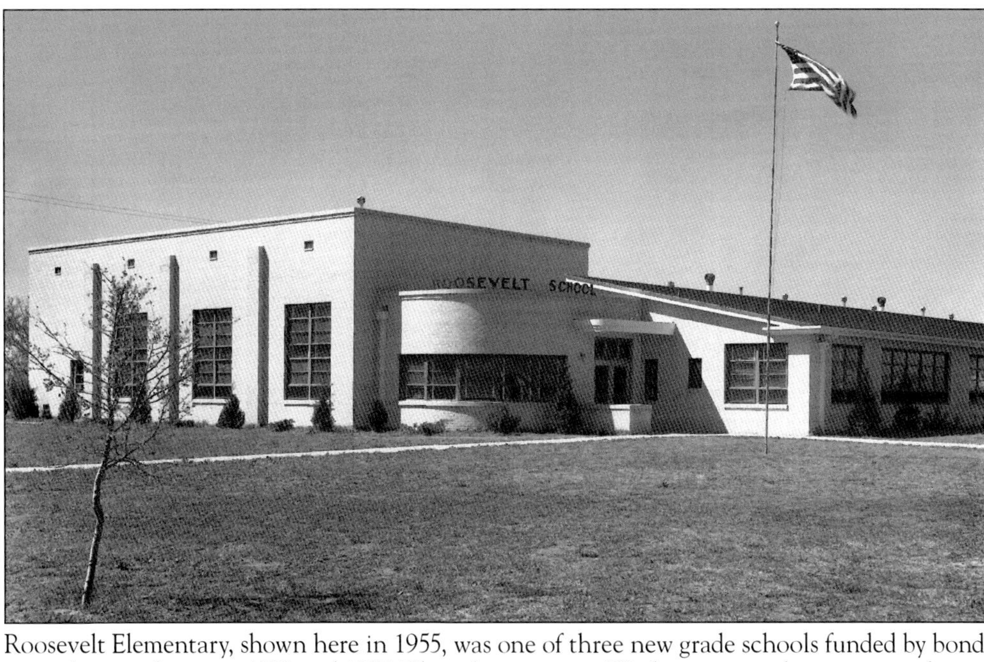

Roosevelt Elementary, shown here in 1955, was one of three new grade schools funded by bond-issue elections between 1953 and 1955. The other two were Washington, in the west part of town, and Jefferson, on the south side. This brought the total number of grade schools to four, with the old Central grade school located downtown.

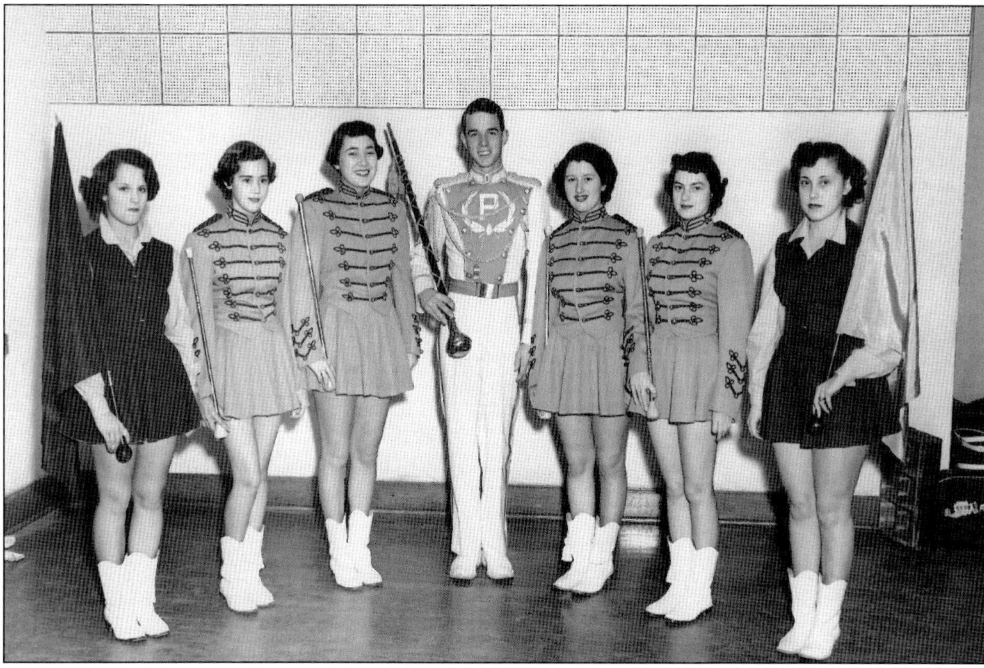

In the 1953–1954 school year, the Pryor High School drum major was Richard Wright. Here, he is flanked by his flag and twirler staff. From left to right are Rosetta Jones, Joyce Wiley, Ernestine Burchett, Wright, Lydia Hawkins, Jean Clayton, and Jean Proctor. (Courtesy of Jean Davis.)

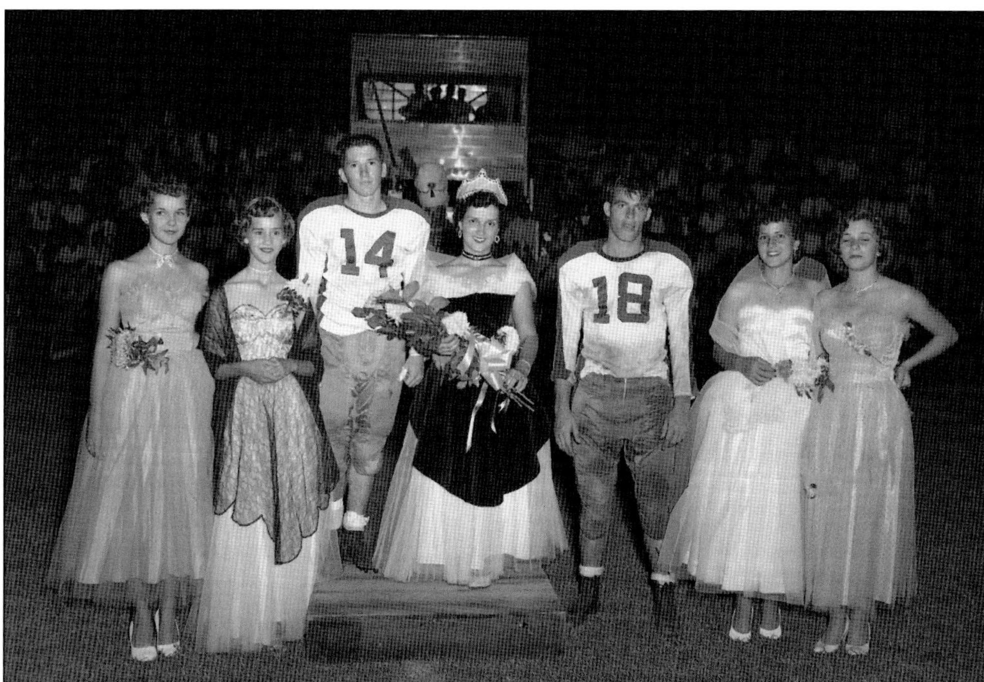

The 1953 football homecoming queen and royalty included, from left to right, Pat Trout, Joyce Wiley, Bob Lanham, Queen Sandra Long, Bert Bowling, Margie James, and Betty Jo Cox.

Pryor cheerleaders for 1955 included, from left to right, (first row) Janette Cloninger, Betsy Gaither, and Peggy Hammer; (second row) Mary Carter, Sherrie Garrison, and Nita Cloninger.

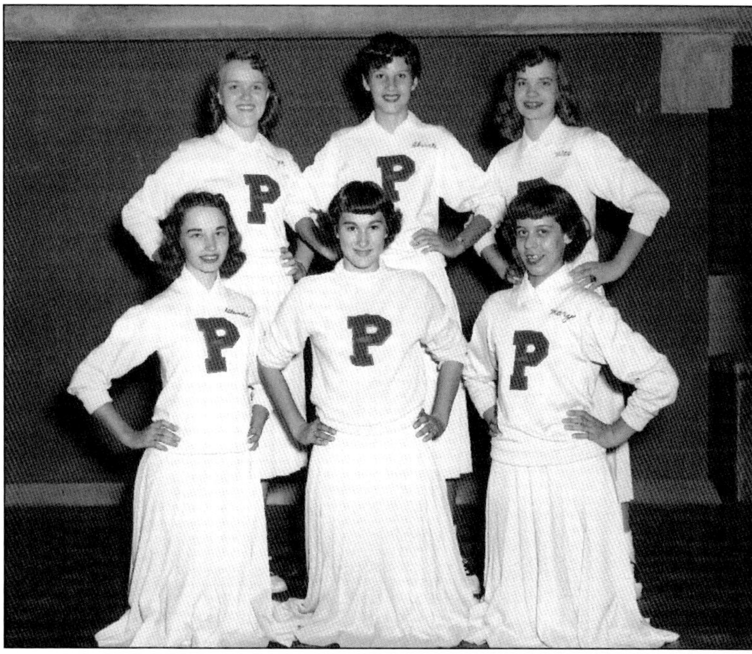

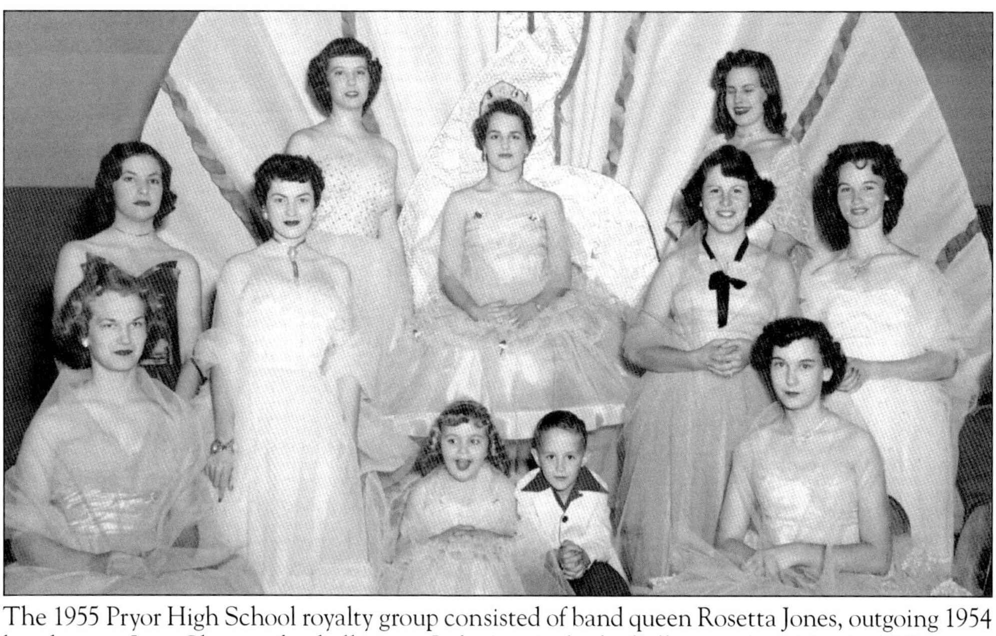

The 1955 Pryor High School royalty group consisted of band queen Rosetta Jones, outgoing 1954 band queen Jean Clayton, football queen Judy Austin, basketball queen Jerri Martin, FFA queen Peggy Lyons, T&I queen Dorothy Burroughs, annual queen Daisy Clayton, attendants Nancy Sheard and Janie Swan, flower girl Vickie Perkins, and crown bearer Kenny Mustain.

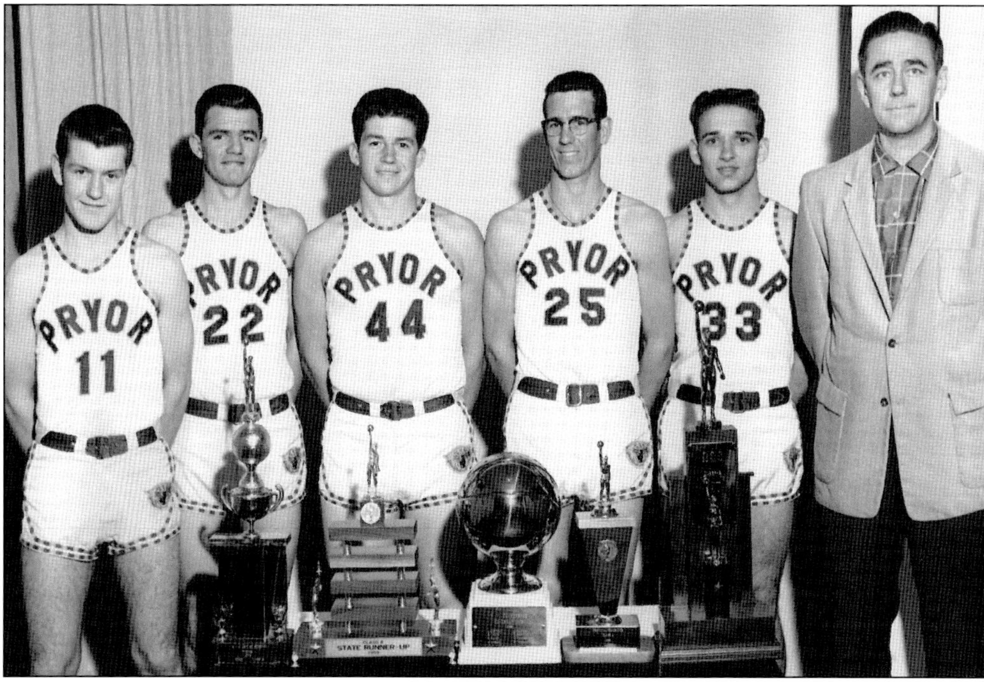

The PHS basketball team defeated Tahlequah 64-51 to become regional champs and advance to the state tournament. After defeating McAlester and Tulsa Webster, the Tigers played Stillwater in the championship game, losing 46-45. Starting team members were, from left to right, Billy George Calvert, Johnny Littlefield, Curt Wheeless, Phillip Bell, and Steve Johnson. The team was coached by Bailey Vanzant (far right). Littlefield was named to the all-state team, and Bell was chosen as an alternate.

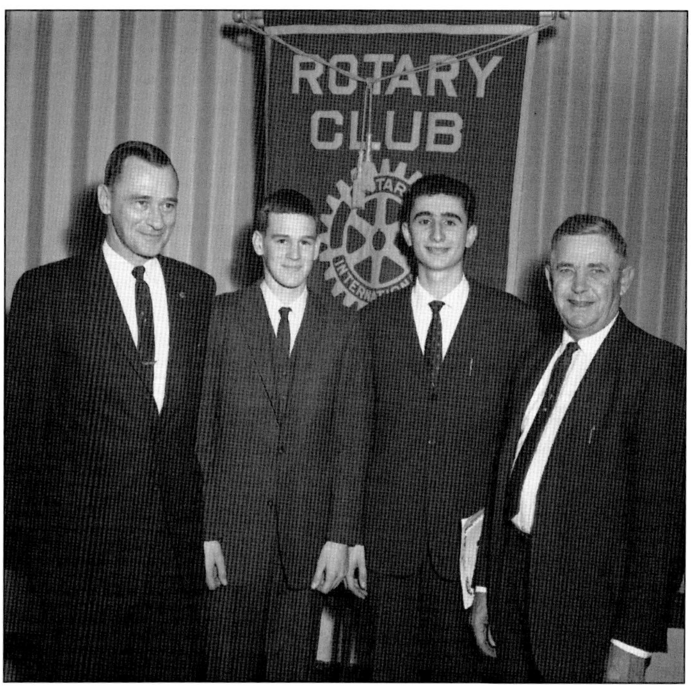

Giorgio Zucchi, of Regio Emilia, Italy, was Pryor High School's first American Field Service (AFS) foreign exchange student. While living in Pryor during the 1961–1962 school year, he was the guest of the Art Costain family. Shown here at a Rotary Club function are, from left to right, Mr. Costain, James Costain, Giorgio Zucchi, and James Vencill, school counselor and sponsor of the AFS program.

Howard Hunsaker (1905–1992) was the longtime principal and coach at Pryor High School before retiring in 1965 to enter the funeral business.

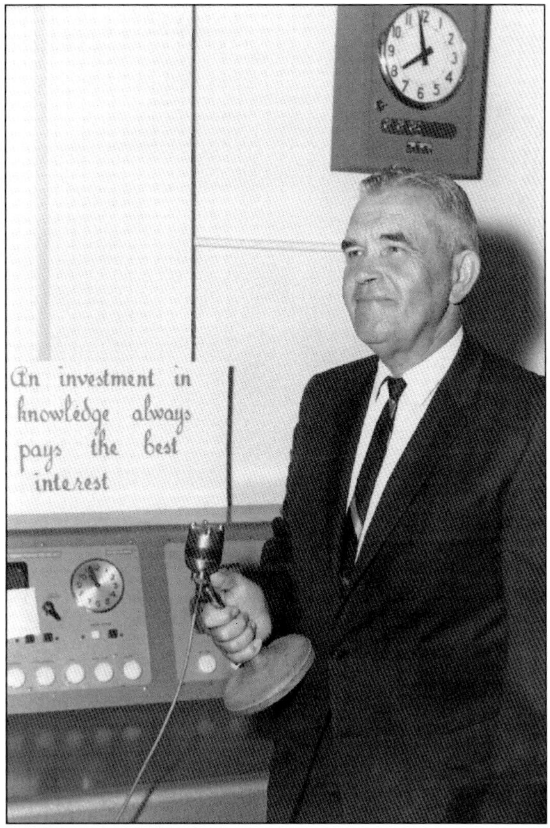

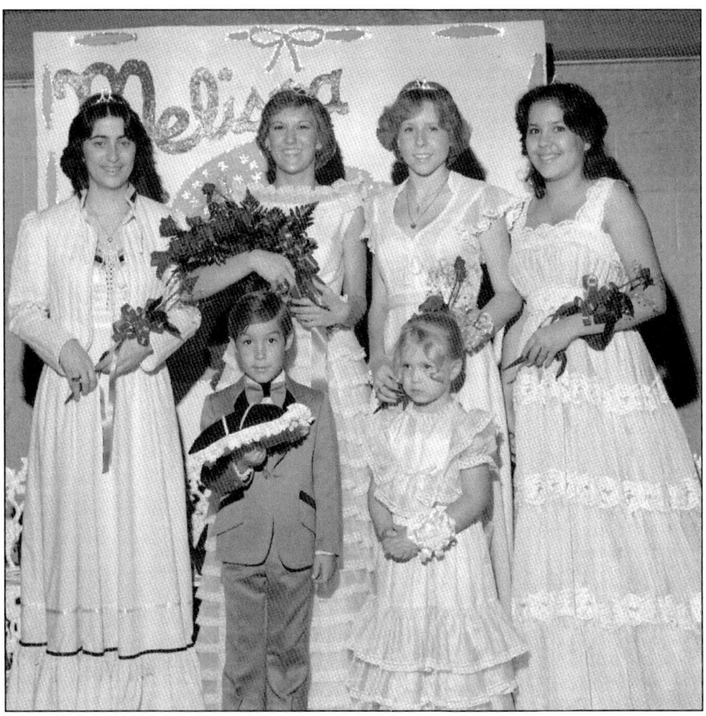

The 1980 basketball queen, Melissa Atkins (second row, second from left), poses with her court. In the second row are, from left to right, Susan McKean, Atkins, Cindy Swank, and Kathryn Martin. The crown bearer and flower girl are unidentified. (Courtesy of Jack Hardy.)

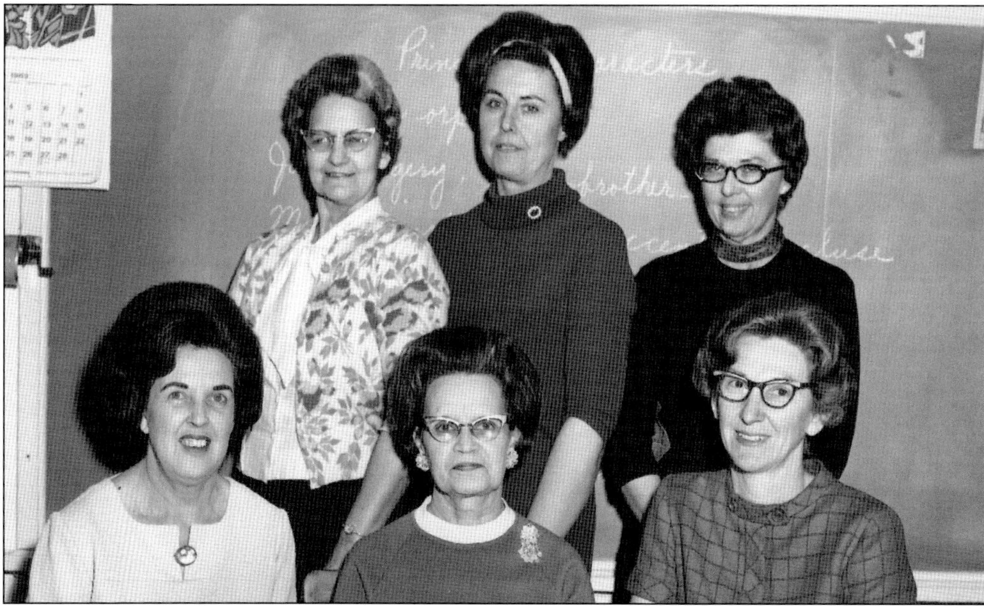

The 1969 officers of the Pryor Classroom Teachers Association pose for a photograph. They are, from left to right, (first row) Neva Goss, Ora Bewley, and Lovis Davenport; (second row) Corrine Horn, Claudine Carver, and Winifred Haddan.

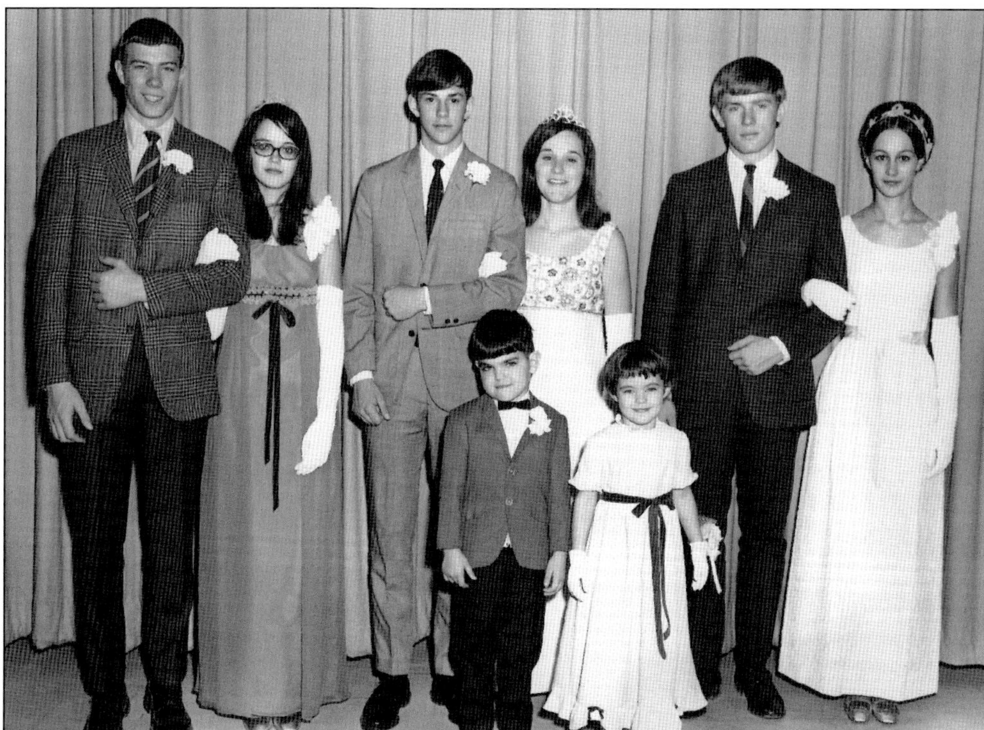

The 1969 Spanish Royalty included, from left to right, (first row) Cash Devers and Kellye Hollis; (second row) Ray Williams, Joni Stafford, Bill Stanford, Susan Prater, Jim Tilly, and Gayla Mayes.

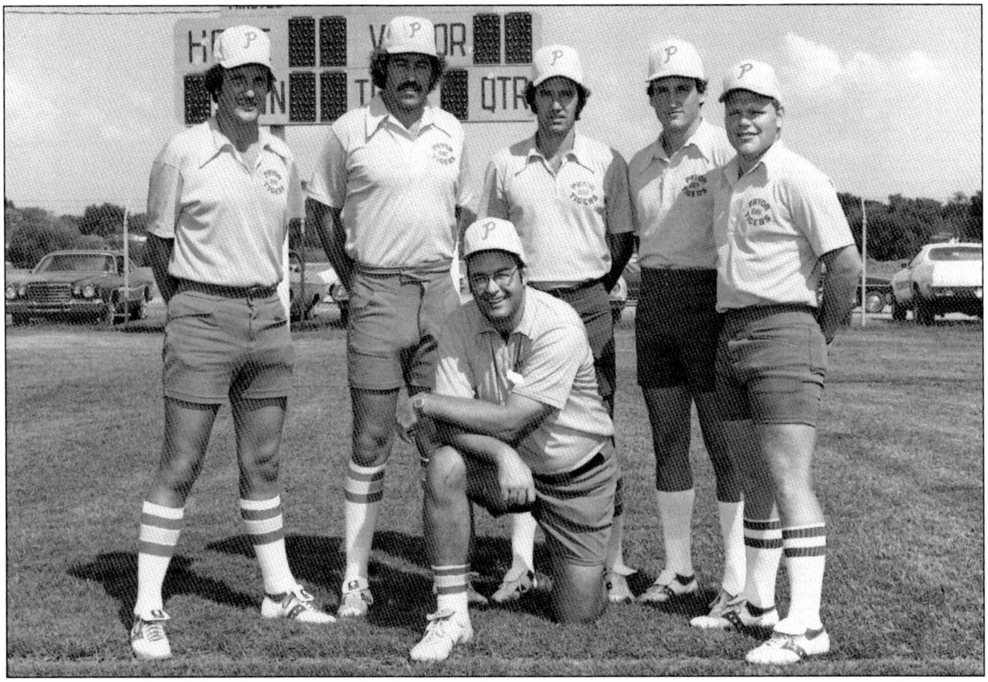

The coaching staff for the 1979 football season gathers for a photograph. From left to right are (kneeling) head coach Bill Defee; (standing) Terry Shrum, Ron Sullivan, Denny Harrell, Bob Walker, and Grant Frankenburg. In his six years at the helm of Tiger football, Defee's record was 38-26.

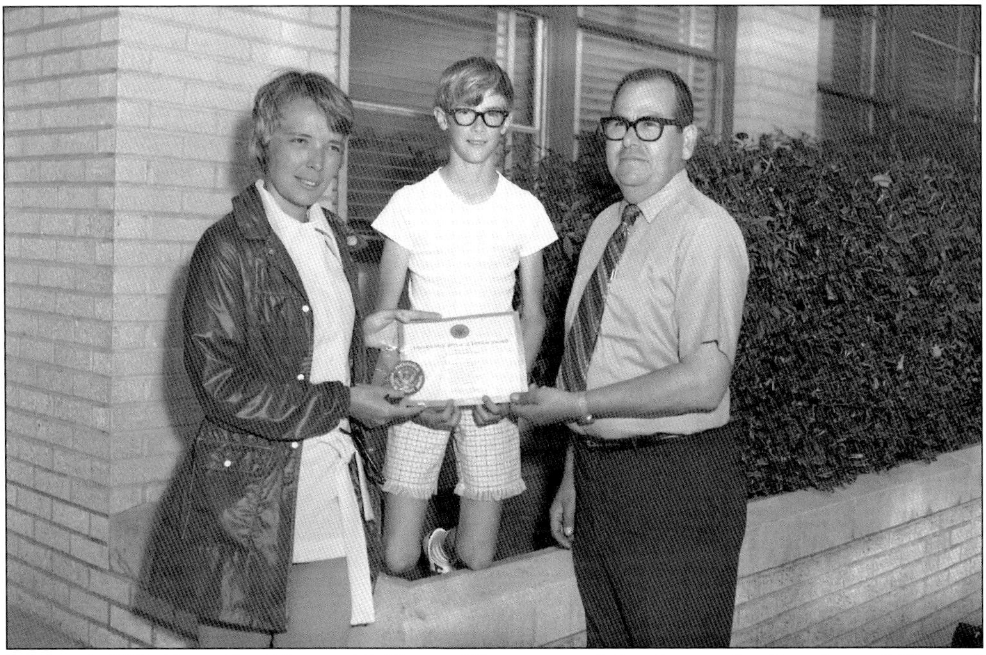

In April 1972, Scott Bradshaw of Jefferson Elementary School won the Presidential Physical Fitness award for the third straight year. Presenting him with the award are physical education teacher Dee Ann Briggs and principal Curtis Barnett.

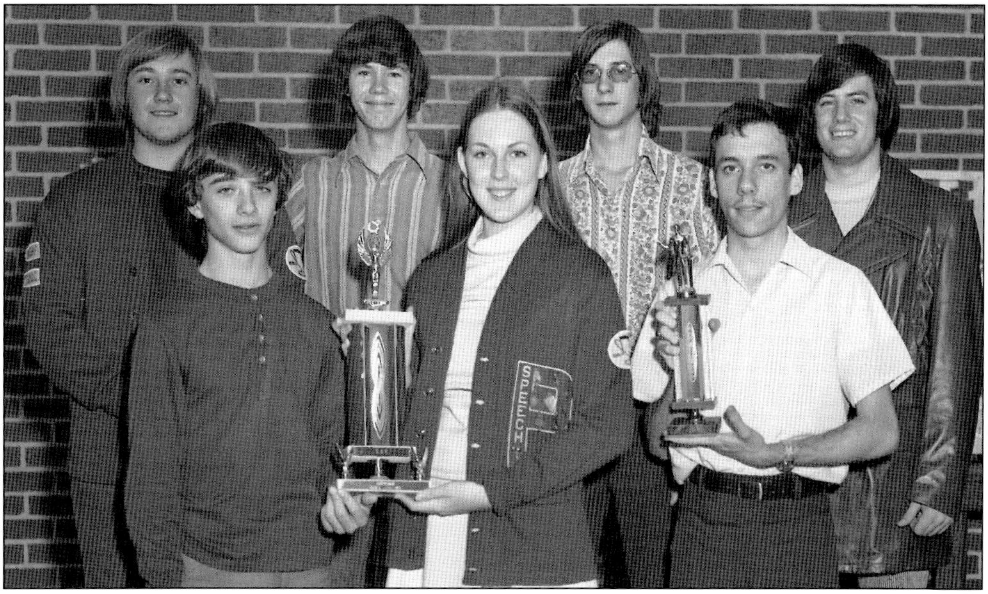

In the late 1960s and early 1970s, Pryor High School's speech department won many speech and debate titles at contests held all over the state. The speech team in the 1971–1972 school year consisted of, from left to right, (first row) Lonnie Thomason, Rita Madole, and Robert Powell; (second row) Jim Stone, Darrell Moore, Chuck Fike, and Mike McCutcheon.

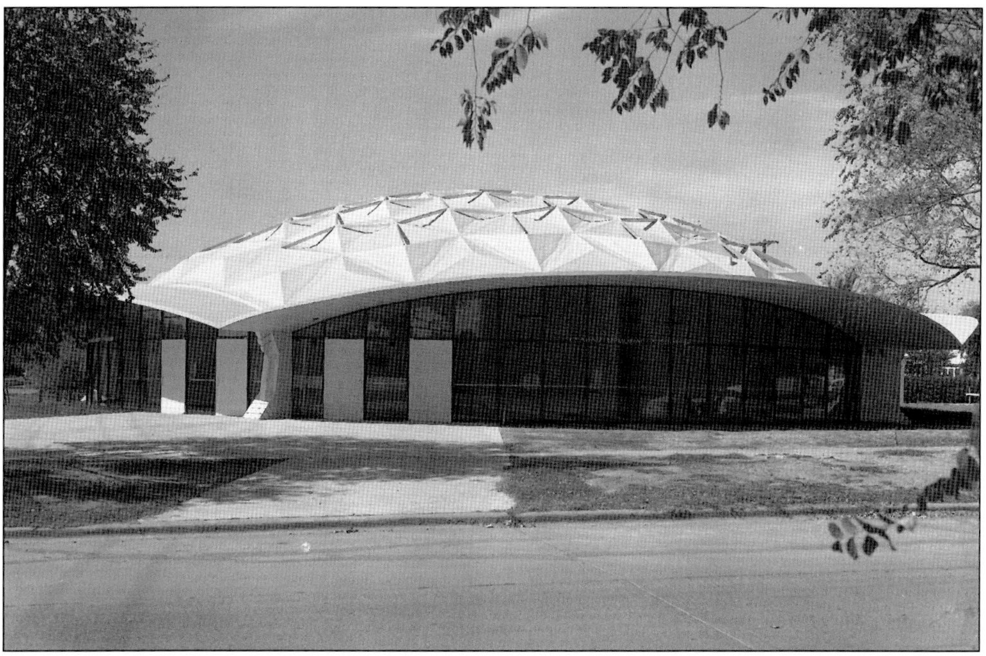

The Graham Memorial Auditorium was dedicated in September 1959 by Oklahoma governor J. Howard Edmondson. Funded by a $214,000 gift from the W.A. Graham estate, the 100-foot-diameter geodesic aluminum dome contained a 10,000-square-foot auditorium with 800 seats. The auditorium was designed by the Oklahoma City architectural firm Bailey, Bozalis, Dickinson & Roloff. In 1984, the facility was condemned and closed due to asbestos contamination. Demolition took place in the summer of 1990.

Four

W.A. Graham

No individual has done more for Pryor Creek and Mayes County than W.A. Graham. While alive, he donated thousands of dollars for library books, streets and sidewalks, buildings, and numerous other pieces of infrastructure for the community.

Graham, a native of Adairsville, Georgia, was born on May 18, 1851, and came to what is now Mayes County, Oklahoma, in 1884. He had $14,000 in his pocket, which he used to enter the cattle business with John C. Hogan, the husband of his cousin. In 1892, he and Hogan entered into partnership in the Hogan Mercantile Company. In 1900, Graham organized the First National Bank of Pryor Creek, Indian Territory.

In 1904, Graham purchased Hogan's interest in the mercantile and changed the name to W.A. Graham Company. His firm dealt in hardware, groceries, dry goods, furniture, grain, and implements. In 1922, he paid to build a new county jail and, in 1938, as a city council member, he paid for construction of a city hall, which was named the Graham Community Building. In 1943, he again came to the help of the town, funding construction of a new city jail.

On his 100th birthday, on May 18, 1951, the city of Pryor held the largest birthday party in its history. A parade was held in Graham's honor, and a party was thrown in the community building that bore his name. Main Street was renamed Graham Avenue, and *Life* magazine came to town, producing a feature titled "The World's Oldest Millionaire Becomes a Centurion."

Graham died on March 28, 1952. In his handwritten will, he bequeathed his estate to the City of Pryor, Mayes County, State of Oklahoma, in addition to specified individuals. Because of the way the will was written, it sparked a legal battle that went on for about five years. In the end, a three-member board of trustees, represented by the city, county, and state, decided how the money was to be spent. As a result, towns throughout Mayes County benefited in the form of utility infrastructure, school improvements, a newly remodeled courthouse, city hall, city-county building, hospital improvements, a new library, a county agriculture facility, and many other items.

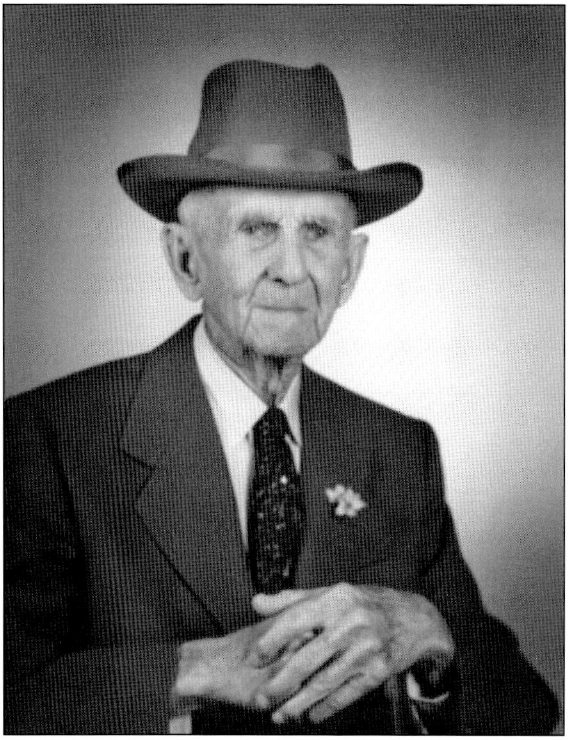

Pryor benefactor W.A. Graham poses for his 100th birthday photograph on May 18, 1951. The banker, businessman, rancher, civic leader, and former mayor bequeathed his multi-million-dollar estate for infrastructure improvements to the city and county that had been his home since 1884.

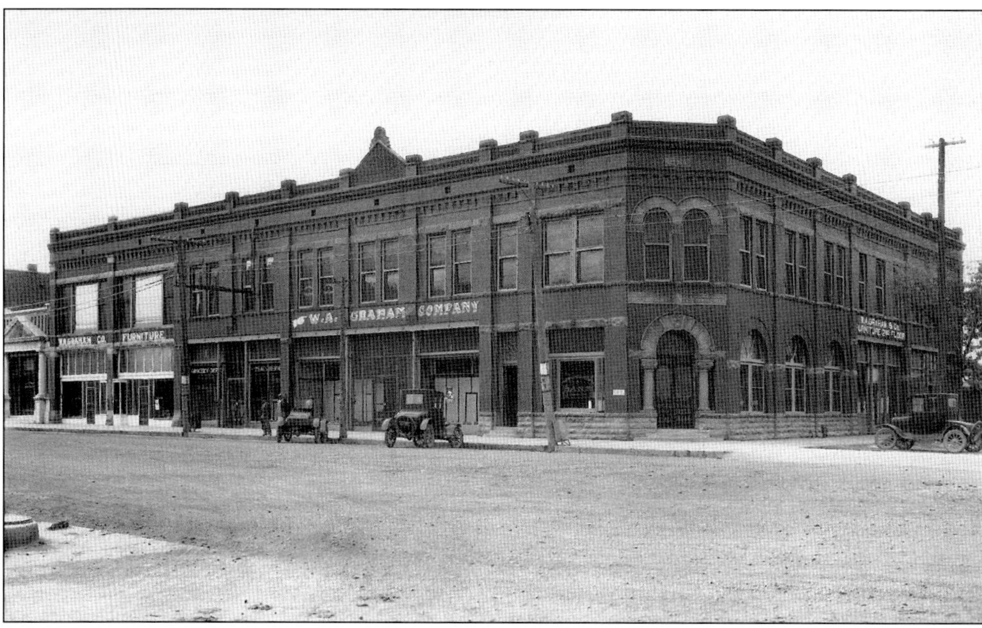

The Hogan Mercantile Company building was constructed in 1900 at what is now the intersection of East Graham Avenue and Mill Street. John C. Hogan and W.A. Graham were partners in the company, which sold dry goods, groceries, hardware, grain, furniture, and implements. The store became the W.A. Graham Company after Graham traded his interest in the cattle business aspect of the partnership for the store in January 1904. The First National Bank was also housed in the building from 1900 to 1957, when a new bank facility was built. (Courtesy of Bill Graham.)

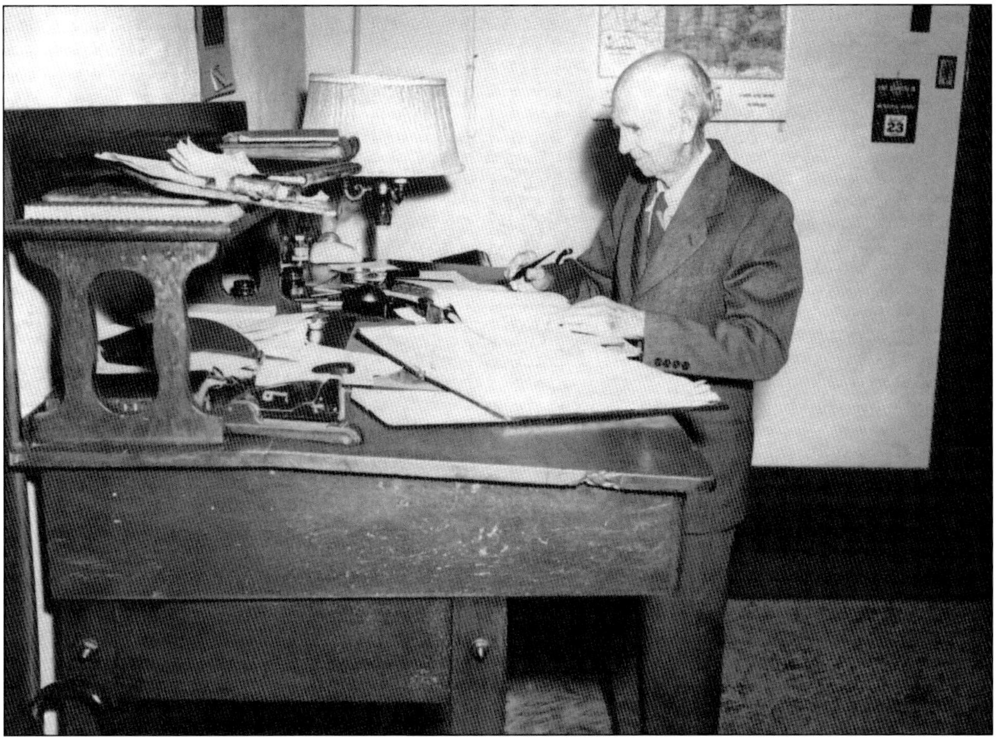

W.A. Graham is shown working at his stand-up desk at the First National Bank on May 15, 1951, just three days before his 100th birthday. Graham's motto was "one man on his feet is worth two on the seat." He was elected mayor in 1913 and served two terms. He also served on the board of directors of banks in Vinita and Eufaula.

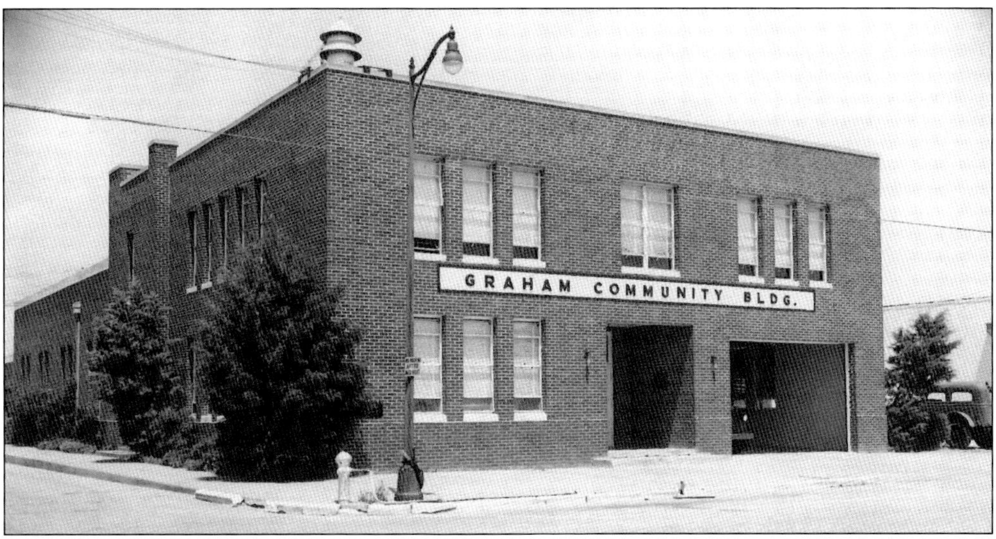

The Graham Community Building was used as Pryor Creek's city hall from 1938 to 2013. The facility, which cost $20,000 and was paid for by W.A. Graham, would house all city offices, a community banquet hall and kitchen, library, and fire station. The city government was located here for 75 years until moving into a multi-million-dollar facility on North Rowe Street in November 2013.

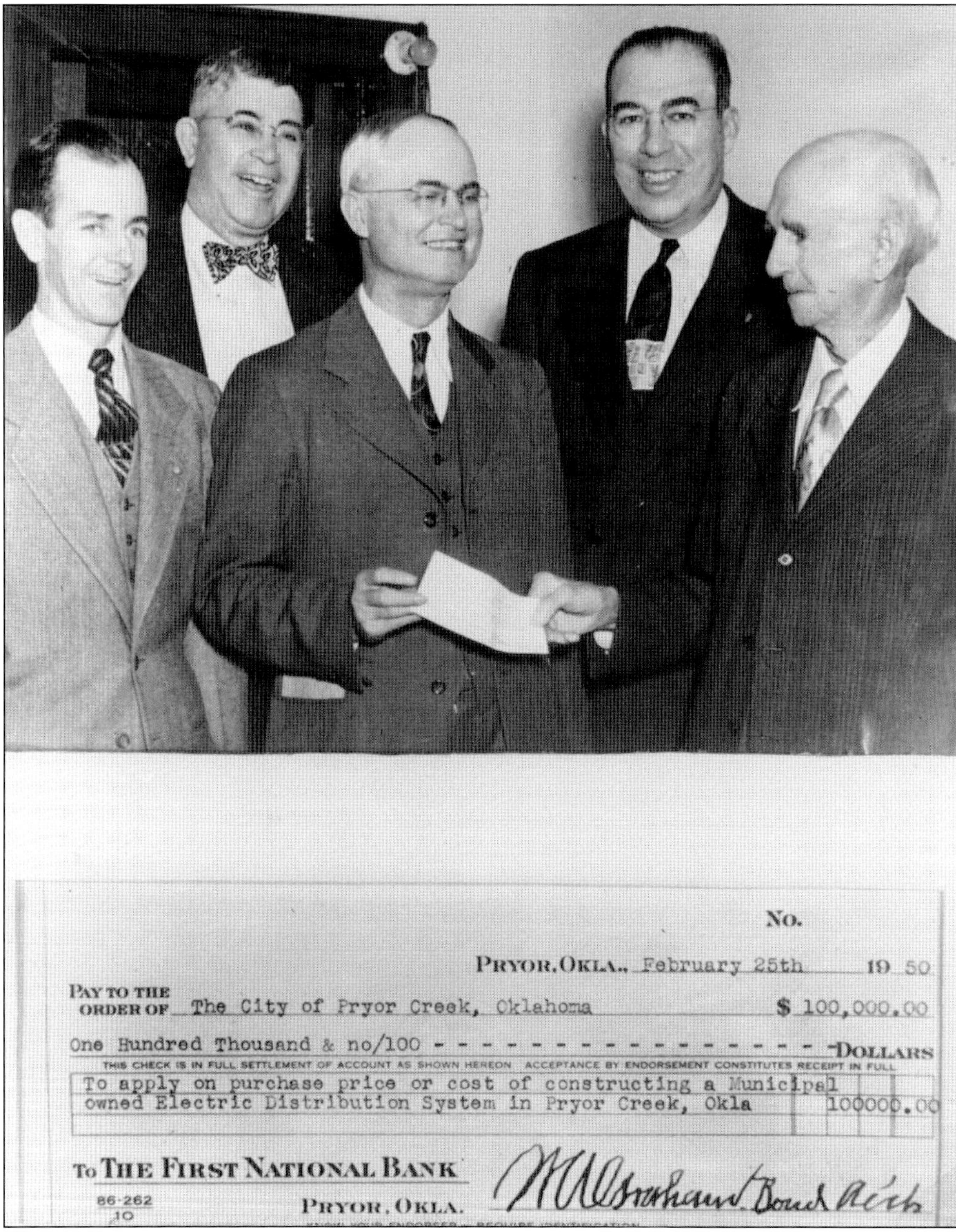

In 1950, Graham saw the need for the city to purchase an electric distribution system from Public Service Company of Oklahoma, an electric utility. He presented the city with a check for $100,000 to apply toward the purchase. After the city passed a bond issue to pay for the remainder, he purchased the bonds and had them burned, thus buying a valuable utility for the town. Here, Graham (far right) presents the check to Mayor Earl Ward (center). Looking on are City Clerk Max Adair (far left), City Attorney Ernest Brown Sr. (second from left), and City Treasurer Jehue Brown.

Five

Recreation

As in every Oklahoma small town, recreation is a vital part of life. Parks, movie theaters, rodeo, hunting, swimming, and Little League baseball are all important recreational activities.

W.T. Whitaker founded what is now the main central park in 1909. Over the past 116 years, the park system has included Bobby Buck Park on the west side, Grace Samuels Park on the north side, Hidden Park in the south central section, and Centennial Park on the far south side. Centennial Park was donated by the Chuck and Gloria Williams family. In addition, a few miles southeast of the city is Earl Ward Park, which contains the Pryor Creek Golf Course. The city also operates an indoor, multi-million-dollar recreation center for exercise and swimming under the management of Laura Holloway.

Pryor's Main Street has been home to four movie theaters since 1915. From 1938 to the early 1950s, three theaters were operating at the same time: Allred, New Pryor–Fiesta, and Castle.

Pryor has been home to two major rodeo groups, the 4-Way Rodeo Association and the Pryor Round-Up Club. The 4-Way group started in 1937 and continues to hold championship events at the Mayes County Fairgrounds. Becky (Hammer) Ramsey has been the club president for the past few years. The Pryor Round-Up Club was started in 1942 by Jess Higgs and Norvelle Green. They built a modern arena on the west side of town in 1949. The club held its last rodeo around 1968 and then was dissolved. For a short time around 1950, the two groups joined together, but they separated due to differences between the leaders of each club.

Little League baseball, begun in town by Frank Hair, has since 1960 allowed thousands of young boys and teens to enjoy the summer sport. They play on several different diamonds owned by the city park department.

From the time of World War II until recently, the community has supported a bowling alley. Bowling leagues were very popular and competitive among business and industry.

For over 70 years, the community has also supported a very popular roller skating rink, located on the west side. The most notable operators of the rink have included Jock Mayor, Bill Kimsey, and Mr. and Mrs. O.J. Miller.

Bowling was also a very popular pastime until the recent closing of the local alley. For many years, the bowling alley operated as Stafford Lanes, originally owned and operated by the late Bob Stafford.

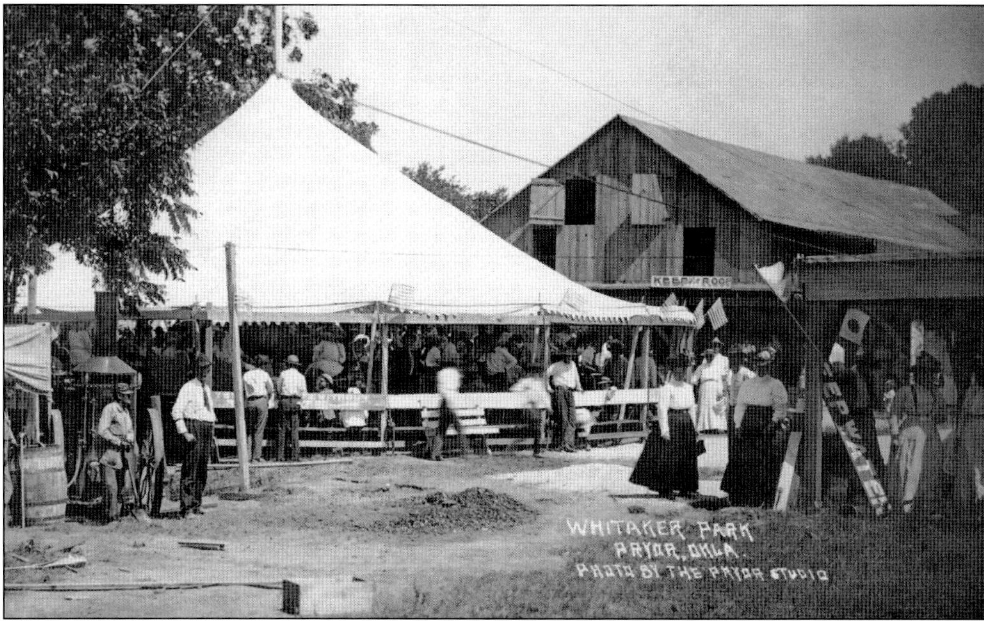

Whitaker Park was opened on June 25, 1909 by W.T. Whitaker, a Cherokee citizen and founder of the Whitaker State Orphan's Home. He originally built a playground, baseball field, skating rink, picnic ground, roping pasture, grandstand, and even a small amusement park near the area of what is now the Sertoma Senior Center. The amusement park included an old-fashioned merry-go-round, hot-air balloon rides, and a small zoo that included a monkey and a snake. There was a theater for plays and moving-picture shows. Children from the orphanage kept the books, maintained the park grounds, ran the amusement rides, sold tickets, and operated the concessions, which included homemade ice cream and lemonade. W.T. Whitaker said, "If everybody doesn't believe that these orphan boys and girls are honest and virtuous and have had the best of training, then watch them and believe." The park is now part of the city park system and contains a swimming pool, fishing pond, tennis and volleyball courts, and picnic facilities.

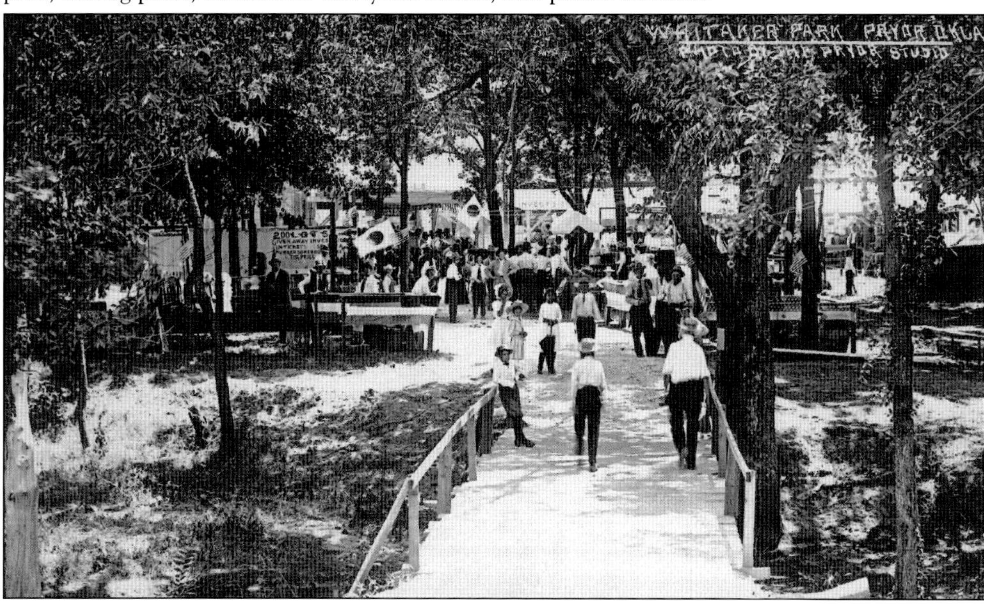

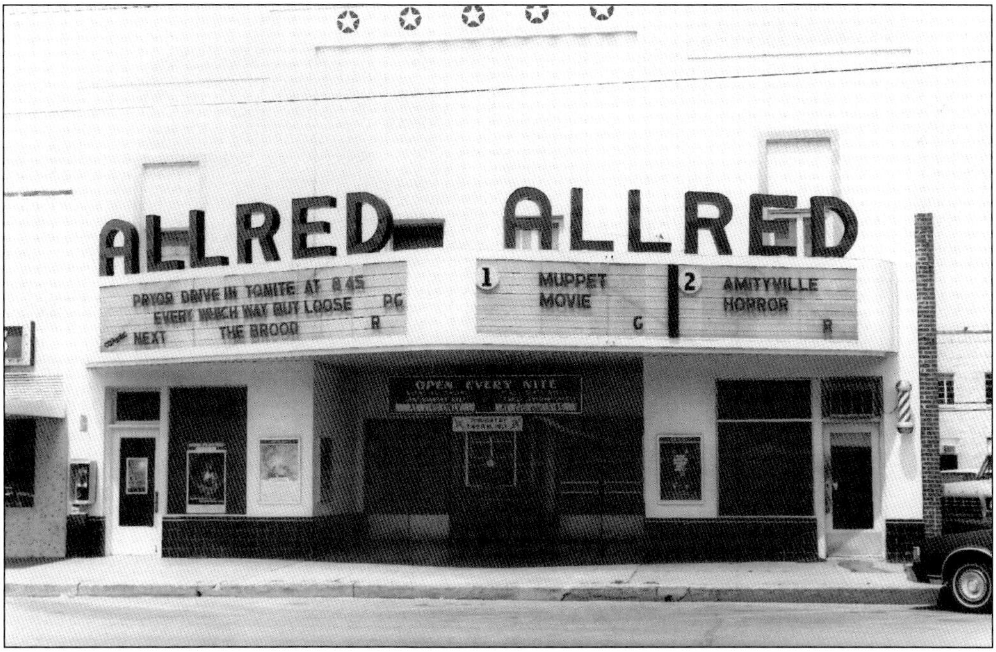

The Lyric, at 225 East Graham Avenue, was owned by Fred Allred. He changed its name to the Allred in the summer of 1937. In 1963, the theater was sold by the Allred family to the Doyle, Kathleen, and Gene Oliver family, who owned it until 2012. Also subleased by the Charles and Willda Townsend family between 1975 and 1987, it is now owned by Robert and Angie Jones. It now contains five digital screen auditoriums.

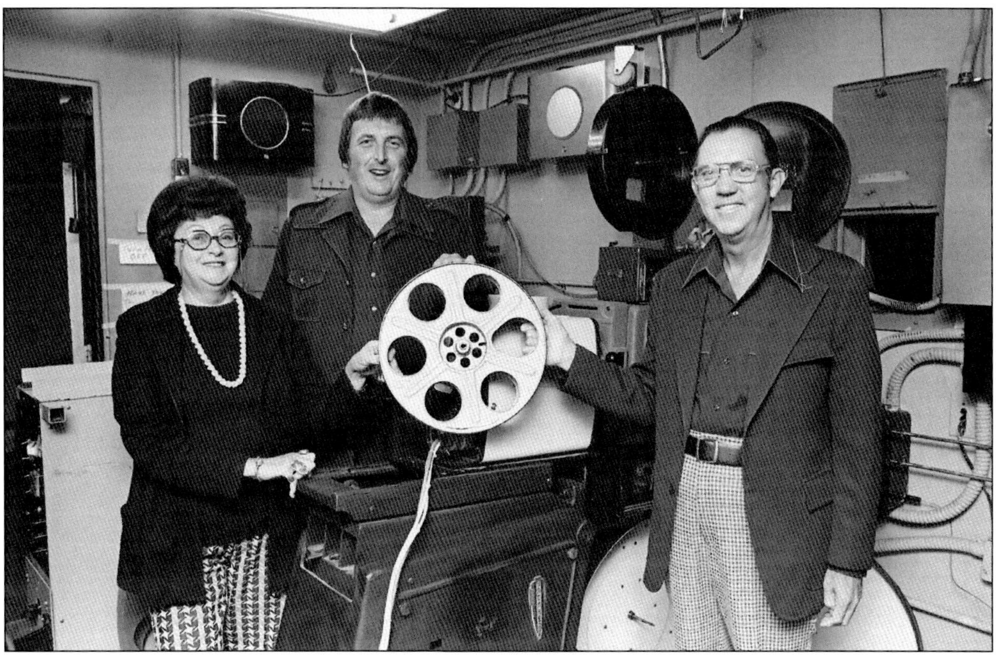
Shown here from left to right are Kathleen Oliver, Charles Townsend, and Doyle Oliver after the Oliver family leased the Allred and the Pryor Drive-in to Townsend. The theater was operated by members of the Charles and Willda Townsend family until the fall of 1987, when Mrs. Townsend retired.

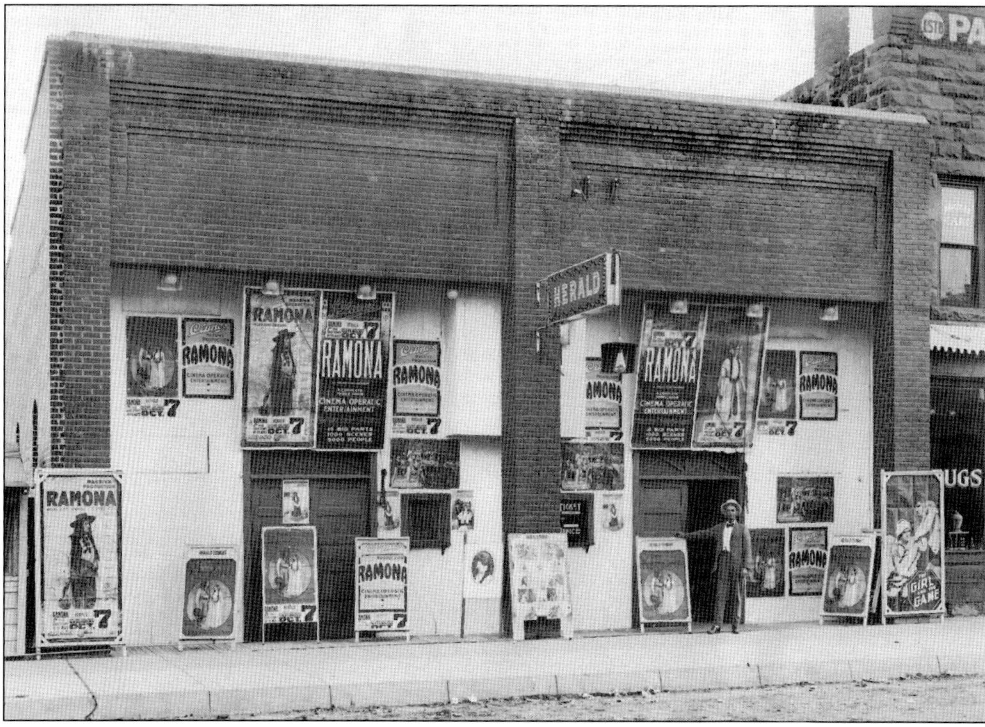

C.E. Herald (1868–1940) was a businessman who operated a store and produce business in what is now the NAPA auto-parts store building. In 1915, on the site of his former store, Herald constructed a modern theater, called the Herald. (Courtesy of Bob Herald.)

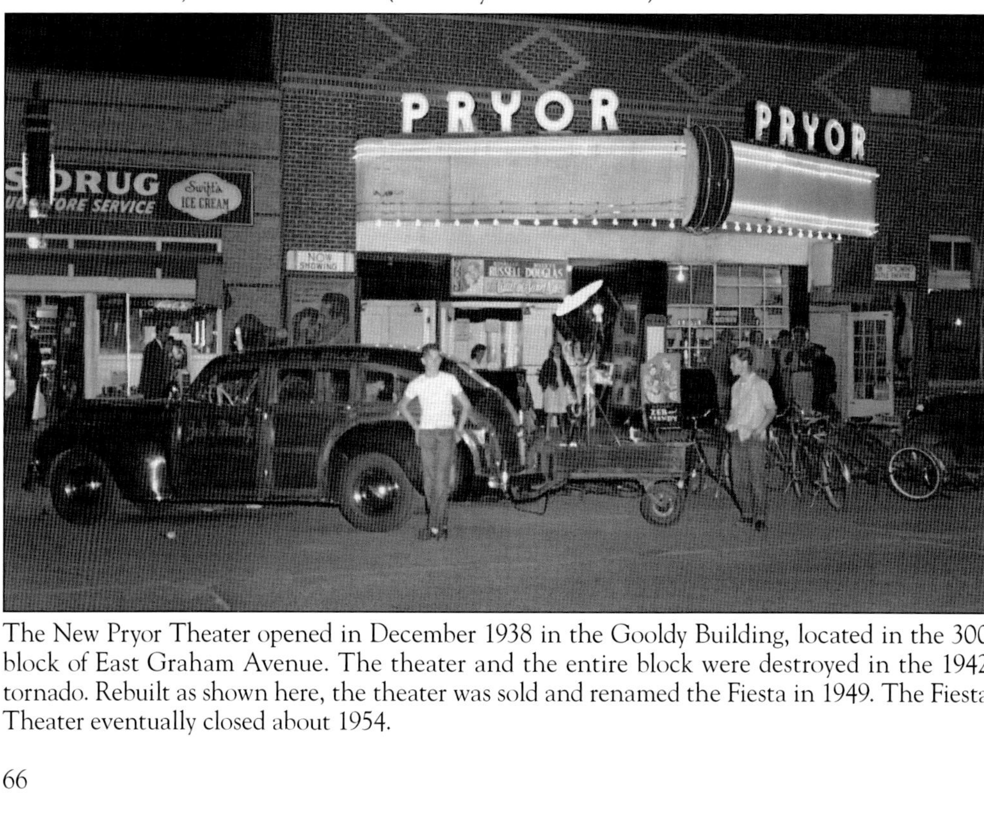

The New Pryor Theater opened in December 1938 in the Gooldy Building, located in the 300 block of East Graham Avenue. The theater and the entire block were destroyed in the 1942 tornado. Rebuilt as shown here, the theater was sold and renamed the Fiesta in 1949. The Fiesta Theater eventually closed about 1954.

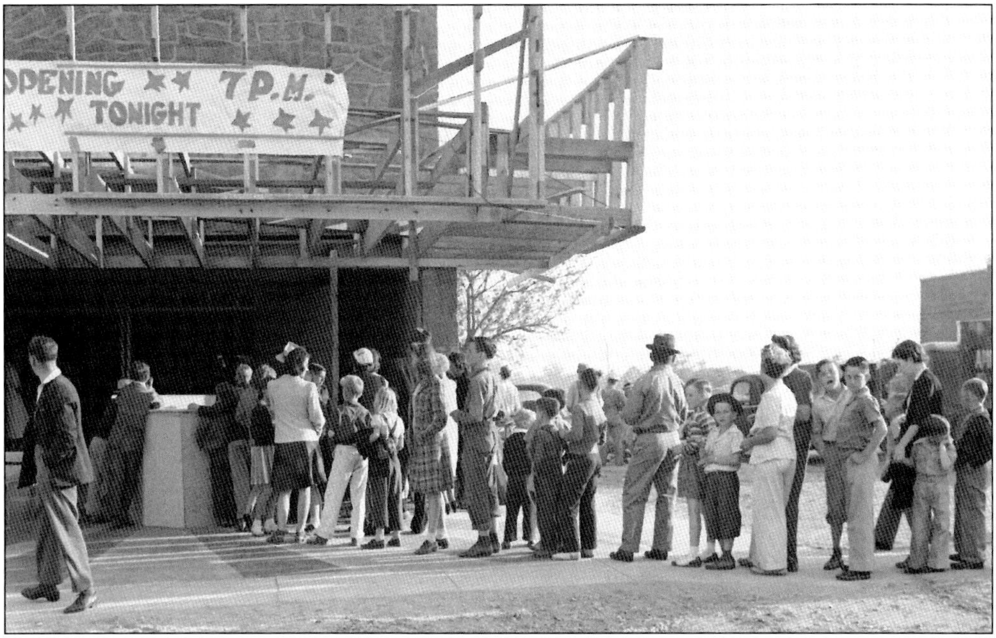

This photograph shows the grand opening of the Castle Theater in May 1942. It was under construction at the time of the disastrous tornado that destroyed the Allred and New Pryor Theaters and much of downtown. The Castle Theater opened its doors before construction was complete in order to get a movie house open for the entertainment of a devastated community.

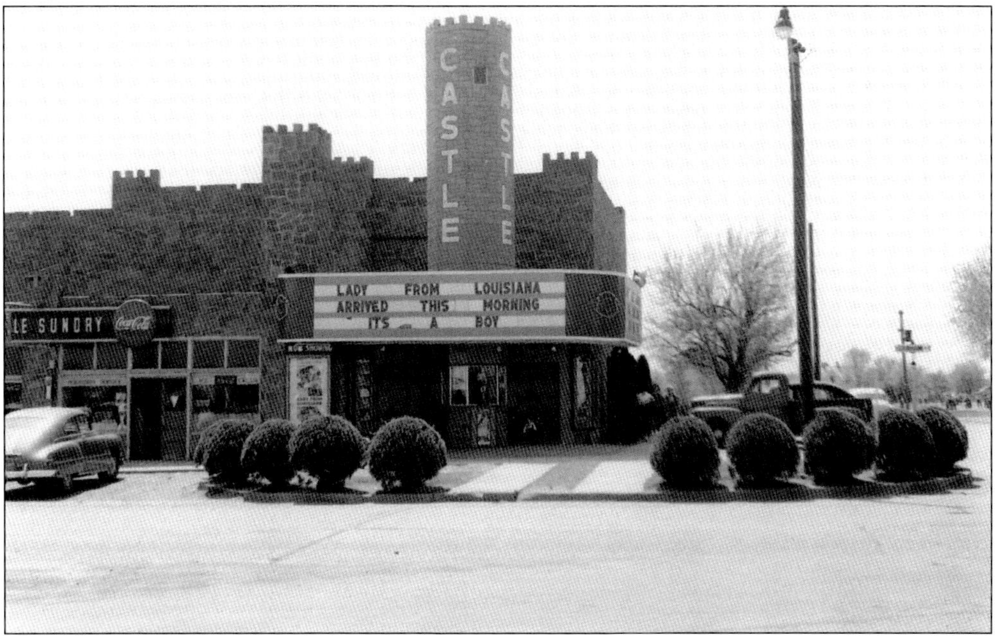

The Castle Theater, located at 700 East Graham Avenue, was opened in 1942 by L.H. Thomas. The venue closed about 1954. The theater building was purchased two years later by the American Legion Post No. 82 and remodeled into the legion hall. In 1958, the building was purchased by the W.A. Graham Estate and given to the City of Pryor Creek for use as the Pryor Youth Organization's Teen Town.

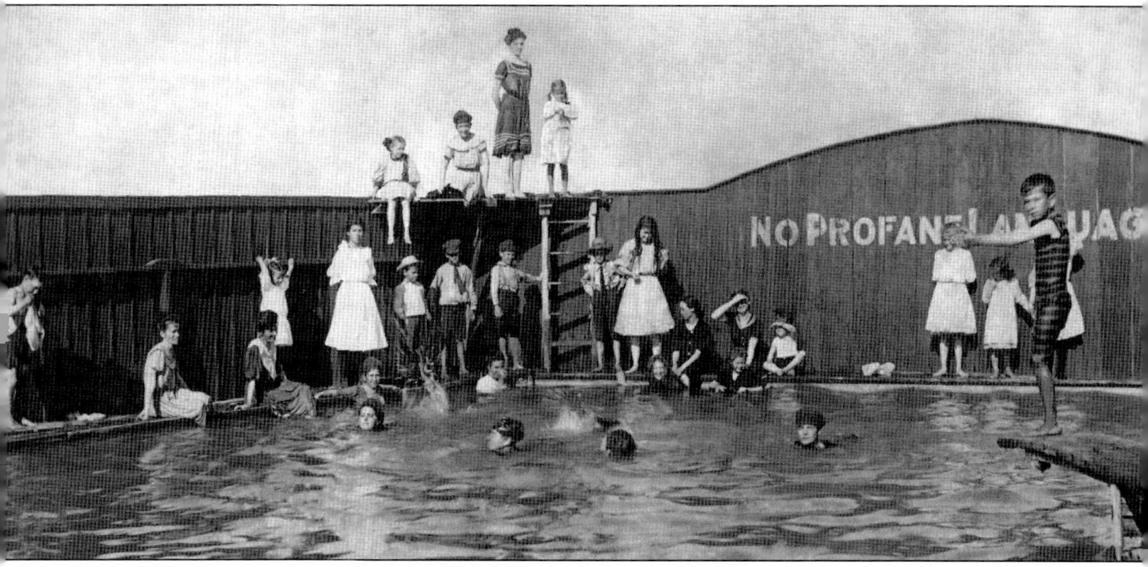

The first swimming pool in Pryor Creek was located near the northeast corner of what are now Elliott Street and East Graham Avenue. The private pool was built by J.A. Quinn about 1909. (Courtesy of Aeileen Harrison.)

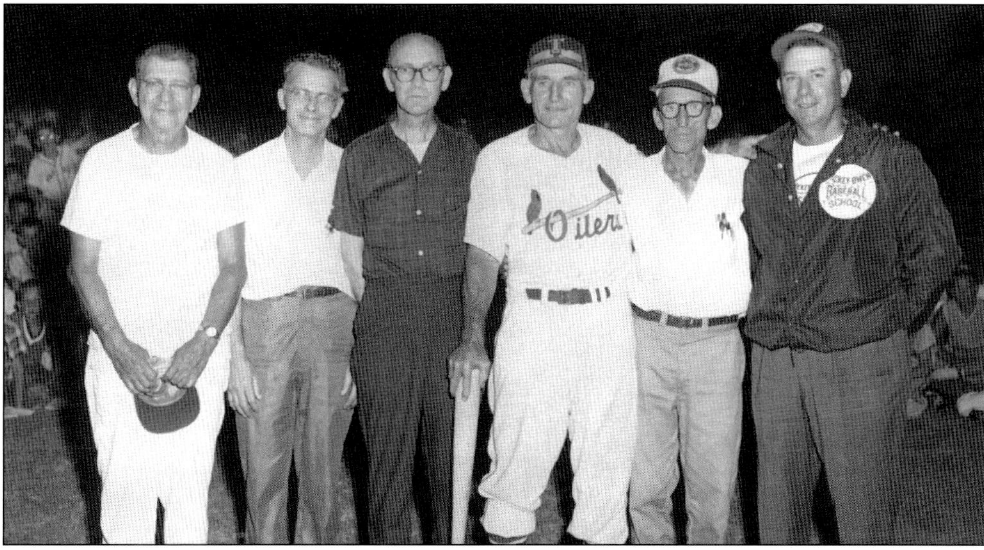

To commemorate the fifth anniversary of the NEO Ok Kids (Little) League baseball, and with over 500 boys in attendance, hall-of-fame baseball player Pepper Martin hosted a baseball camp in Pryor in July 1963. Shown here are, from left to right, Frank Hair, Woody Littlefield, Harold Addington, Martin, Sam Baker, and Mickey Owen. Martin was a star with the St. Louis Cardinals from 1928 to 1944. Later, he was a player-coach in the minor leagues, including for the Tulsa Oilers.

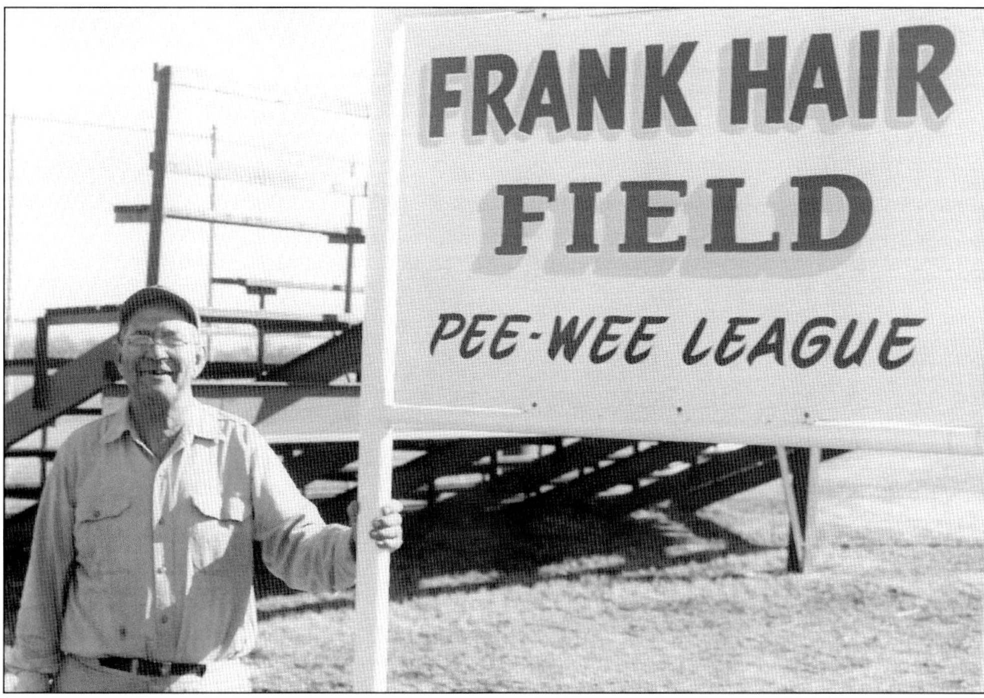

Frank Hair (1896–1980) was considered the father of Little League baseball in Mayes County. A barber by trade and a longtime school board member, he was a mentor to hundreds of aspiring ballplayers. He also worked for the city park department as groundskeeper for the baseball program. While he was mowing the grass, he suffered a fatal heart attack. He died while taking care of the "field of dreams."

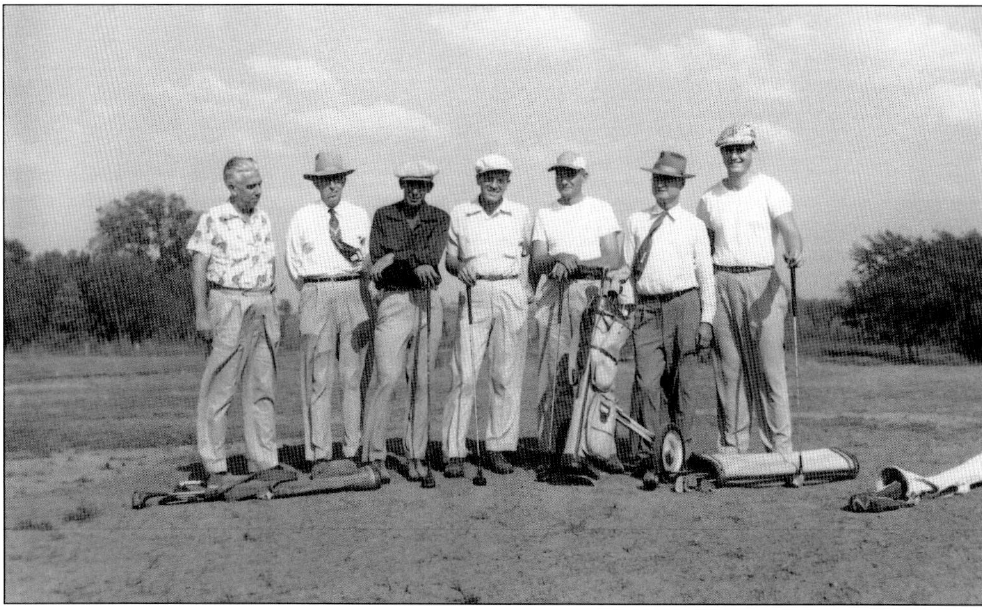

The first golfers to play a round at the Earl Ward Park Golf Course, in October 1953, were, from left to right, Bayliss Graham, Judge Tom Landrum, Bill Cobler, Al Middleton, H.B. Roy, Mayor Earl Ward, and Quentin Poe.

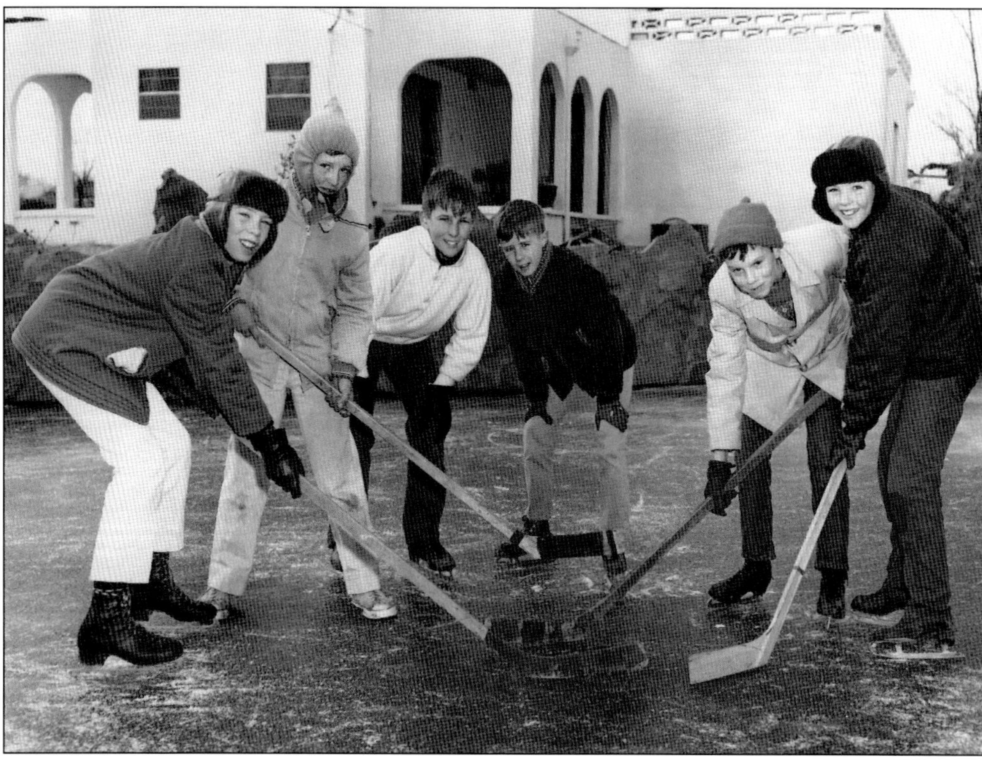

Neighborhood hockey players take advantage of a frozen stream near the city park in December 1964. From left to right are Ray Williams, Tom Kinion, Mike McCollough, Jim Schardein, Jody Burnett, and Charles Williams.

Winners of the February 1973 city men's bowling tournament included, from left to right, Conard Gaither, Gene Abdoo, Carl Gaither, Luke Wilkerson, and Harry Schaefer. The team, sponsored by Chupp Implement Company, had a collective score of 2,977.

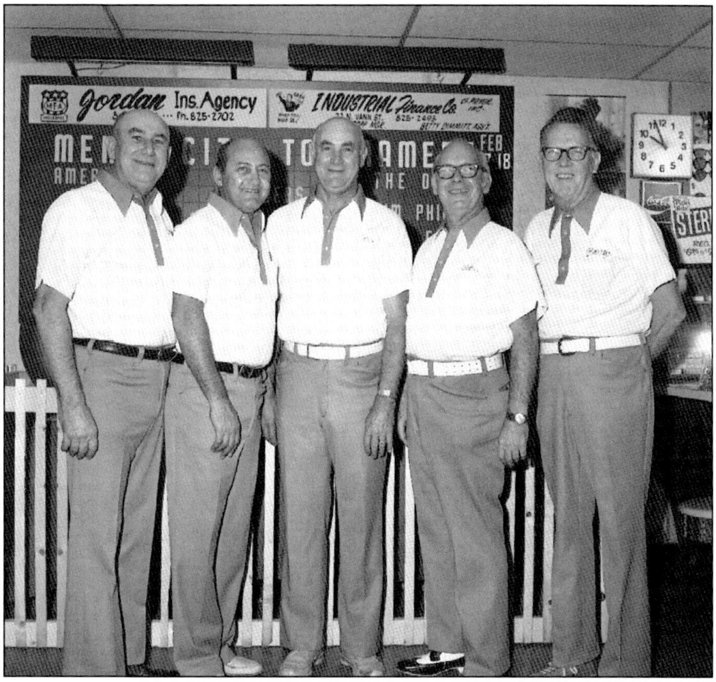

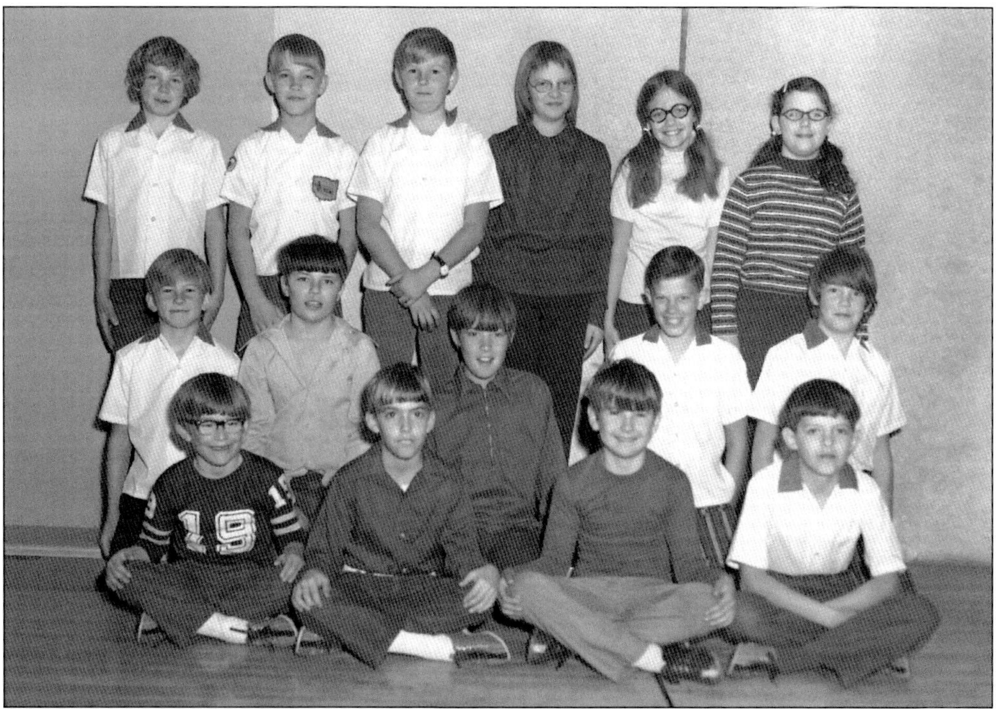

In March 1972, Pryor youth bowlers at Stafford Lanes included, from left to right, (first row) Greg Arnold, Scott Ray, Lynn Wallis, and Greg Southern; (second row) Curt Cranford, Mark Hartman, Randy Palmer, Randy James, and Leonard Ward; (third row) Larry Ward, Ray Shivers, David Going, Connie Miller, Angelia Southern, and Stephanie Shearer. The team was coached by Ardis Shepherd and Daisy Shivers.

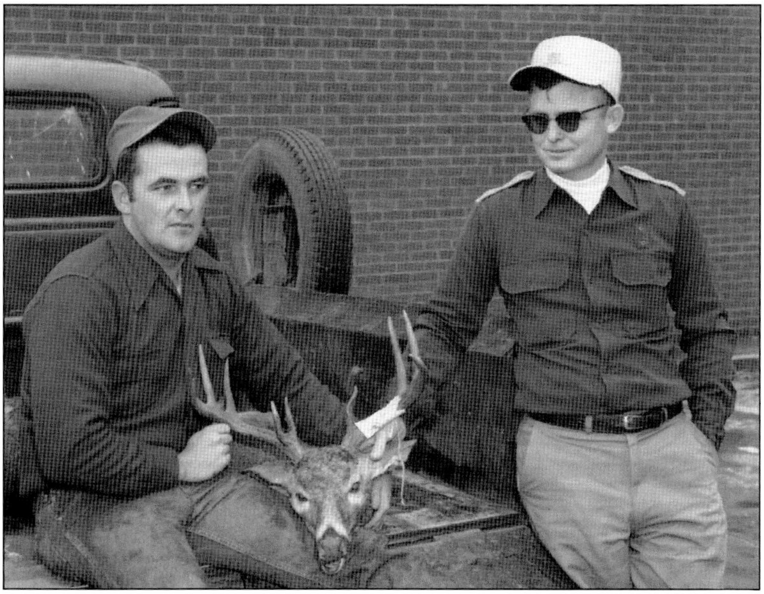

Pryor policemen Bill Dickey (left) and Leroy Crow took a couple days of vacation to go deer hunting. They show their trophy around 1963.

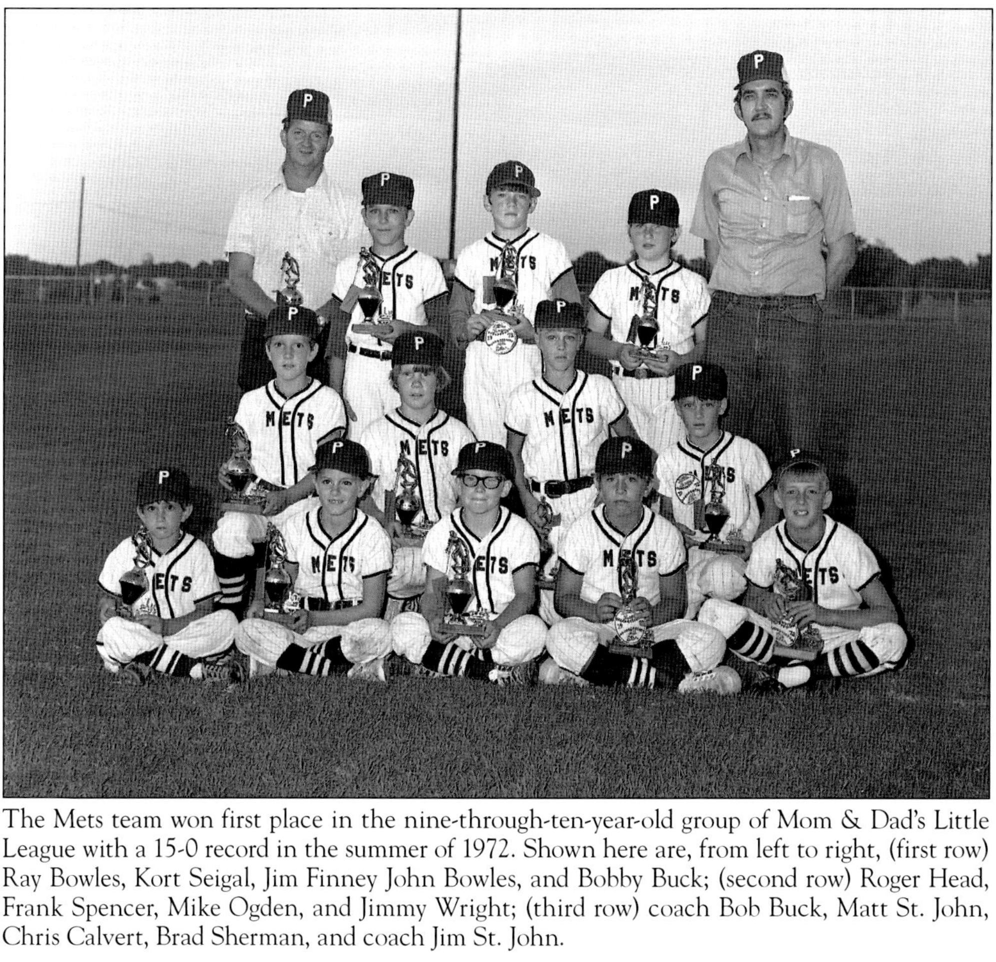

The Mets team won first place in the nine-through-ten-year-old group of Mom & Dad's Little League with a 15-0 record in the summer of 1972. Shown here are, from left to right, (first row) Ray Bowles, Kort Seigal, Jim Finney John Bowles, and Bobby Buck; (second row) Roger Head, Frank Spencer, Mike Ogden, and Jimmy Wright; (third row) coach Bob Buck, Matt St. John, Chris Calvert, Brad Sherman, and coach Jim St. John.

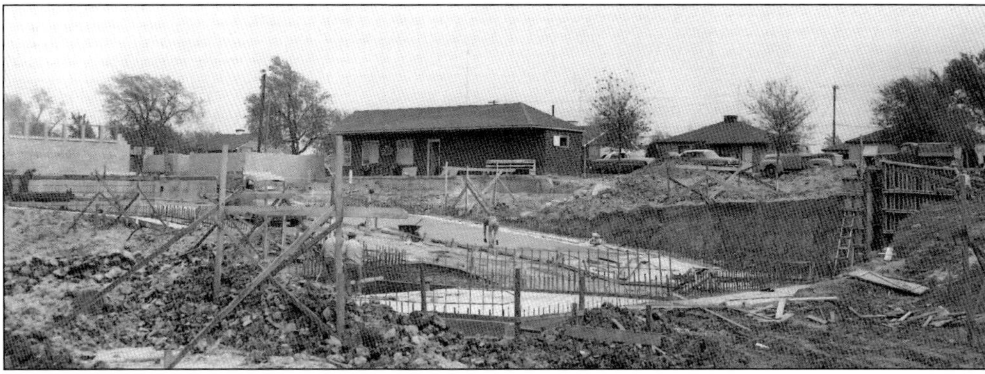

Construction of a new $100,000 swimming pool in Whitaker Park is shown here in April 1955, four months before it opened in August 1955.

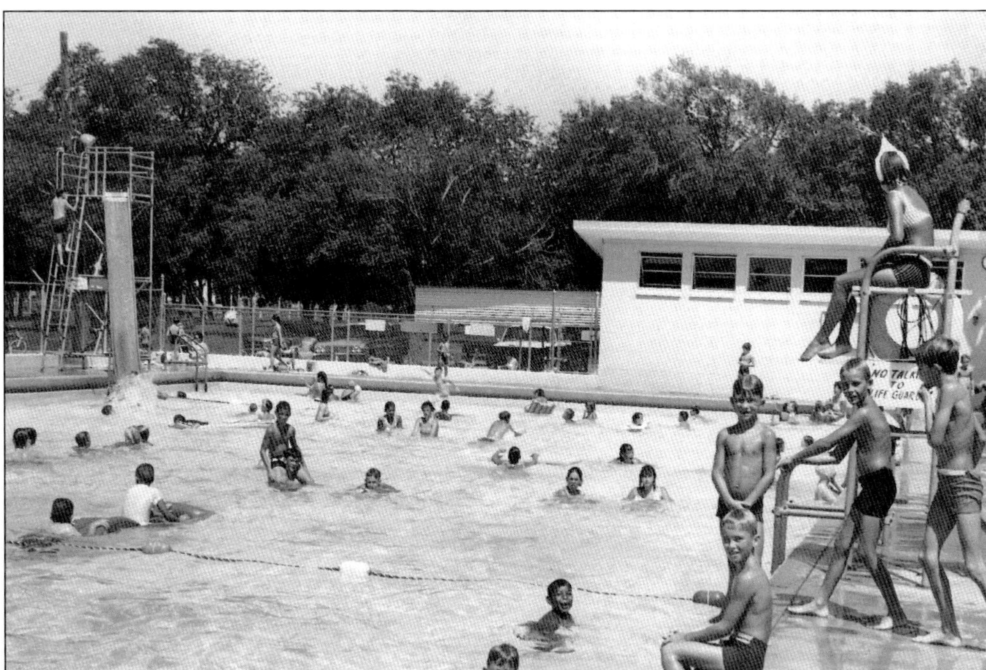

Young people enjoy the Whitaker Park swimming pool around 1968.

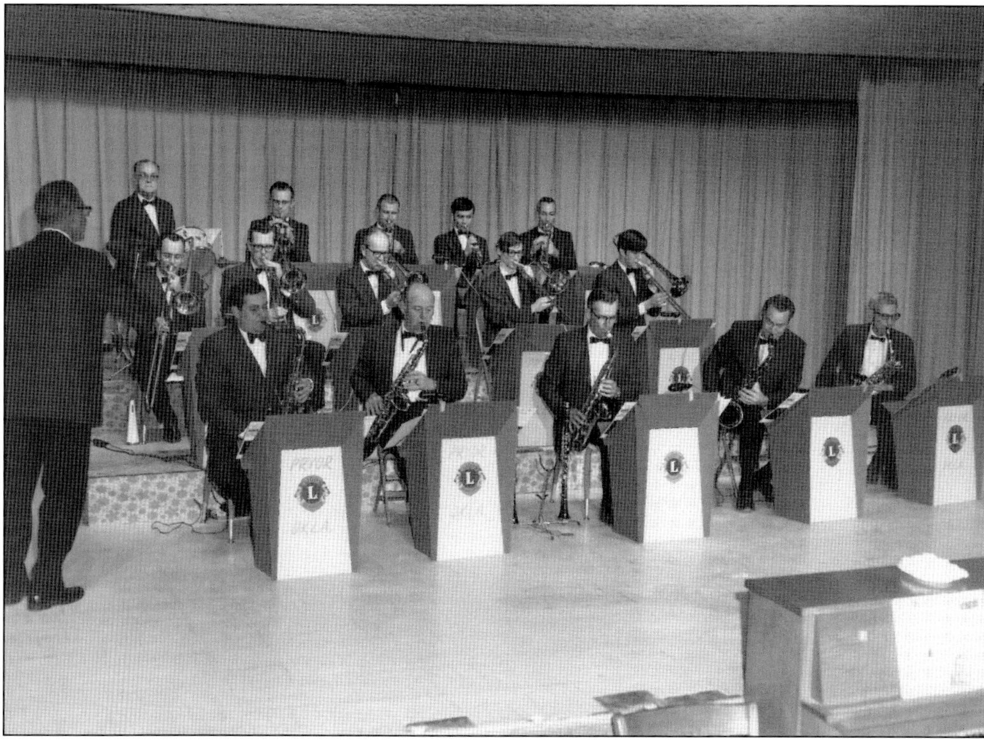

The Lions Club orchestra included, from left to right, Red Carpenter on drums; Doug Brown, Cecil Agnew, and Don Webster on trumpet; Dr. Burt Frazier on trombone; and Richard Medlock, Dr. Pat Williams, and Charlie Cooper on saxophone.

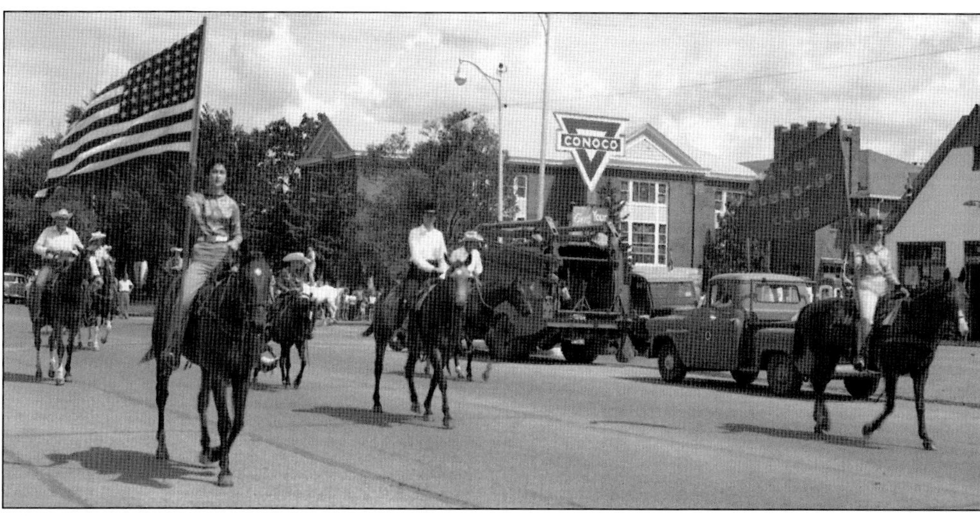

The Pryor Round-Up Club rodeo parade in July 1959 features color bearers Jessie Carole Higgs (left) and Kaye Dee Harris (right) escorting Queen Karen Kimsey.

Six

Municipal Government

The city government of Pryor Creek began in 1894 when the town was incorporated under the laws of the Cherokee Nation. James Lee Mills was elected the first mayor, and James L. Taylor was elected city clerk. In 1911, the city government was designated as a city of the first class and incorporated under the laws of the State of Oklahoma.

Pryor Creek has a strong mayor-council form of government. The citizens choose a mayor, clerk, treasurer, police chief, and eight council members, two from each ward. Services are provided by police, street, park, cemetery, and fire departments.

The history of the police department does not begin until 1901, but it is known that John Ingram served as city marshal at some point in the late 1890s. The fire department was officially formed in April 1904 as a volunteer department, with L.H. Tolbert, a local pharmacist, as the first chief. The present department, run by fire chief Tim Thompson, comprises full-time and volunteer members.

The Pryor Public Library was founded in September 1939, with Irma Dee Springer as the first librarian. Since 1955, Cornelia Sifferman, Thomasine Ward, David Johansson, Kim Risner, Susan Newberry, and Cari Rérat have filled that position.

The city operates two cemeteries, Fairview Cemetery and Graham Memorial Cemetery. Both are located on the east side of the city.

The City of Pryor Creek is unique in that it also has a municipal utility board, which operates the gas, water, and sewer operations, as well as a municipally owned electric distribution system. General managers of the Municipal Utility Board have included Al Middleton, Bob Shafer, Bob Pierson, and Gary Pruett.

In December 1962, citizens went to the polls to vote on a proposed city-charter change to drop the word "Creek" from the city's official name. The referendum was defeated by a vote of 583-297. Then, a few months later, the US Post Office took a survey vote of postal customers about the name of the post office. Voters were asked whether the name should remain Pryor, or be changed to Pryor Creek. Postal customers voted to leave the post office as Pryor.

Current elected officials are Mayor Jimmy Tramel, City Clerk Eva Smith, City Treasurer Lois Thompson, Chief of Police Steve Lemmings, and council members Cheryl White, Roger Willcut, Yolanda Thompson, Houston Brittain, Randy Chitwood, Greg Rosamond, Ryan Rains, and Drew Stott.

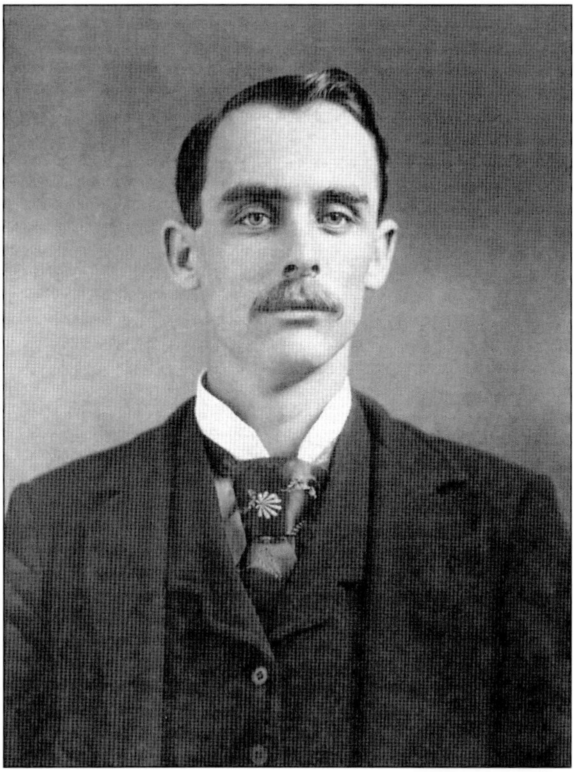

James Lee Mills (1867–1936) was the first mayor of Pryor Creek, serving from 1894 to 1896. Mills, a Cherokee citizen, started the community's first newspaper, the *Enterprise*, and later worked as a lawman for the Cherokee Nation and as undersheriff of Mayes County. (Courtesy of Lorene Keys.)

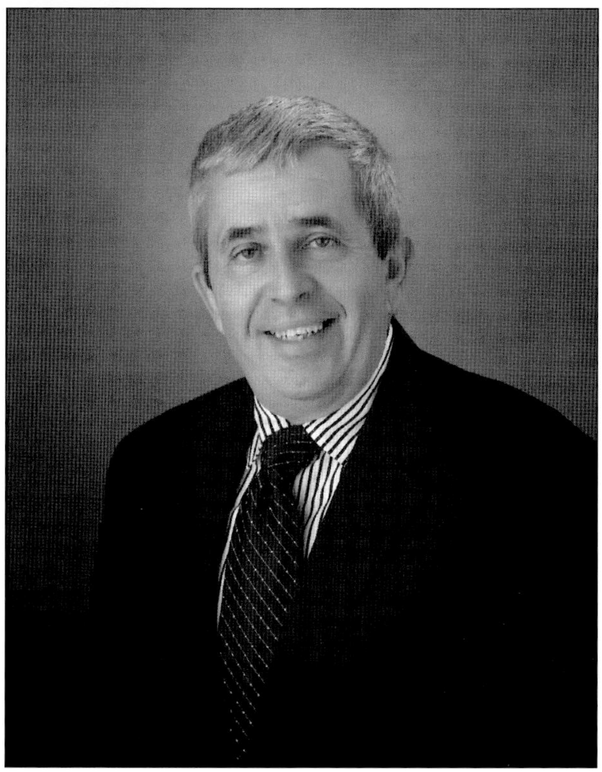

Jimmy Tramel, the current mayor of Pryor Creek, is a former city councilman and American Airlines retiree. First elected in 2003, he was subsequently reelected in 2005, 2007, 2011, and 2015. (Courtesy of Terry Aylward.)

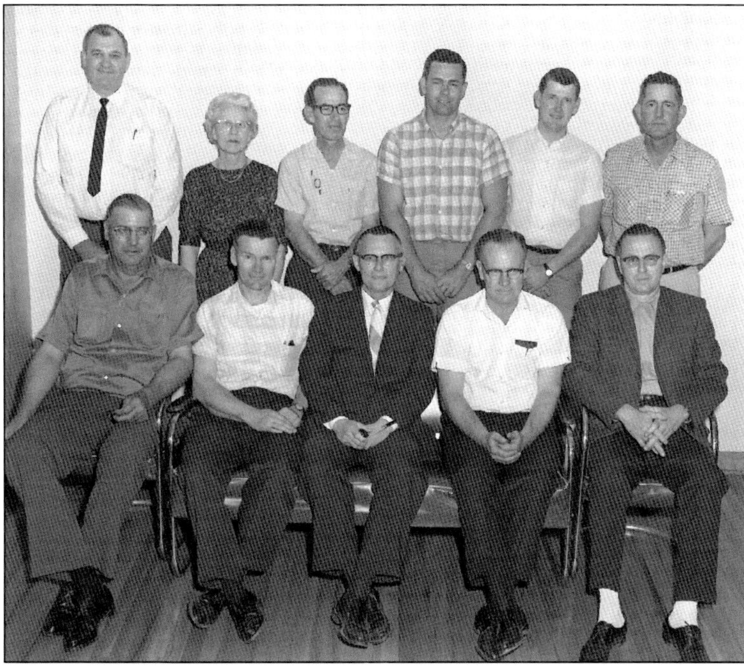

Pryor Creek elected city officials pose for an official portrait in April 1965. From left to right are (seated) Slim Weaver, Jim Bradley, Mayor Stewart Robertson, Charles Cass, and John Prather; (standing) Mutt McArtor, Martha Wilson, Elmer Swan, Ernest Young, E.A. Borrer, and Dick McNair.

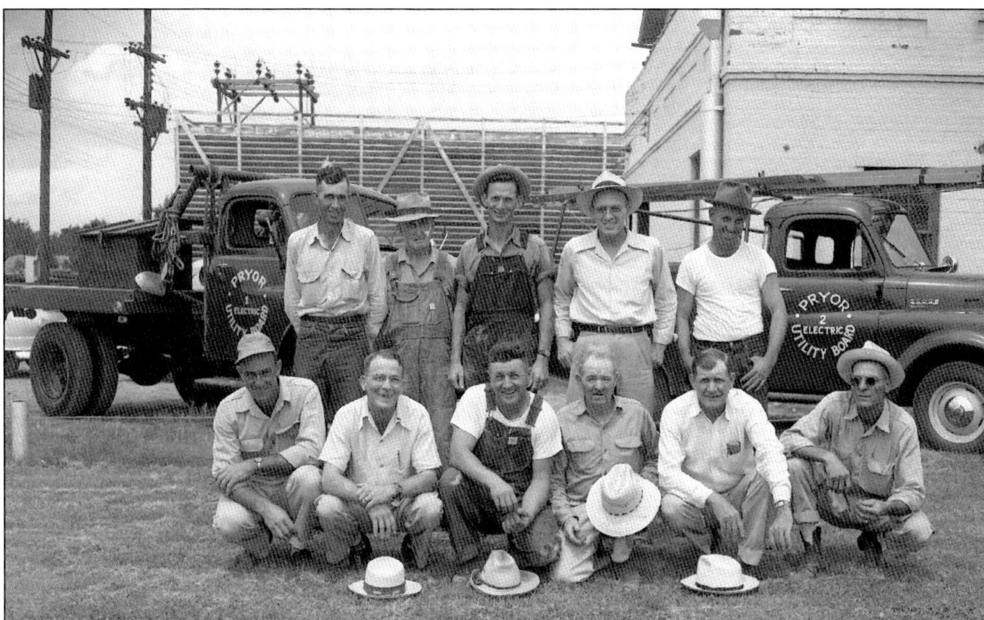

Municipal Utility Board employees in July 1951 included, from left to right, (first row) Bob Shafer, Ted Livingston, Chester Goss, Henry Hale, Joe Greenfield, and Jim Lawhorn; (second row) Albert Walker, Jack Barnes, J.E. Hess, Al Middleton, and Vernie Willis.

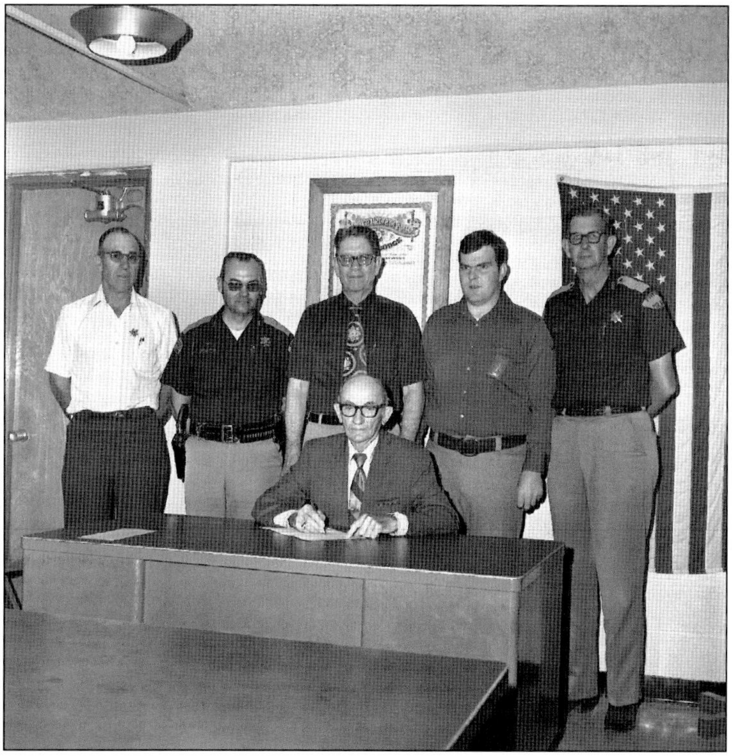

In May 1973, Mayor Ramon Bewley (seated) signs a proclamation recognizing National Police Week. Looking over his shoulder are, from left to right, Pete Weaver, Harlan Lamar, Earl Proctor, Mike Coatney, and Buster Ogilvie.

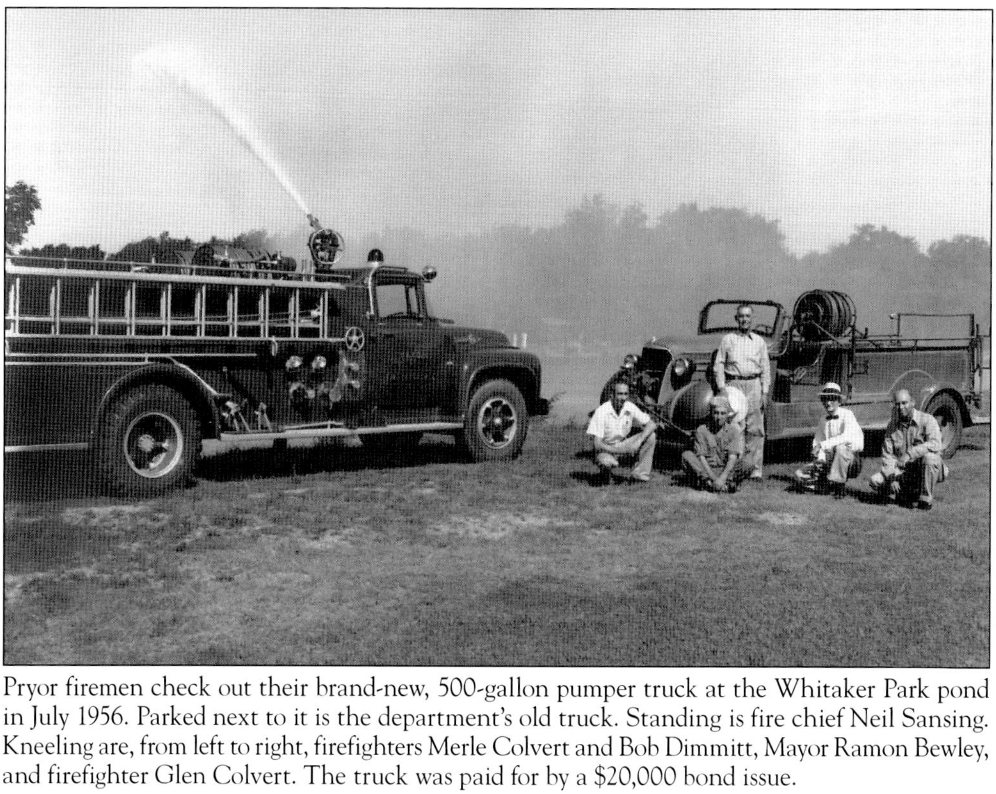

Pryor firemen check out their brand-new, 500-gallon pumper truck at the Whitaker Park pond in July 1956. Parked next to it is the department's old truck. Standing is fire chief Neil Sansing. Kneeling are, from left to right, firefighters Merle Colvert and Bob Dimmitt, Mayor Ramon Bewley, and firefighter Glen Colvert. The truck was paid for by a $20,000 bond issue.

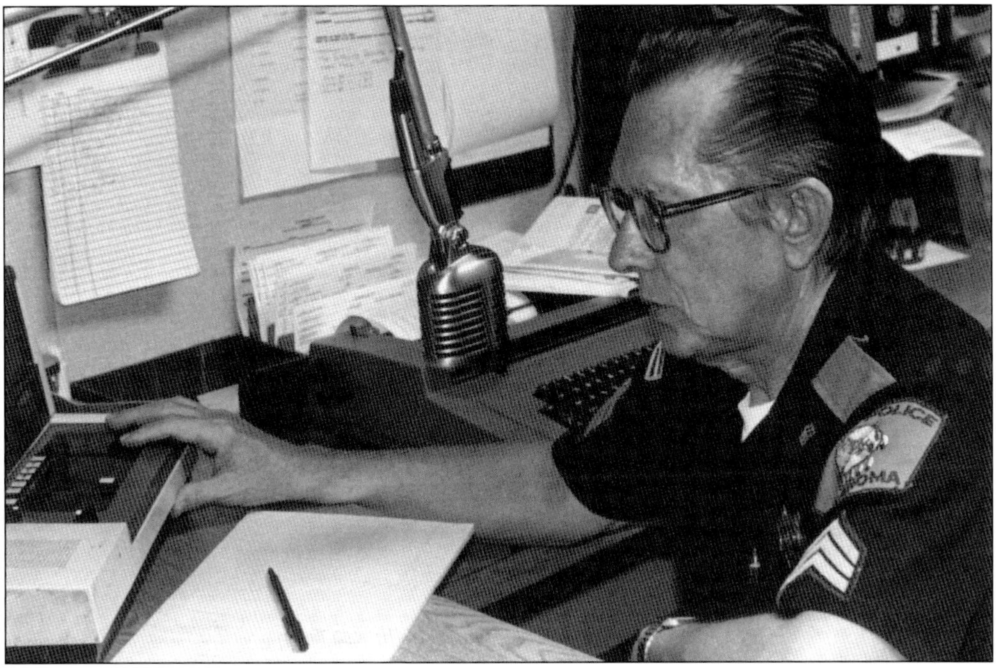

Sgt. Jim Moore (1926–1999) was a living legend at the police department, working as dispatcher for over 30 years, as well as four years with the Mayes County sheriff's office. He was also 1972 police officer of the year.

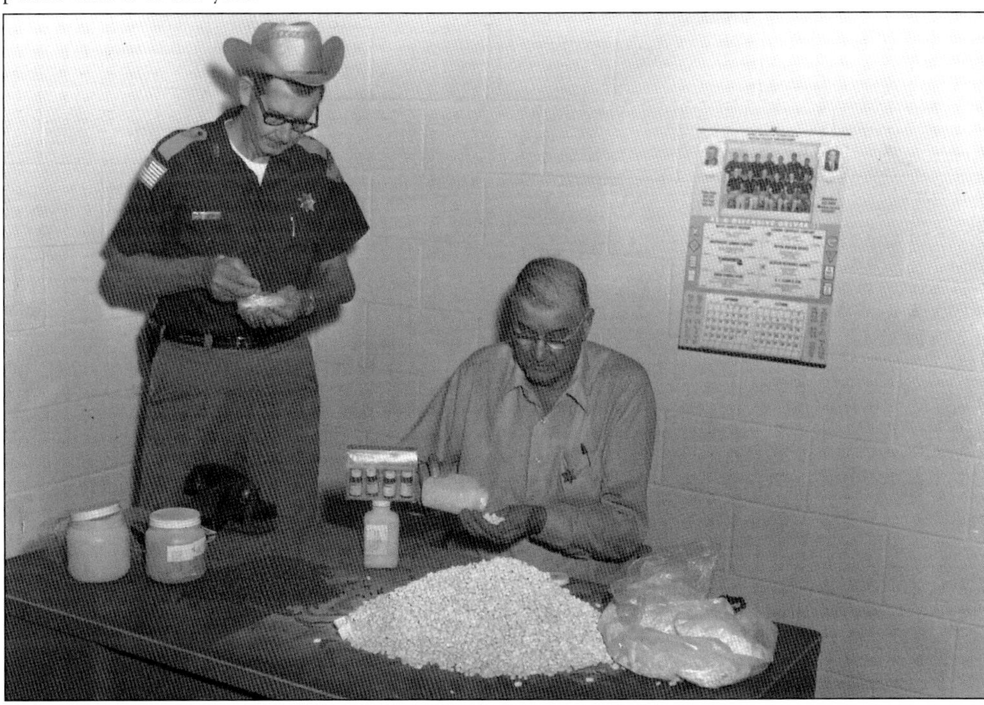

Assistant police chief Buster Ogilvie (1915–2001) and Chief Slim Weaver (1910–1983) inventory stolen narcotics recovered during a pharmacy burglary in May 1971. Weaver was the elected chief of police from 1965 to 1973 and sheriff of Mayes County from 1953 to 1965.

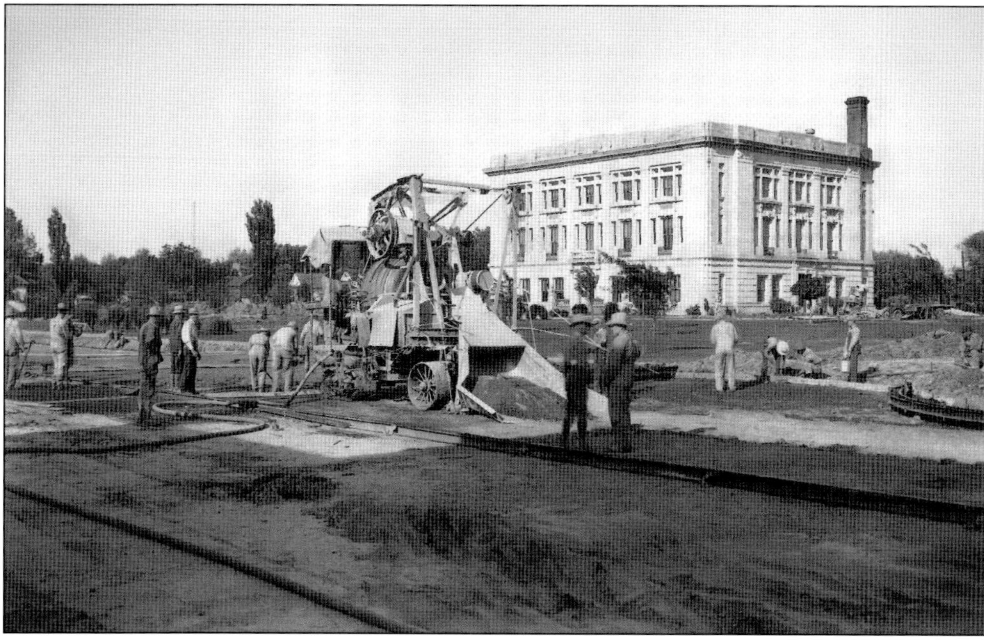

This 1930s photograph shows the paving of North Adair Street for the first time. In the background is the Mayes County Courthouse. (Courtesy of Aeileen Harrison.)

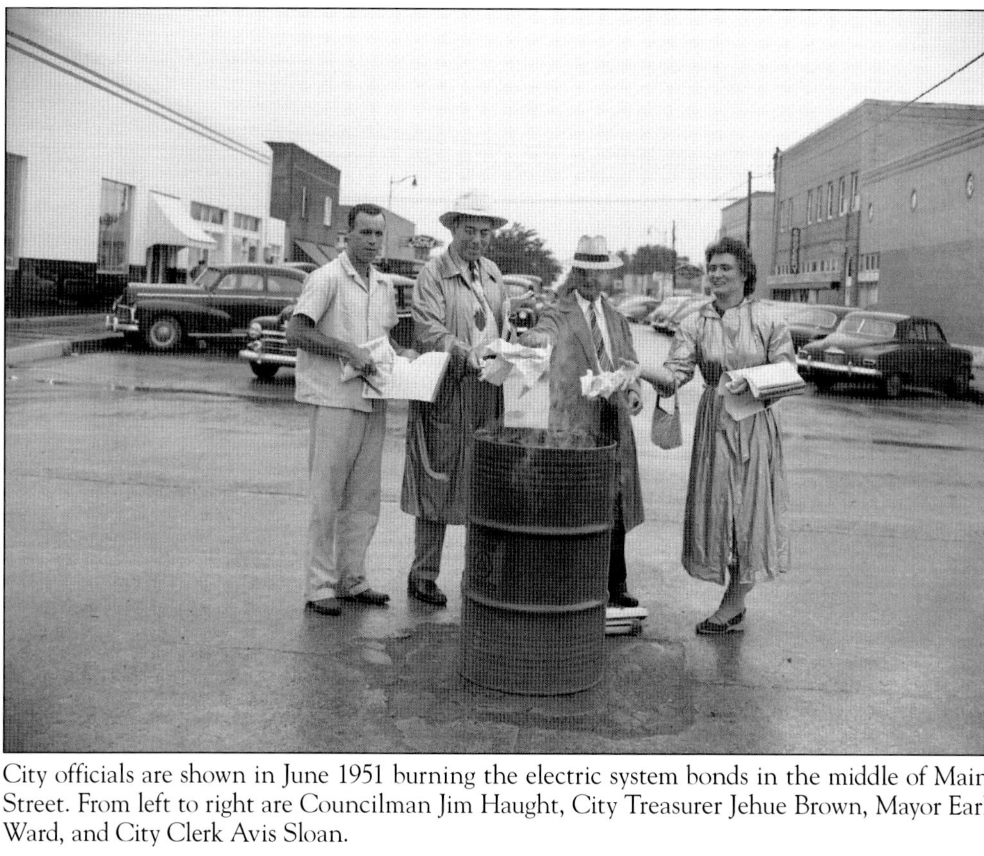

City officials are shown in June 1951 burning the electric system bonds in the middle of Main Street. From left to right are Councilman Jim Haught, City Treasurer Jehue Brown, Mayor Earl Ward, and City Clerk Avis Sloan.

Lucy Belle Schultz (1922–2013) was the first and only woman to be elected mayor of Pryor Creek, serving from 1991 to 1997. In 1992, she was selected as the Oklahoma mayor of the year by the Oklahoma Municipal League. The retired businesswoman and former city council member was a very active and prominent civic leader and community volunteer.

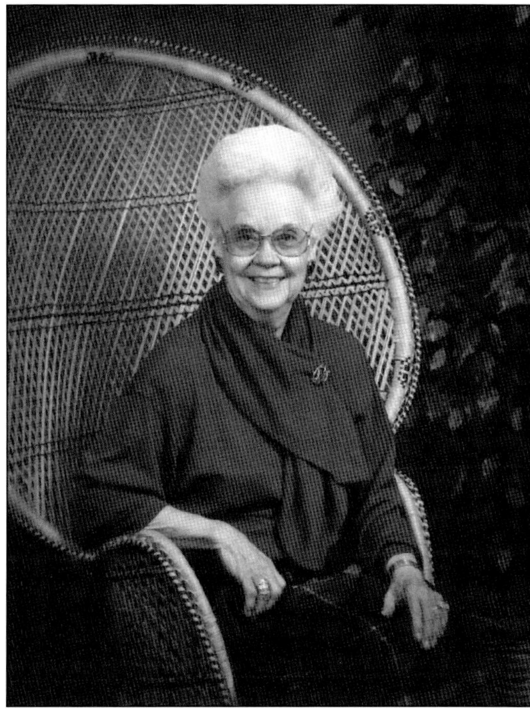

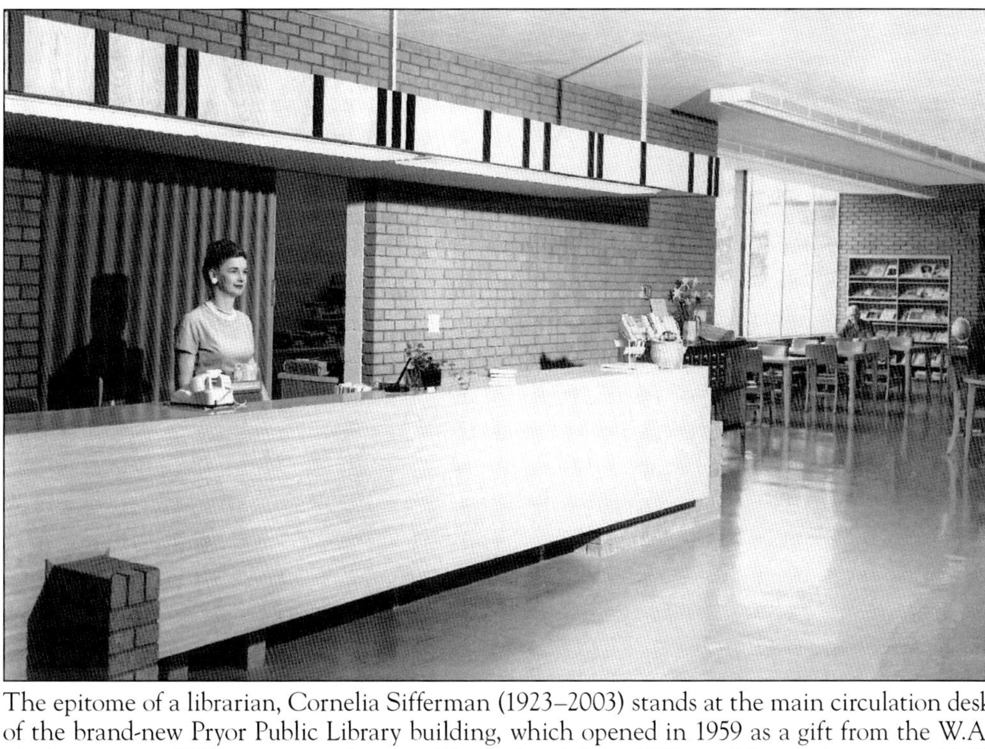

The epitome of a librarian, Cornelia Sifferman (1923–2003) stands at the main circulation desk of the brand-new Pryor Public Library building, which opened in 1959 as a gift from the W.A. Graham estate. Sifferman served as city library head from 1955 until her retirement in 1989. She was also selected Citizen of the Year for 1988 by the Chamber of Commerce. (Courtesy of Thomas J. Harrison Pryor Public Library.)

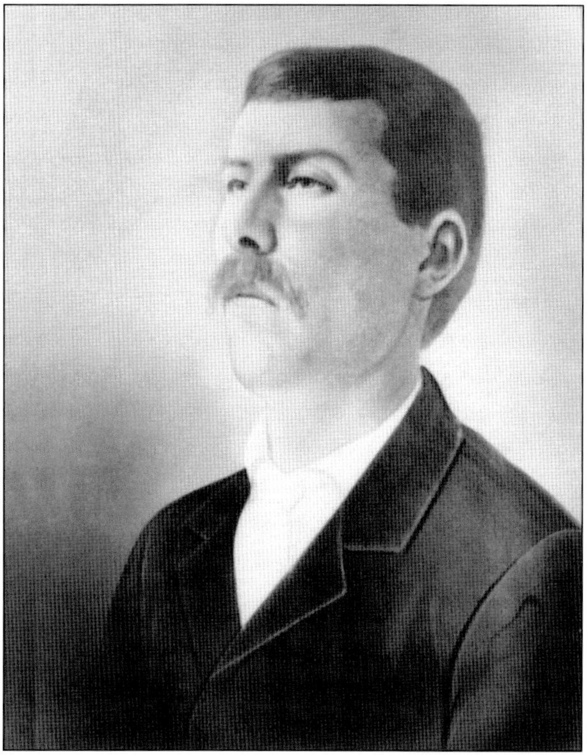

James Coates (1866–1914) was the chief of police from 1913 until his death in 1914. Coates was the only Pryor Creek police officer to die in the line of duty. On December 17, 1914, he was shot multiple times while serving a municipal arrest warrant on Jesse Moore in the Mayor Hotel, located in the 100 block of East Graham Avenue. He is buried in Fairview Cemetery. (Courtesy of David Coats.)

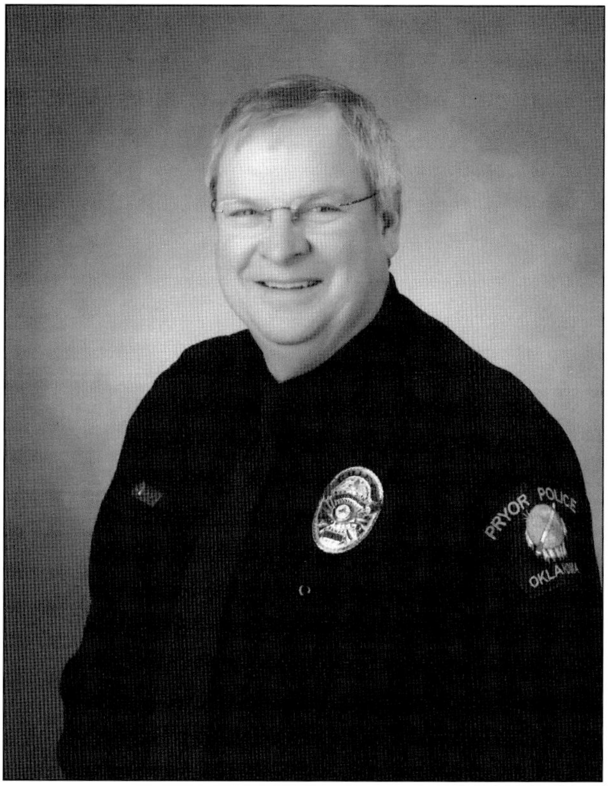

Dennis Nichols served as the elected police chief longer than anyone in history, from 1987 to 2015. Overall, he gave over 40 years of service to the citizens of Pryor Creek, serving as patrolman and detective prior to his election to the top-cop job. (Courtesy of Terry Aylward.)

Seven

DuPont Powder Plant

Just four months before the attack on Pearl Harbor, the US War Department announced plans to build a mammoth smokeless powder plant between Pryor and Chouteau in what is now the Mid-America Industrial Park. The plant would be constructed and operated by the DuPont Company, at an estimated cost of about $51 million.

The Mayes County facility would be the first such plant west of the Mississippi River, and also the fourth and last nationwide. The others were located at Charlestown, Indiana; Radford, Virginia; and Childersburg, Alabama.

In September 1941, an $84,235,594 contract for construction was let. An estimated 15,245 acres of land would be needed; the properties were condemned, and landowners and tenant farmers were evicted, some given just one week to vacate. The property owners were eventually paid an average of about $66 per acre for the land. The government took bids on the sale of the farmers' crops, both harvested and still in the field.

On December 18, 1941, work was completed on 100 of 400 planned buildings and 15 miles of interior roads. In addition, 15 miles of electrical wiring were installed, a 30,000-square-foot administration building was finished, and over 100 railroad cars of building materials were unloaded per day.

Following the surrender of Germany in May 1945, the plant received a cutback order, reducing production by 25 percent. Following the surrender of Japan in August 1945, a shutdown order affected about 2,700 workers over a period of five or six months. All of the plant-maintenance force and other key employees were to be retained until all buildings and equipment were cleaned and decontaminated. On September 10, 1945, the last line of powder was packed. In all, the plant produced 408,036,249 pounds of smokeless powder; the plant operated for about three years and 45 days.

In addition, a prisoner-of-war camp was constructed to house German prisoners just east of the powder plant. It opened in the fall of 1944. One of about 30 such sites in Oklahoma, the Pryor camp was closed shortly after a March 1945 escape by a German naval officer and an enlisted man. The two men were captured while camping in a group of cedar trees in Pryor's Fairview Cemetery.

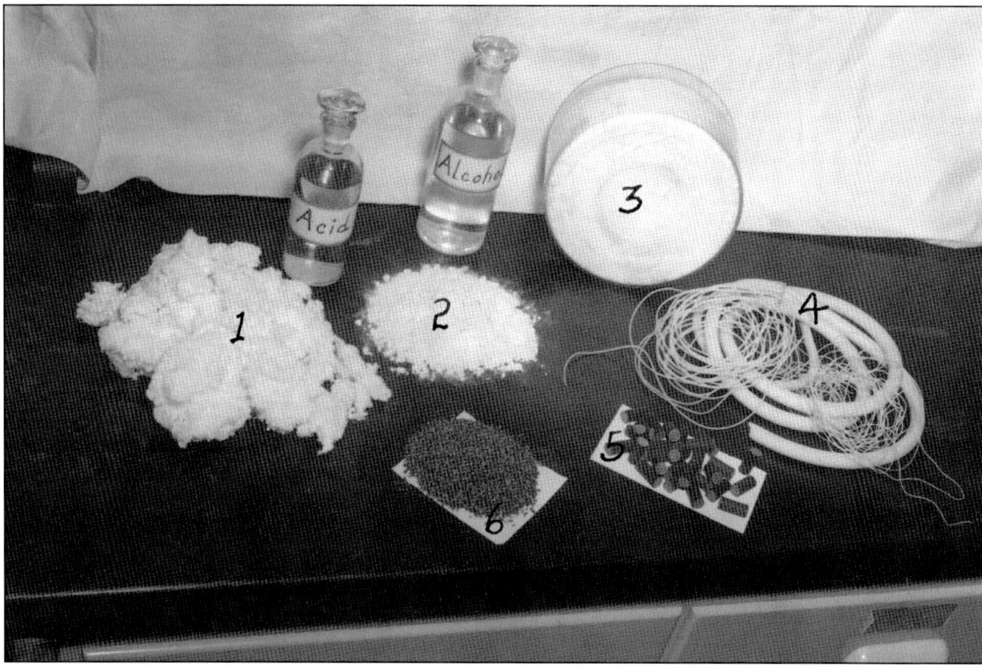

Materials used in the manufacturing of cannon powder and gunpowder include cotton linters; nitrocellulose; colloid block; 50-millimeter, 30-millimeter, and 155-millimeter strings; 155-millimeter Howitzer finished powder; and 50-caliber finished rifle powder. Smokeless powder is nitrocellulose, which is obtained by treating cellulose with nitric acid. The reaction then becomes a propellant, which drives the bullet of a rifle, pistol, or machine gun. The bullets are also filled with a form of TNT, to blow them into fragments. Cotton linters are also vital in the process of making the powder, as they absorb parts of the nitric acid. Cotton linters are the hair-like fuzz that clings to the cottonseed after the long fibers are removed in ginning. (Courtesy of Thomas J. Harrison Pryor Public Library.)

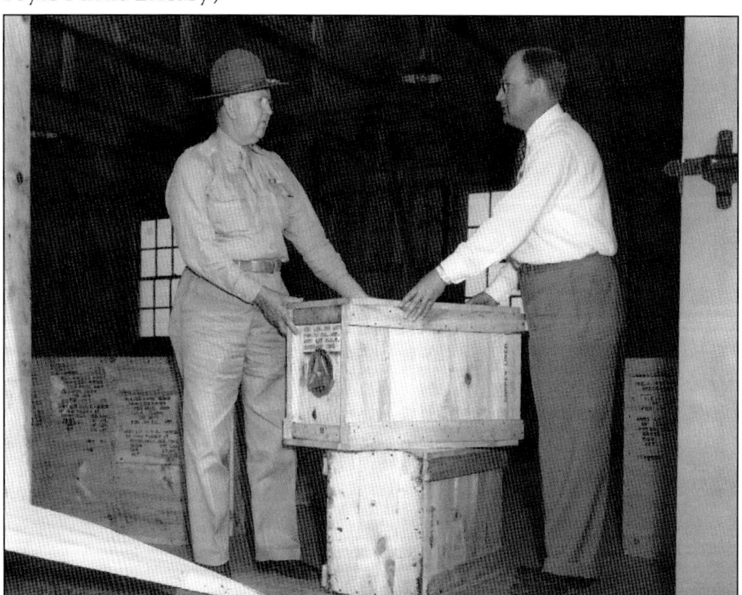

The first box of powder was delivered by DuPont manager G.R. Cantwell to Lt. Col. S.R. Kimble, nine months after the start of construction. By the summer of 1942, full production of rifle and cannon powder lines was in full swing. An estimated payroll of $2,985,568 was paid out to plant employees by year's end. (Courtesy of Thomas J. Harrison Pryor Public Library.)

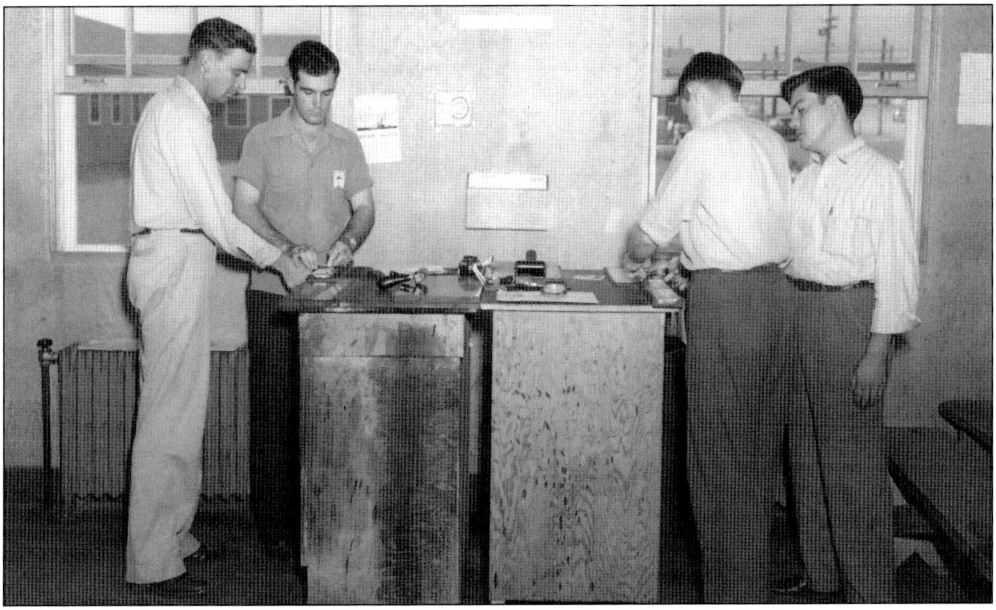

Newly hired employees at the plant were fingerprinted as part of an extensive background check. An estimated 15,000 to 20,000 people were expected to be employed during construction, and then 5,000 people for production. By February 1, 1942, there were 13,000 employees, with shuttle trains carrying one-seventh of the workforce. Service was added to the site from Vinita, Big Cabin, Adair, and Pryor. Fees were 25¢ round-trip from Pryor and 50¢ round-trip from Vinita. (Courtesy of Thomas J. Harrison Pryor Public Library.)

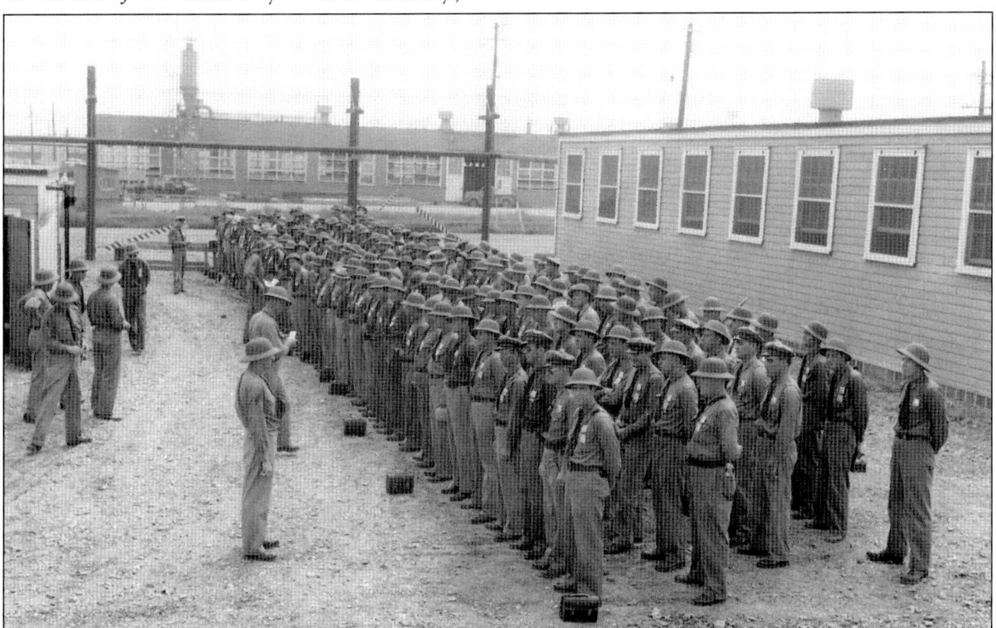

Plant patrolmen receive shift-change information prior to assuming their posts. On November 27, 1941, DuPont moved its offices from downtown Pryor to the plant site; 5,000 people were working, including 105 security guards. It was estimated that 15,000 would be employed by January 1942. (Courtesy of Thomas J. Harrison Pryor Public Library.)

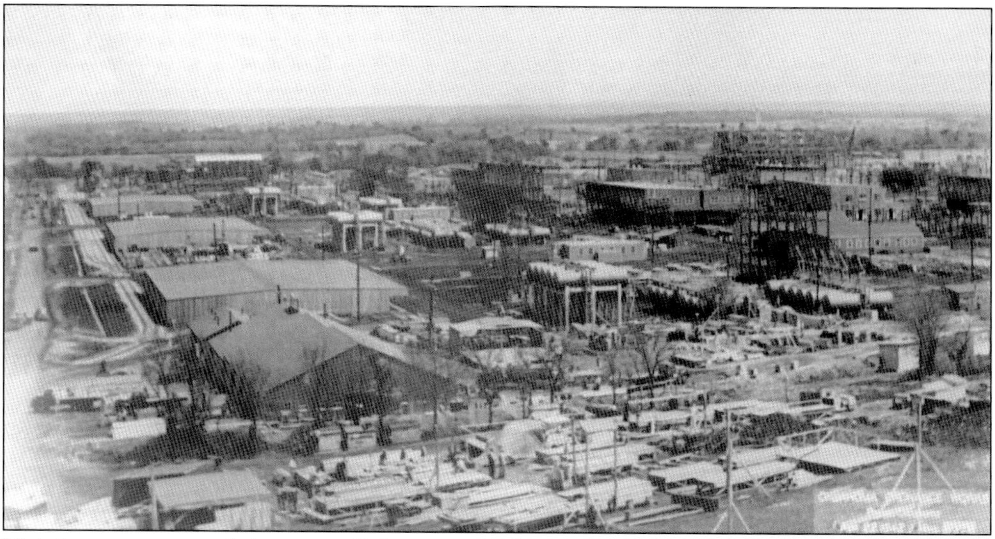

This is an overview of the nitrocellulose area and powerhouse under construction on April 22, 1942. (Courtesy of Thomas J. Harrison Pryor Public Library.)

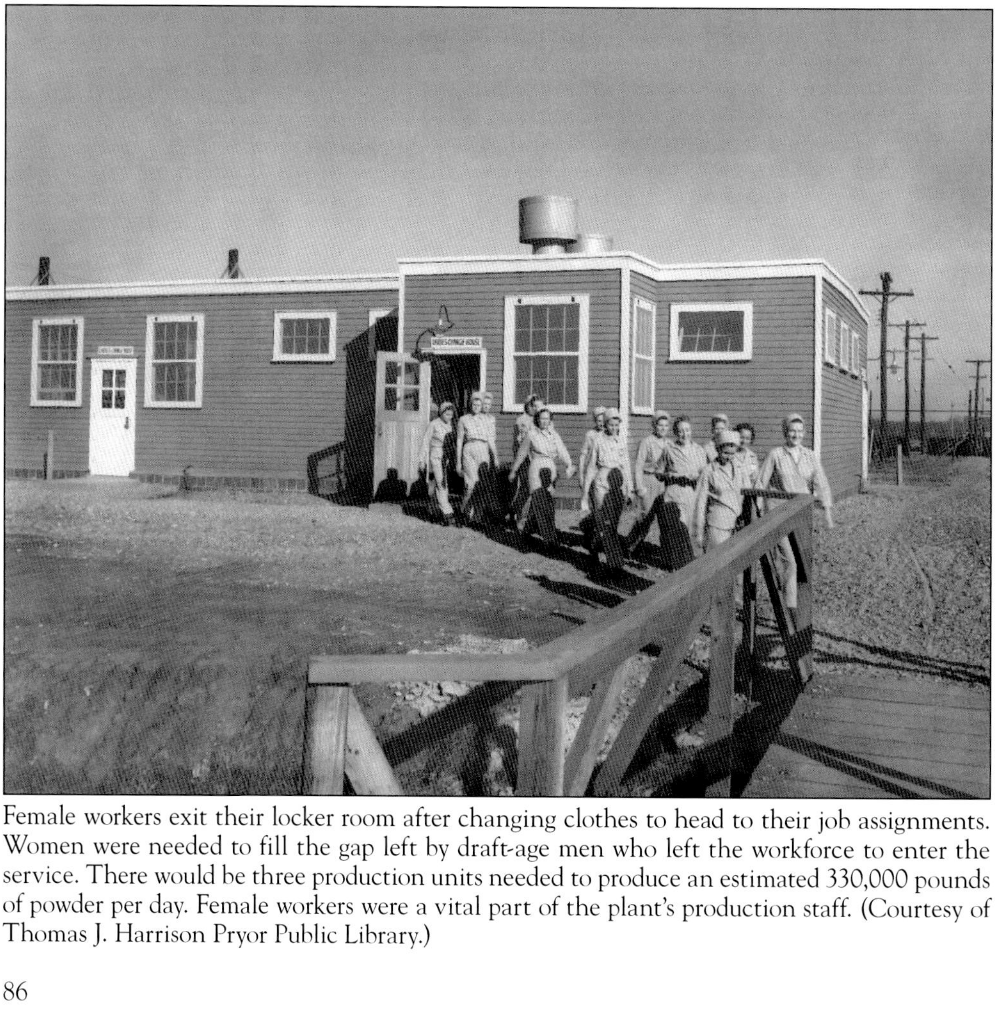

Female workers exit their locker room after changing clothes to head to their job assignments. Women were needed to fill the gap left by draft-age men who left the workforce to enter the service. There would be three production units needed to produce an estimated 330,000 pounds of powder per day. Female workers were a vital part of the plant's production staff. (Courtesy of Thomas J. Harrison Pryor Public Library.)

This photograph shows the granulation-cutting process of the cannon powder. Smokeless powder is actually a cylindrical grain about 1/32 of an inch by 1/12 of an inch for .30 caliber ammunition, and 9/10 of an inch by 2 inches for 16-inch artillery shells. (Courtesy of Thomas J. Harrison Pryor Public Library.)

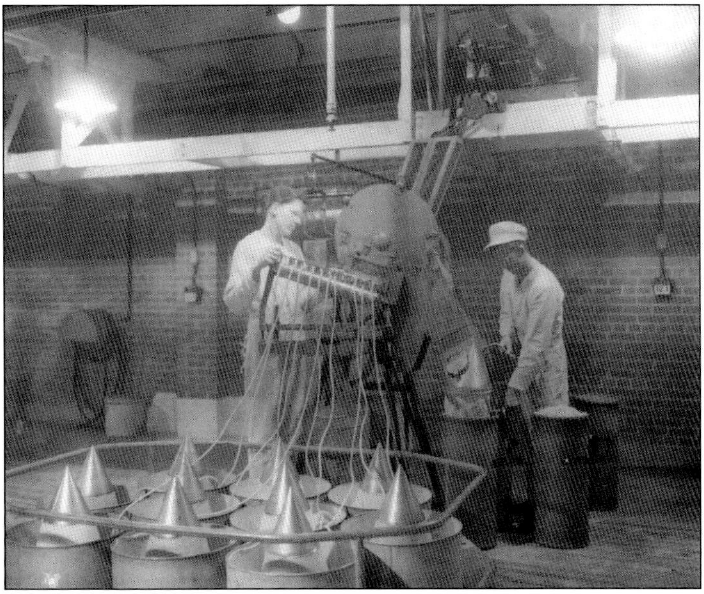

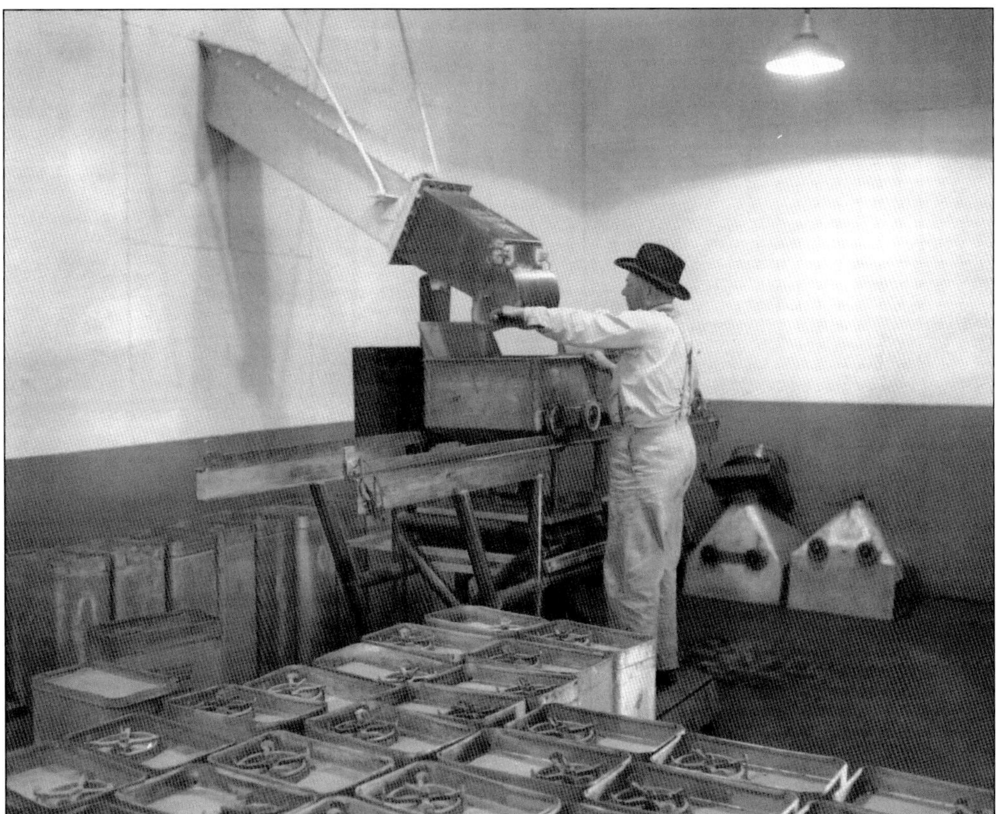

This photograph shows final packing of the cannon powder. The plant had been one of the Army's primary manufacturers of small-arms ammunition. Cannon-powder production centered on the 75-millimeter and 90-millimeter antiaircraft guns, as well as the 155-millimeter and 240-millimeter Howitzer. (Courtesy of Thomas J. Harrison Pryor Public Library.)

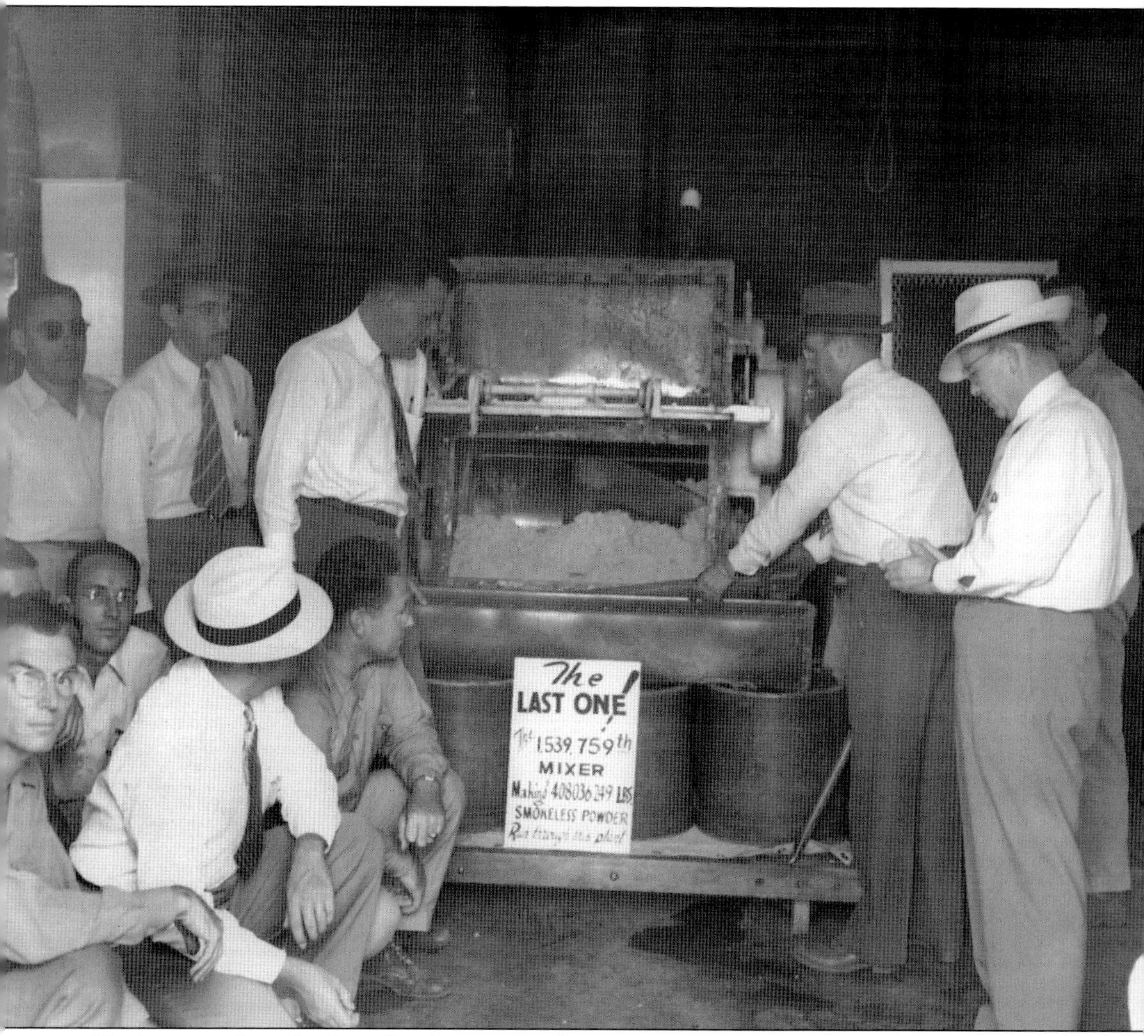

The last mix of powder from the plant was made on August 23, 1945. All total, the plant produced 1,539,759 mixes of powder, totaling 408,036,249 pounds of powder since production began in the summer of 1942. (Courtesy of Thomas J. Harrison Pryor Public Library.)

Eight

Tornado

The face of downtown Pryor was destroyed by a tornado on April 27, 1942, at 4:45 p.m. The storm killed 52 people and injured 400. It is believed that two tornados, originating in Rogers County, to the west of Pryor, came together to form one massive funnel. The tornado followed Oklahoma Highway 20 in an easterly direction as it struck downtown Pryor, destroying everything in its path. At the east end of Main Street, the twister turned north and followed the "S curve" back east, following the highway to the east edge of the city limits. The tornado lifted up as it passed over Cemetery Hill and disappeared.

Within two hours, officials from the DuPont Company, operating the government gunpowder plant south of town, had arrived downtown to bring aid and rescue workers. Laborers brought in heavy equipment, potable light units, and medical teams. Within two hours, streets were being cleared of debris with bulldozers in order to allow emergency crews to have free movement of the streets.

Medical personnel from out of town arrived within about three hours to assist the two local hospitals, Herrington and Whitaker. The injured were also taken to hospitals in Vinita, Miami, Tulsa, Muskogee, and Wagoner. The Salvation Army and Red Cross also played a major role in assisting with relief efforts, providing food and drink and bedding. Within three days, an Army field kitchen detachment from Fort Sill at Lawton, Oklahoma, was on the scene, providing hot meals 24 hours a day.

Utility superintendent R.D. Morgan was credited with saving more lives and preventing fires, as he was able to cut off the main gas-line valve for the city just as the storm hit.

Damage was estimated at $2 million by some, and the National Weather Service lists the storm as the fifth deadliest tornado in Oklahoma history.

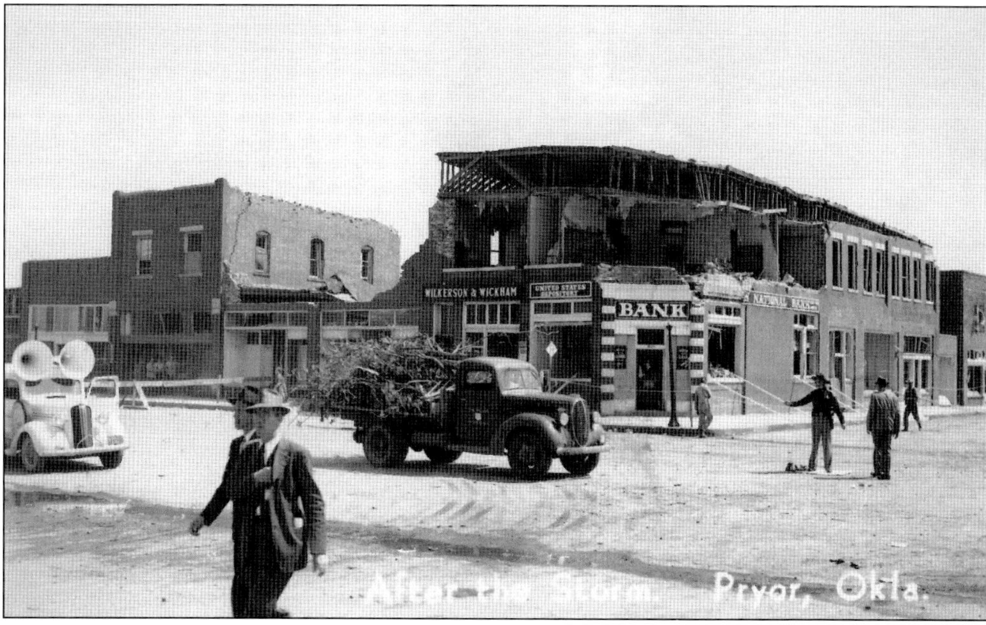

Taken several days after the tornado, this photograph shows the American National Bank and, to the left, Dougherty's Dime Store and Gatewood's Drug Store. Note the highway patrolman directing traffic in the middle of the intersection and the mobile radio-station broadcast van on the left.

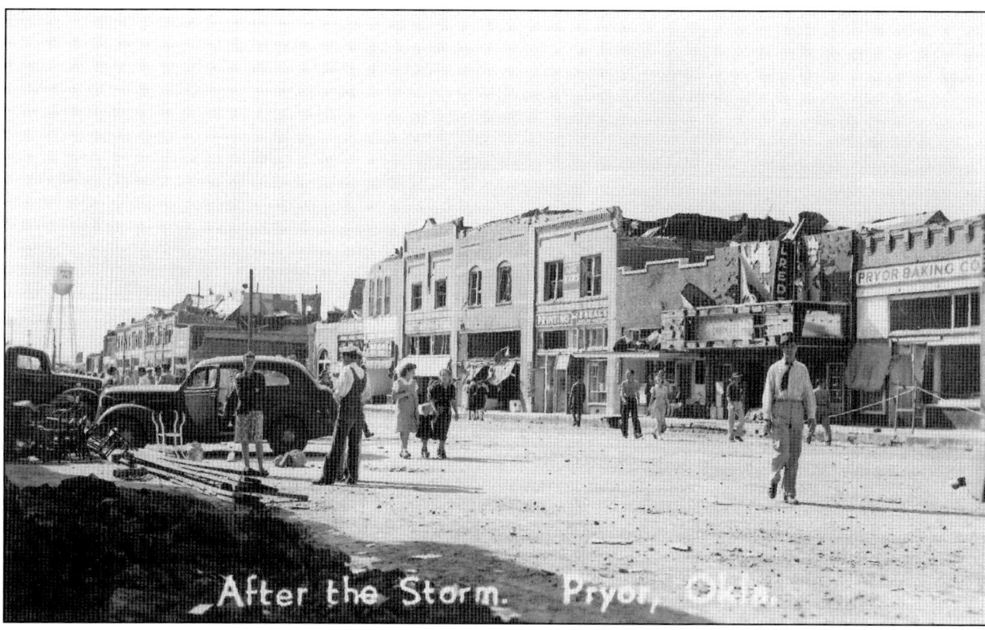

A few days after the storm, damage can be seen to the north side of Main Street, looking west from Vann Street. As can be clearly seen, the Allred Theater was destroyed, as was the Pryor Baking Company.

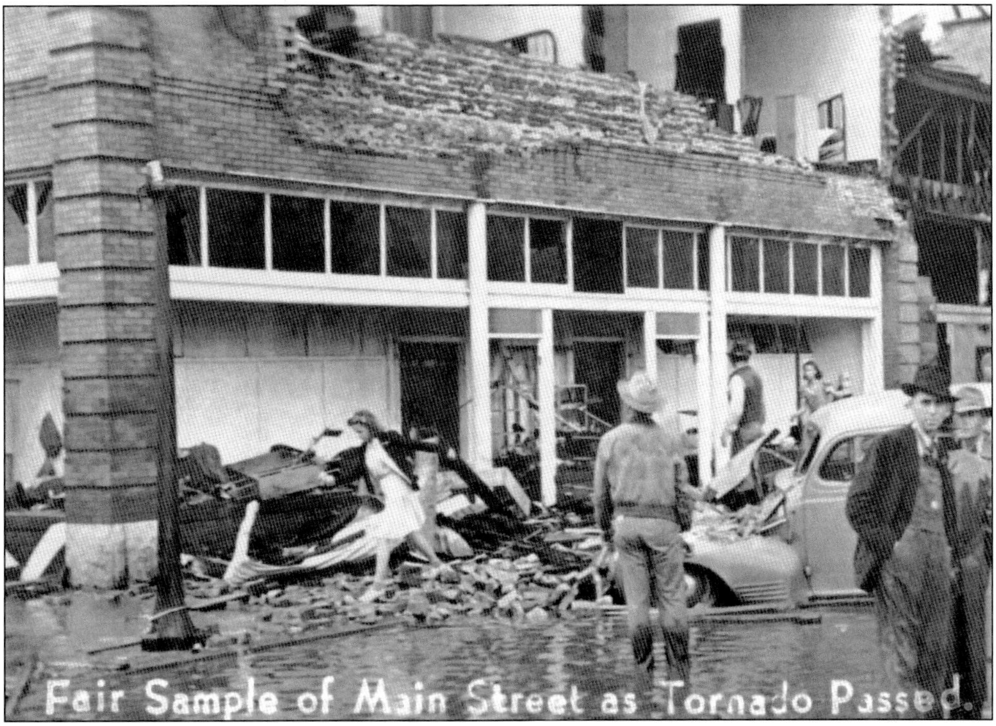

This photograph, taken a few hours after the tornado destroyed Main Street, shows the front of the Mayes Mercantile Company store and flooded street.

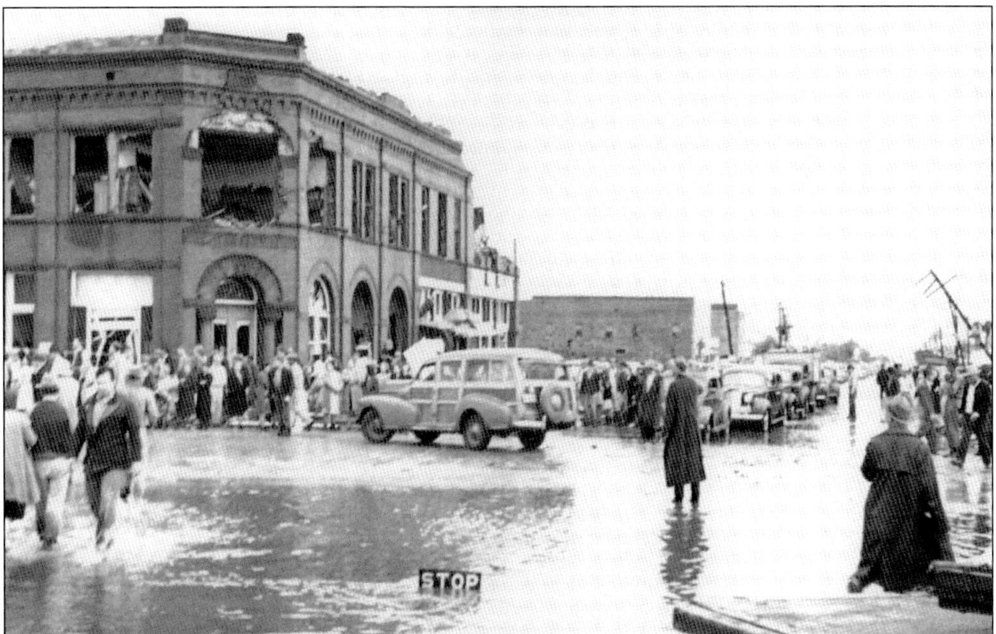

Townspeople wade through water at the intersection of Main and Mill Streets (US 69). The damage to the First National Bank and W.A. Graham Company is clearly visible at left. (Courtesy of Becky Hawkins.)

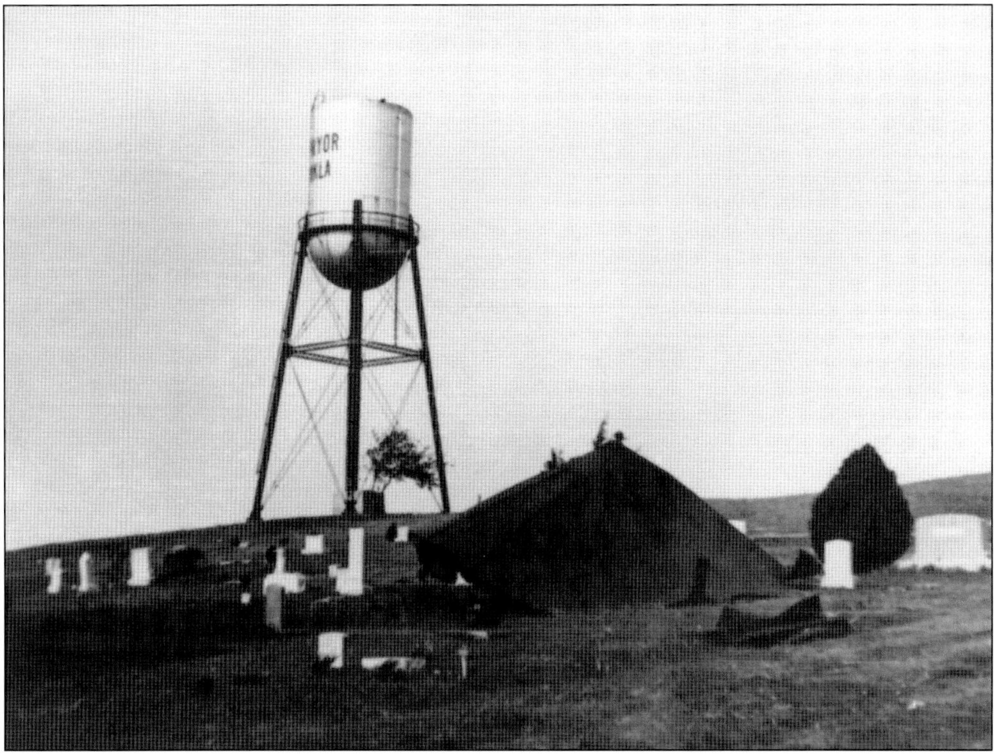

The tornado lifted off the ground at the top of Cemetery Hill, east of town, taking off the top of the city's eastside water tower.

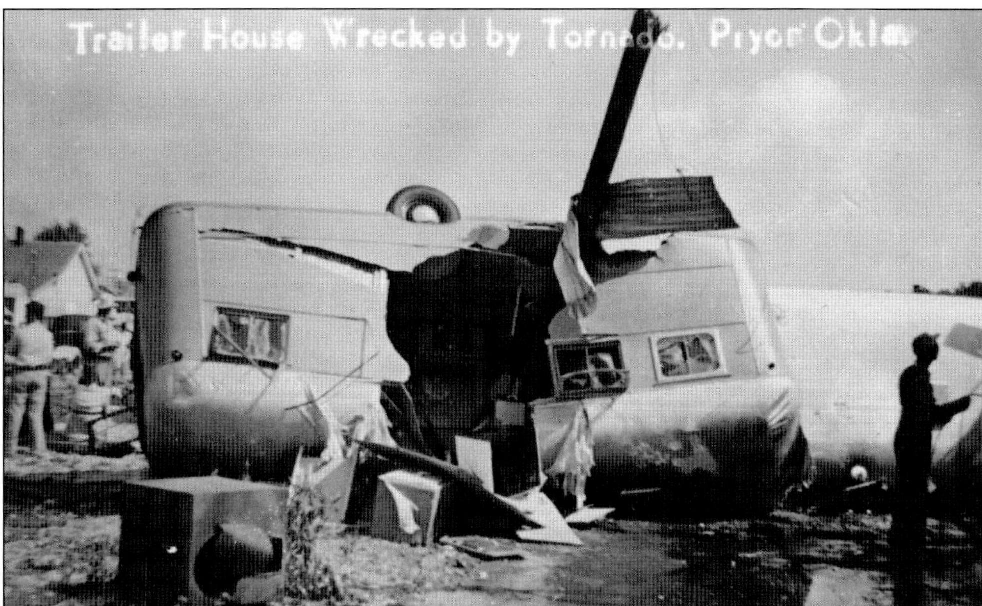

The destruction of this travel trailer, located on West Main, illustrates the amount of force a tornado possesses. The trailer is wrapped around a telephone pole.

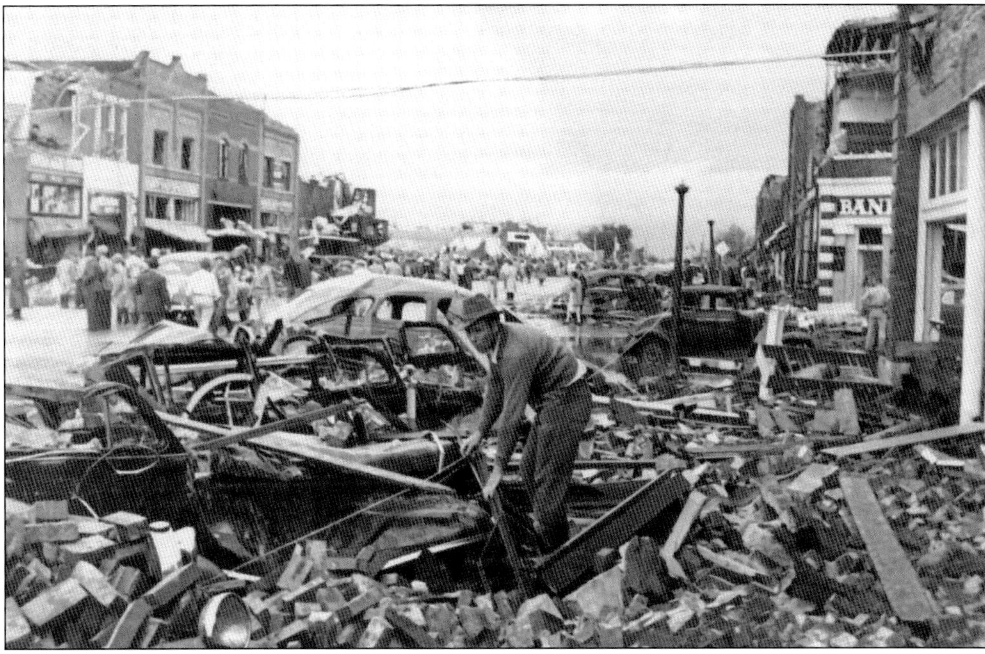

This east-facing photograph was taken from the front of Mayes Mercantile. The man is standing on the bumper of the destroyed car, indicating the depth of debris on the sidewalk.

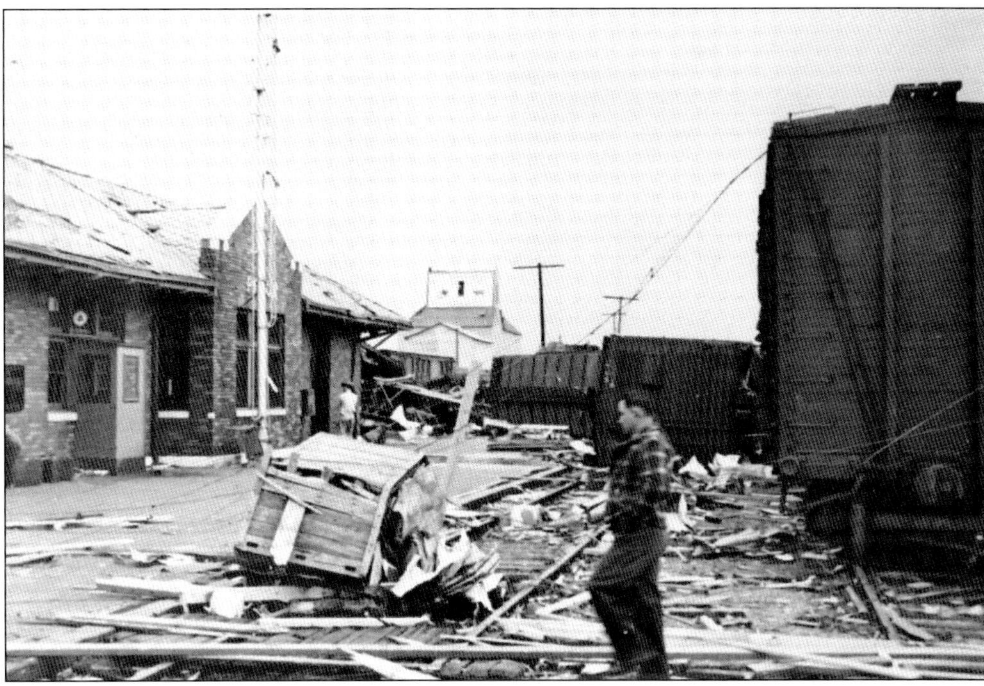

This photograph shows an overturned railroad boxcar on the west side of the Katy Depot.

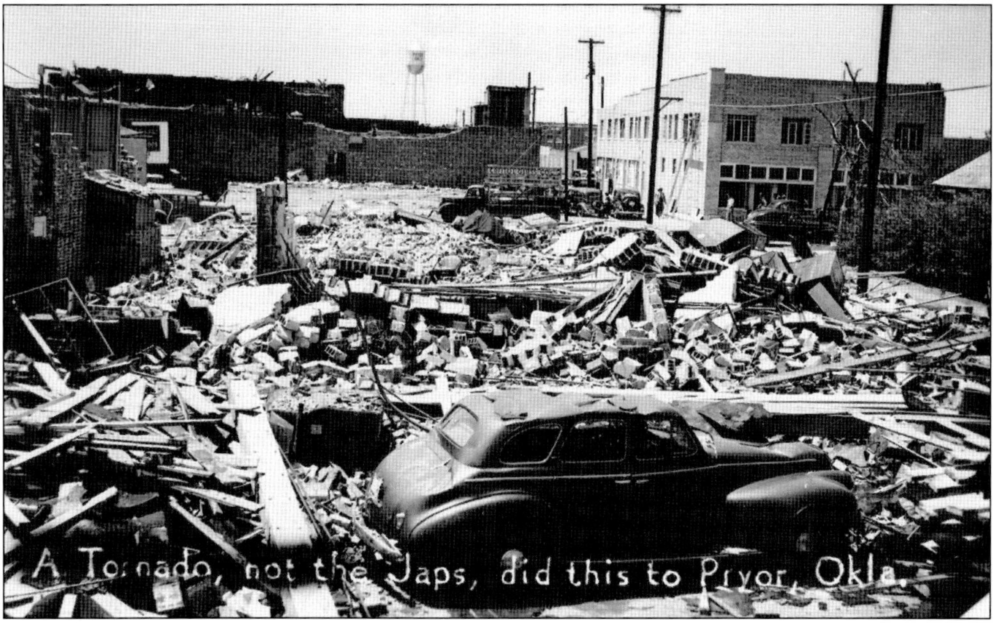

Damage was severe along the alley behind Gooldy Chevrolet and the New Pryor Theater. The photographer noted that "a tornado, not the Japs, did this to Pryor, Okla."

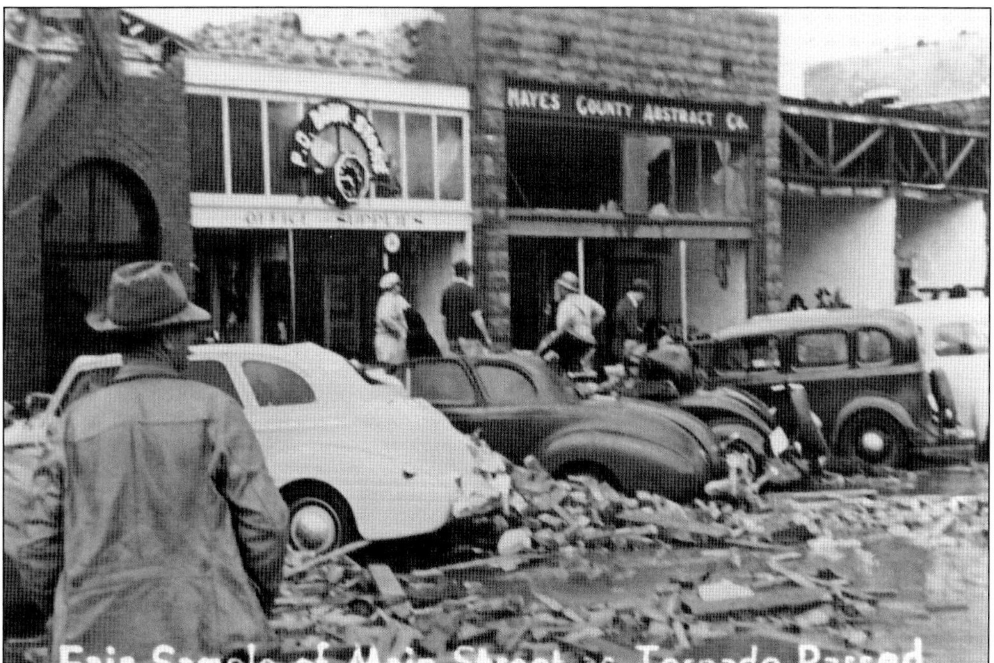

Damage to the Post Office Book Store and Mayes County Abstract Company is shown here. Note that the clock on the bookstore's facade has stopped at 4:45 p.m., the time that the deadly tornado roared through downtown.

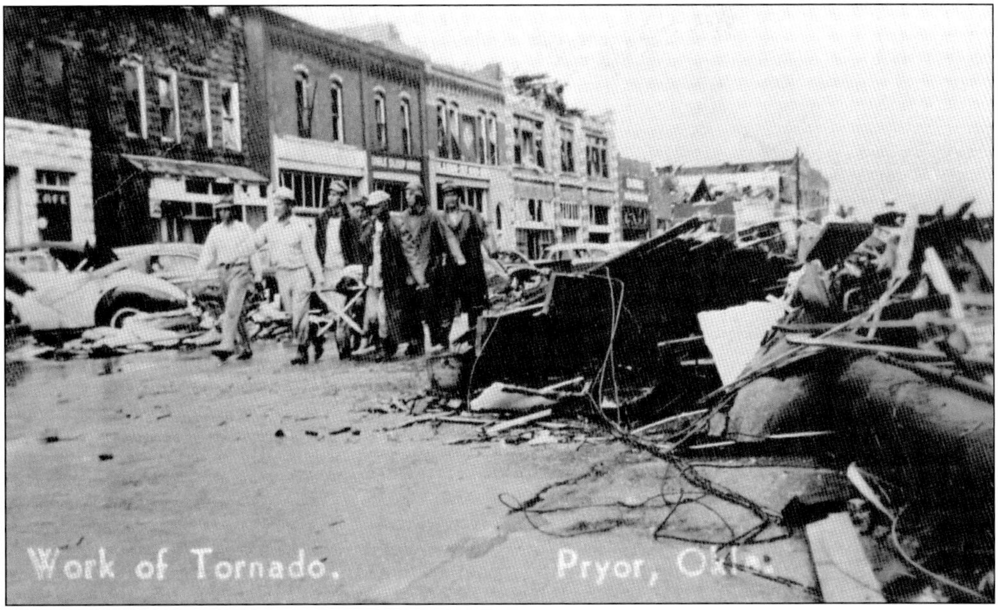

Rescue workers carry the wounded through a debris-strewn Main Street.

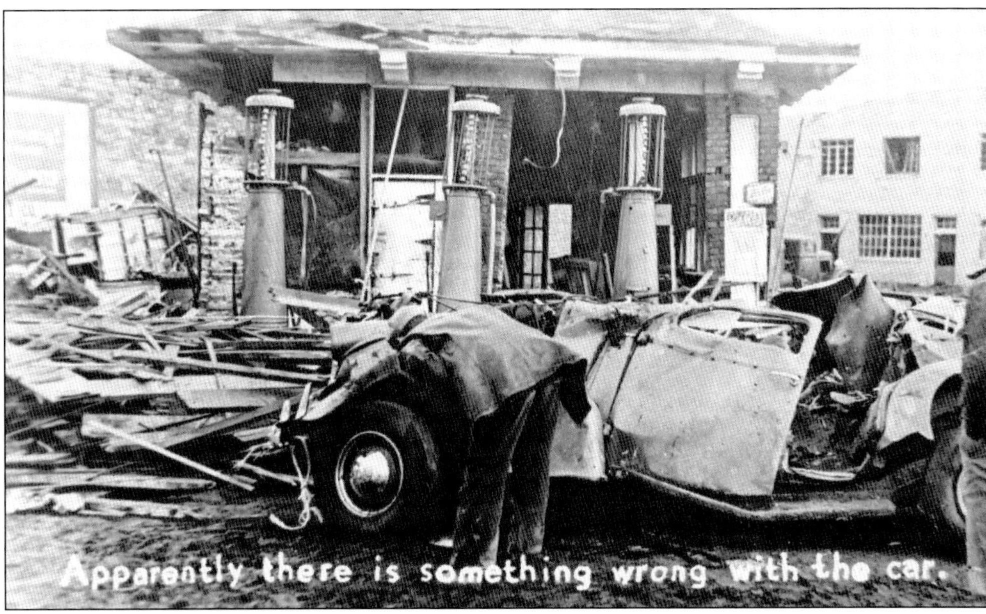

Located on the northwest corner of Main and Vann Streets, this gasoline station, along with the car, was destroyed by the tornado.

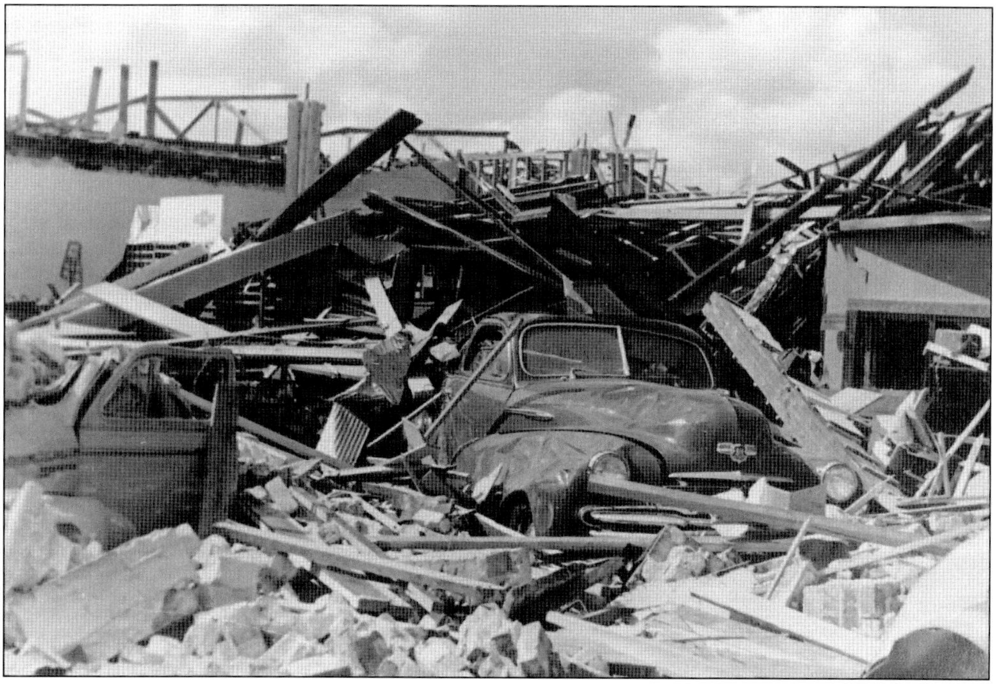

The showroom floor of Gooldy Chevrolet took a direct hit from the deadly storm. One of the Gooldy garage mechanics died when he was trapped underneath a car as the garage floor filled with water, drowning him.

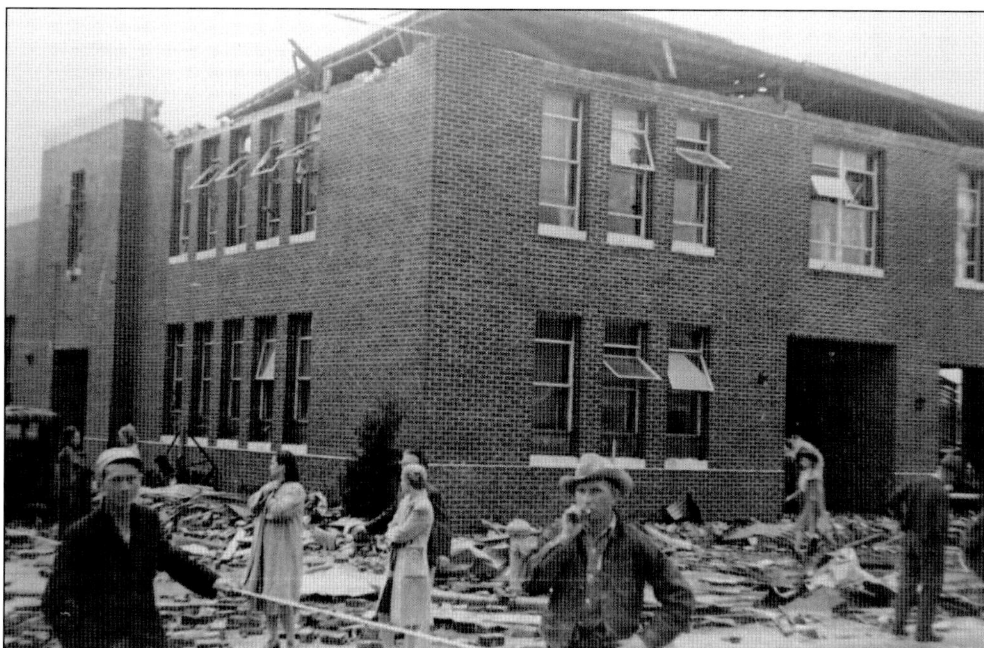

The tornado tore off the roof of the Graham Community Building (city hall) and broke out windows throughout the building.

Nine

Fires

The history of the Pryor Fire Department dates to April 1904, when the modern department was organized. The first volunteer firemen were Chief L.H. Tolbert, G.E. Hendrix, John J. Holt, P.A. Beyers, William McFarland, Ben Elliot, J.A. Quinn, Ed Hyde, Edgar Langley, W.W. Herron, S.A. Duncan, William Wright, Walter Hairston, F.R. Morgan Jr., J.J. Riddle, Thomas J. Harrison, and T.R. Crookshank. Former chiefs of the fire department since Tolbert have included John J. Holt, Albert Davis, Neil Sansing, Ted Blakemore, Eugene Rudd, Benny Donahue, David Harrison, and present chief Tim Thompson.

There have been about 44 major business fires over a 101-year period (1909–2010). Those include the following fires in the first half of the 20th century: Samuel & Poffenbach Building (August 1909), Merchants Café gas explosion and W.A. Graham Corn Crib Warehouse (June 1911), John Holt Building (Pool Hall and Plumbing Shop, May 1913), Mayes County Motor Company (September 1923), Farmer's Elevator (October 1930), John Shutt Cotton Gin (November 1930), Bouldin-Thornton Grain Elevator (April 1931), Samuel Bros. Hardware (January 1932), Gooldy Chevrolet (April 1938), Antrim Lumber Company (May 1943), Mayes Mercantile/Roberts Apartments (December 1943), Cities Service Warehouse (July 1945), *Daily-Times Democrat*/ Dr. Taylor Office/Victory Cab Company (September 1947), Mayor Hotel (November 1948), Ed Hamilton's Service Station (November 1951), Pryor School Gymnasium (December 1952), Jones Hardware explosion (December 1953), Gay Paree Nightclub (September 1954), Bill's Skating Rink (April 1957), and Packard Bros. Motor Co. Garage (October 1959).

The following major fires occurred in the second half of the 20th century: Cherokee Drug Store (January 1960), MidWest Carbide explosion (December 1960), Gabel's Ranch House Sausage Plant (January 1961), Dimmitt's Garage (January 1964), Old City Jail explosion (January 1964), Sears/ Sherwin-Williams Paint Store (August 1967), Pryor High School and OTASCO/Skel-Gas/ Mule-Skin Brown Furniture/Avenue TV (January 1969), Cherokee Nitrogen explosion/fire (January 1973), Pryor Rescue Mission (October 1973), Ken's Red Barn Café (Old Hereford House/Cattleman's Café) (August 1979), Wallpaper Barn (January 1980), Pet Parade Pet Shop (Old Prairie Schooner Café) (June 1980), Moose Lodge (Old Polly's Restaurant) (February 1985), Pryor Rescue Mission (August 1985), Moots Hospital (August 1994), and Pryor Lumber Yard (April 1996).

The town has experienced the following fires in the 21st century: Thomas Restaurant (May 2006), Kla-Mart Warehouse (January 2008), Second Impressions retail shop (December 2009), KFC (December 2009), Boom-a-Rang Diner (January 2010), and Western Auto store (March 2010).

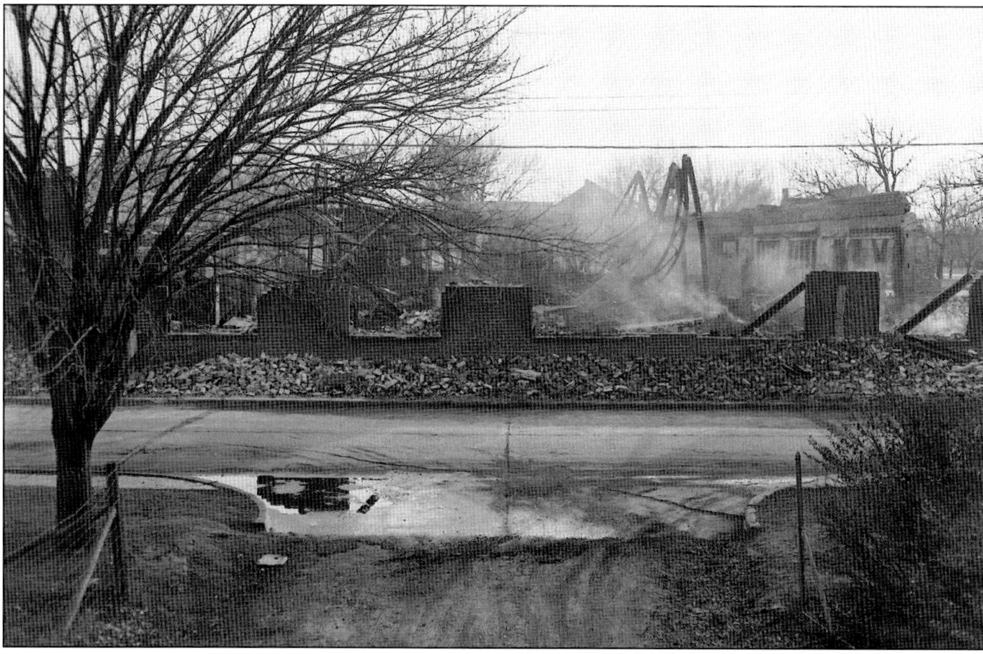

The Pryor High School gymnasium, built in 1921, was destroyed by fire on December 29, 1952. Also destroyed were the school's industrial arts shop and FFA classrooms and equipment. Those classes, as well as the athletic activities, were moved to the Whitaker State Home campus until a new gymnasium was completed in 1954. The devastating blaze, thought to be electrical, caused over $150,000 in damage. The school board only carried about $64,000 in insurance coverage on the facility. Firefighters from three area departments had a difficult time bringing the fire under control, battling stiff winds, which caused various grass fires in yards within a two-block radius of the school campus. Several thousand dollars in damage to telephone lines resulted in multiple phone outages throughout the neighborhood.

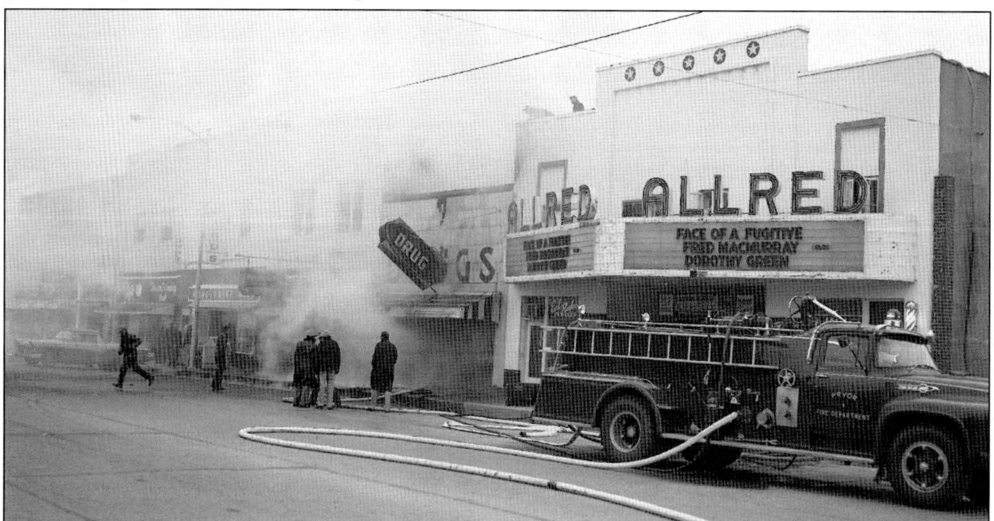

In January 1960, a major fire destroyed the Cherokee Drug Store and caused smoke damage to adjoining businesses. Firms affected by the smoke and water damage included Wallis Men's Wear and Earl Ragland Jewelry.

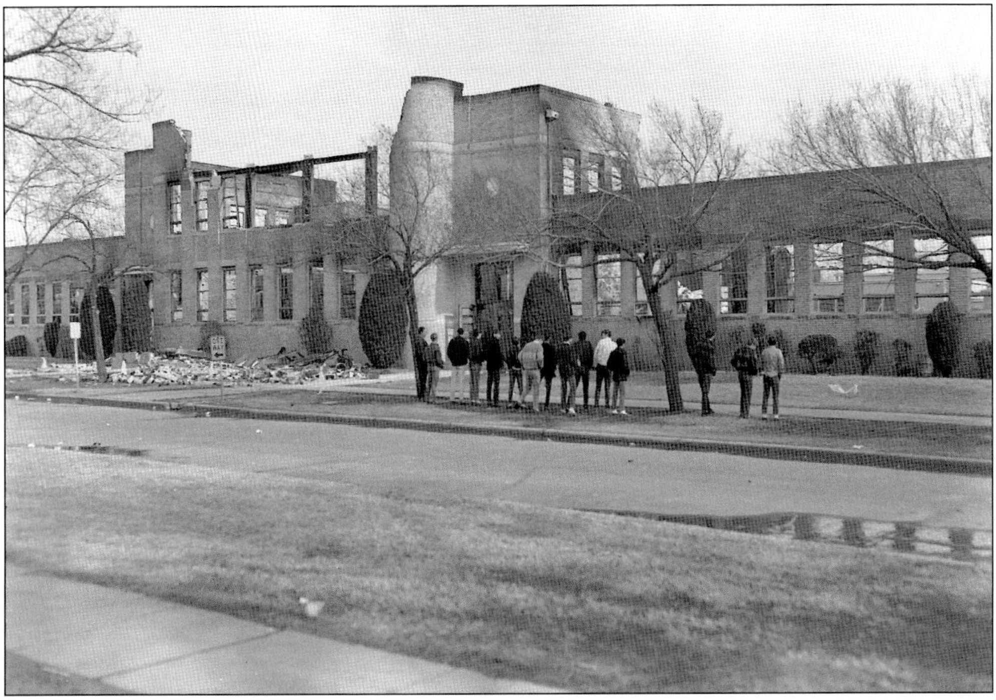

Pryor High School was destroyed by fire in the early morning of January 12, 1969. It was suspected that the blaze was set to cover up a burglary of the building. Damages were estimated at $800,000, and two dozen firefighters from three departments spent hours to bring the blaze under control. Here, students observe the school building that they will attend no more.

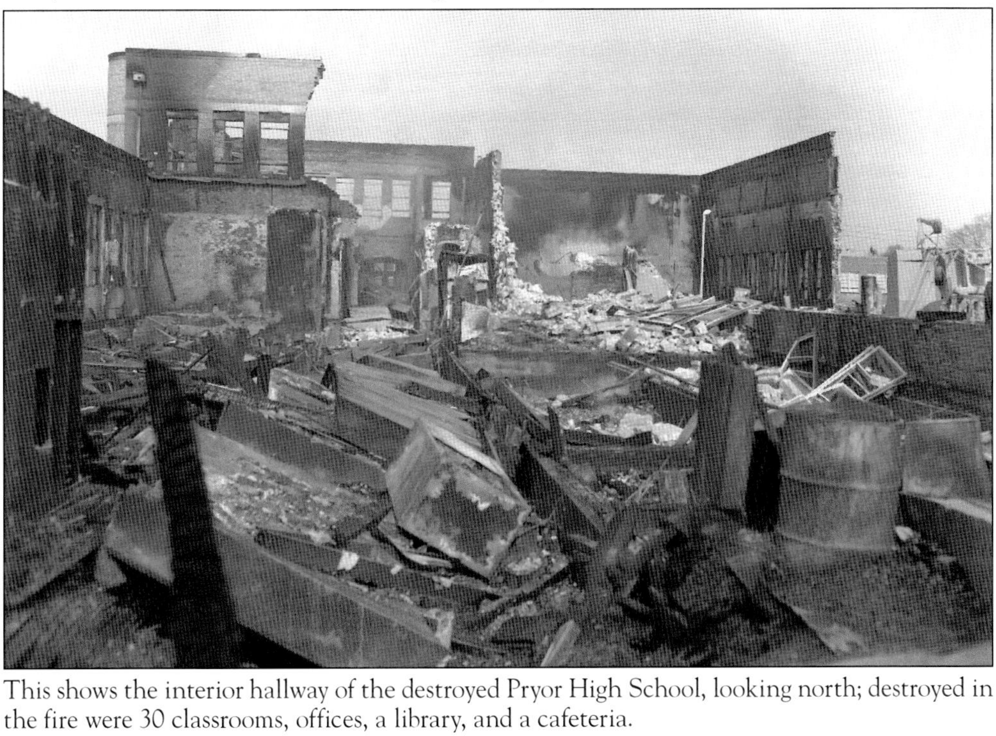

This shows the interior hallway of the destroyed Pryor High School, looking north; destroyed in the fire were 30 classrooms, offices, a library, and a cafeteria.

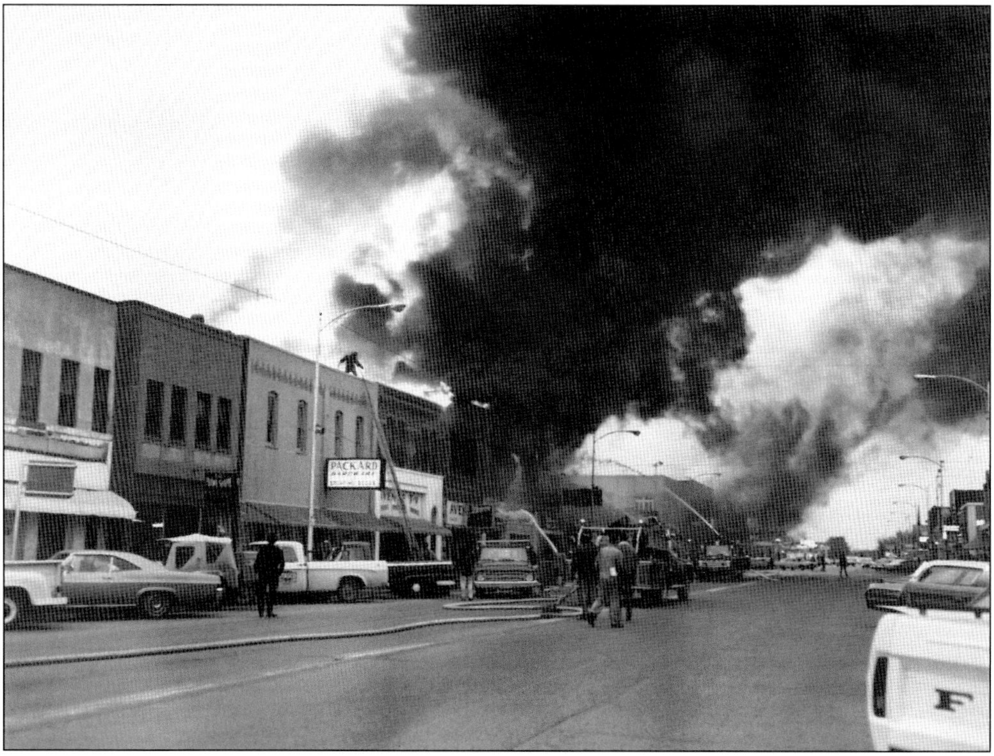

A half block of downtown Pryor Creek was destroyed by fire on the afternoon of January 23, 1969. The blaze was suspected to have started with a gas leak in the Skel-Gas store before spreading throughout the former Mayor Hotel building, erected in 1910. That building had earlier been damaged by fire in 1948. Businesses destroyed were Vandevort Accounting, Farm Bureau, Avenue TV, OTASCO, and Mule-Skin Brown Furniture.

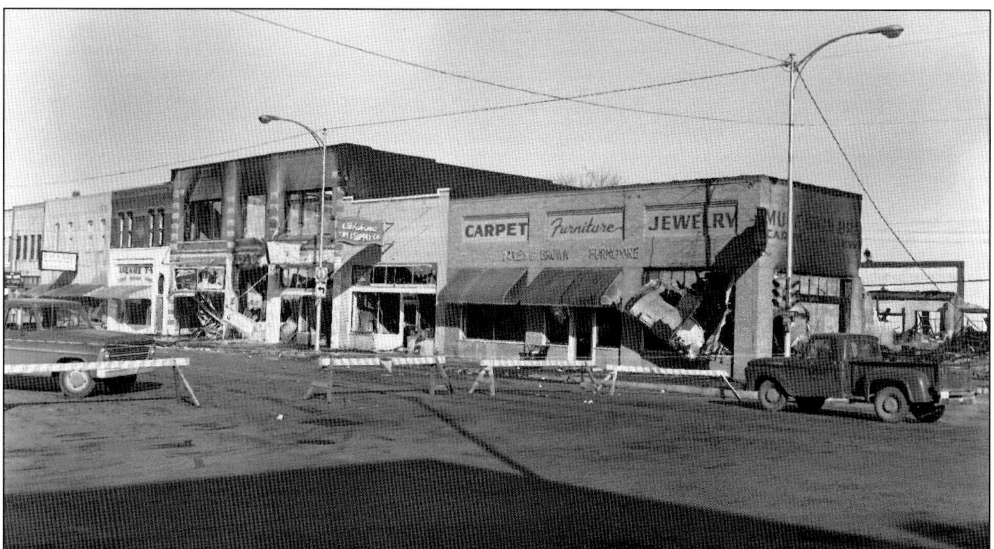

The aftermath of the 1969 downtown fire is visible a week later. This photograph shows the destruction of half a city block.

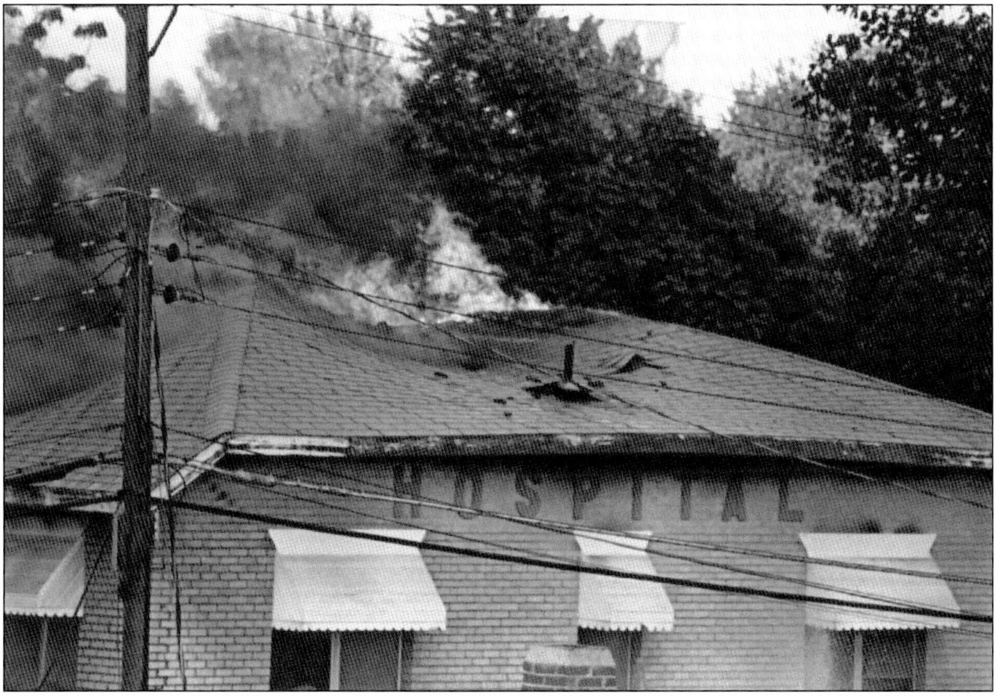

Flames breaking through the roof of the closed Moots Hospital are clearly visible on August 15, 1994. The former medical center had stood empty for a few years. It was the birthplace of many Mayes County residents. The fire, thought to be arson but never solved, quickly spread through the 52-year-old structure. (Courtesy of Terry Aylward.)

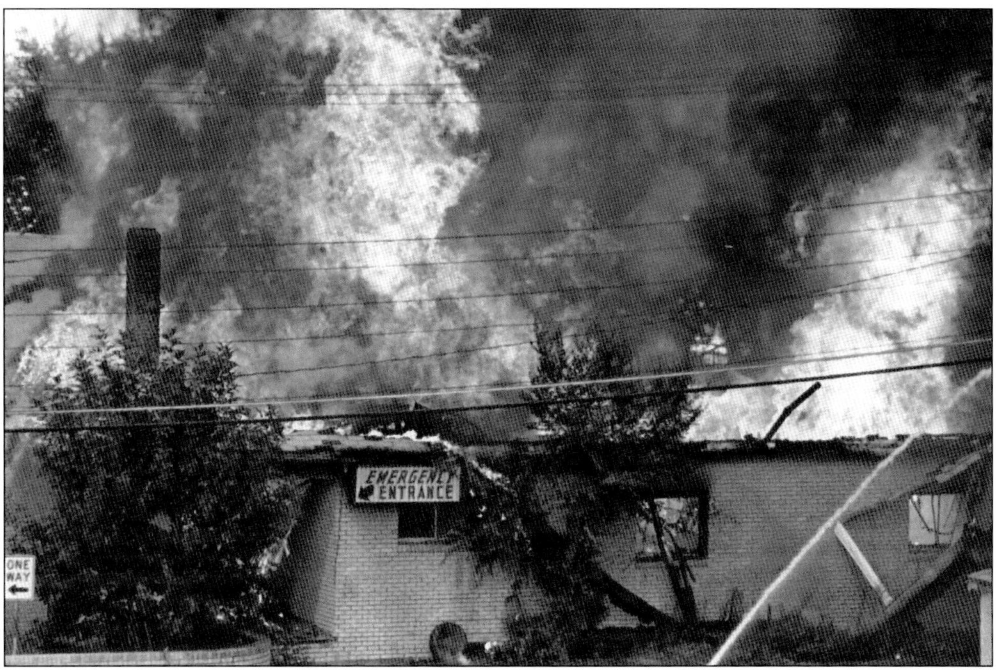

The west wing emergency room area is a blazing inferno as the former Moots Hospital is destroyed on August 15, 1994. (Courtesy of Terry Aylward.)

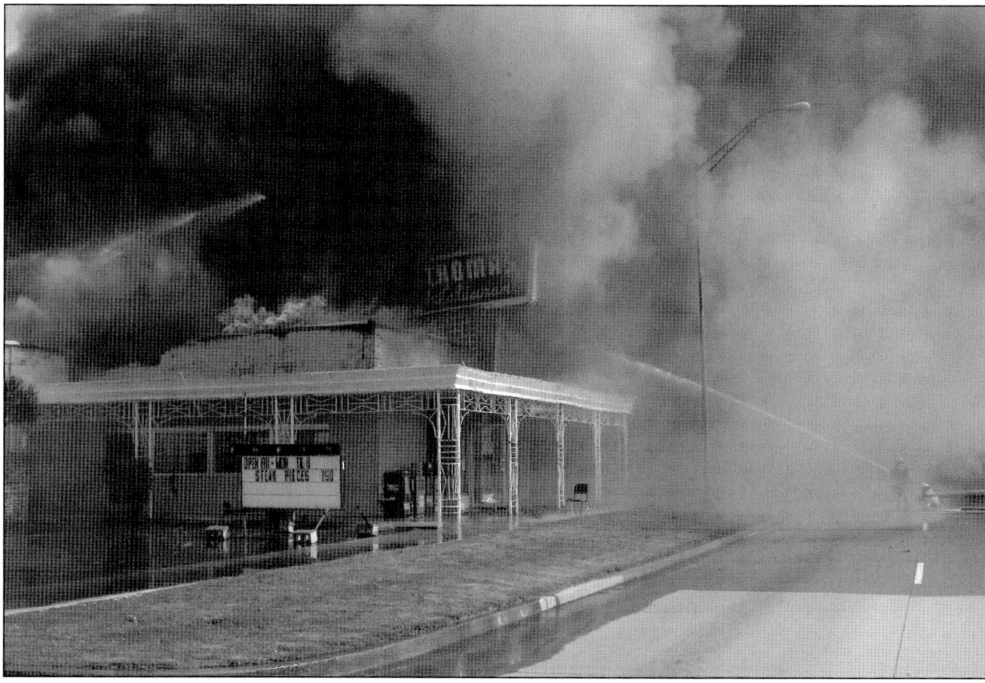

Thomas Restaurant, a regional landmark since 1954, was destroyed on the afternoon of May 18, 2006. The blaze, which started in the kitchen, quickly spread through the attic. Firefighters were unable to stop it. Dozens of firefighters from several fire departments worked for hours to bring the fire under control, but not before the building was a total loss. (Both, courtesy of Terry Aylward.)

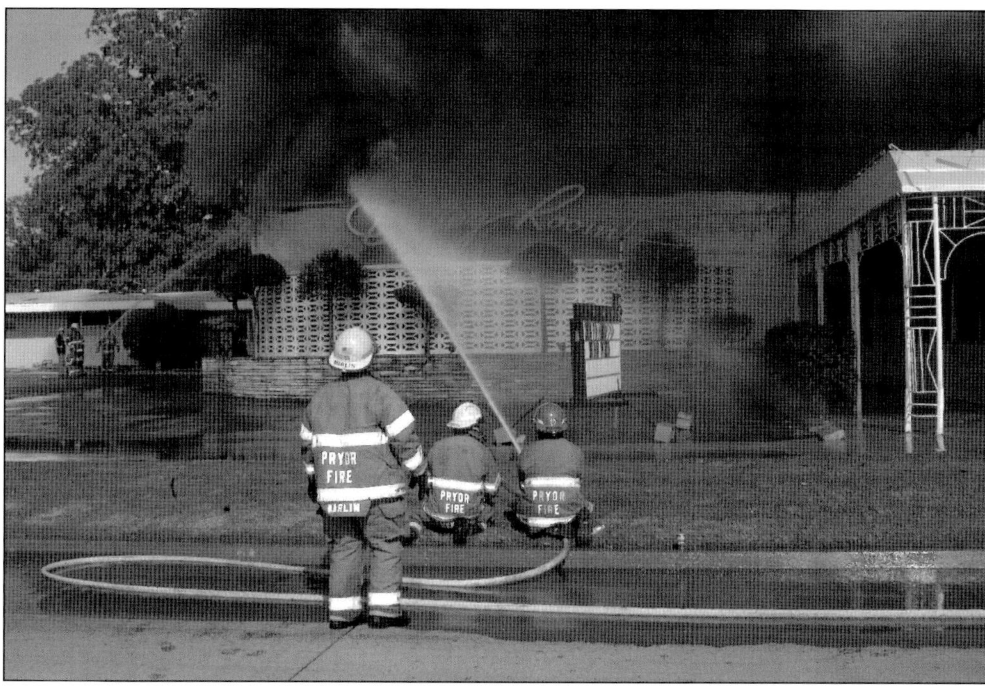

Ten

People

The people of a community make an impact on others, whether through business, politics, church or school activities, civic or scouting groups, or the military. Just a few of Pryor Creek's citizens are featured in this chapter.

Many people are left out of this chapter due to space restraints or the lack of available photographs. Among these memorable people are clothing-store owners Retta Crawford, Chuck Saunders, Tommy Thompson, Ken Spencer, and Boyce Wallis; agriculture-related businesspeople such as Riley Low, D.A. George, Red Powell, Orbie Lair, Churchill Stanislaus, and Leslie Sandusky; and service-station operators Herb Sansing, E.G. Wise, Brice Wallis, Roy Conn, Ralph Ables, Ted Cagle, Cliff Allen, Ralph Powell, Emery Martin, Pat Curtsinger, and George Price.

The town's car dealers include Jay Martin, Jack Norman, Jim Phillips, Ralph Moore, J.D. Cox, Jim Fleming, Bill Gooldy, Guy Hedrick, and Merle and Glen Colvert. Grocers not able to be highlighted in these pages include Raymond and Margaret Gable, Les and Lea Horner, Raymond Dyer, Connie Pullen, Charlie and Clara Engle, and Jerry and Agnus Stafford. Those involved in banking are R. Kenneth Crain, Mutt McArtor, Nolen Jacobs, Pat Robinson, Lynn Hudson, George Tilly, Tom McFarland, Roy Lawson, Lester Moore, Jehue Brown, and Doug Brown.

Other important people in town include church leaders Rev. C.E.A McKim, Forrest Jackson, Wendell Lange, Father Patrick Murtagh, and Ray Gwartney; school personnel Dean and Jean Robertson, Mary Louise Janz, Wanda Gore, Dorothy and Curtis Barnett, Ward Neal, Patsy Gore, Dee Ann Briggs, Ken Pierce, Angelina Rickey, Ida Mae Phillips, John Livengood, and Rick and Jana Elliot; and political leaders Lisa Melchior, Joe Faircloth, Pat Morgan, Erma Rogers, Hokie Foreman, Chief Jordan, Wiley Backwater, Frank Cantey, Larry Rice, J.D. Whorton, John Mozingo, and Judges Bill Thomas and Edwin Moore.

Local photographers include Herb Thompson, William Parker, Jack Hardy, Tommy Parker, Tim Bonea, and Charles Quiatto. Area doctors are Pat Williams, Don Collins, Robert Bissell, William Dieker, R.L. Detjen, O.R. Nunley, Gary McClure, G.W. Tilly, and James Jones. Café operators include Pop Delay, Larry Yancey, Pat Roberts, Searcy Ritch, Pat Curtsinger, Joe Littlefield, Jess and Dovie Higgs, Otis Whipkey, and Pete Stamper.

And finally, the following people have not been able to be included here: Gene Schultz, Harry Schaeffer, Leroy Melton, Lee Morgan, Lester and Virginia Gatewood, Dale Hardy, Paul Venamon, Bob Stafford, Maurine Walsh, Ruth Hogan, Merrill Stott, Monty Summy, Henry Neftzger, Tony Jack Lyons, Herb Hale, Bob Dimmitt, "Citizen" Doug Carson, Bill Kimsey, Gerald Clack, J.C. Wilkerson, K.C. and Jean Hesler, David Greer, Ronnie Ramsay, Mike and Mary Ann Guadagno, Red Carpenter, Dutch Longenbaugh, Ivan Pace, Tim Key, Warren Hadley, Blair Doolin, J.W. Gatewood, and Gene Jones.

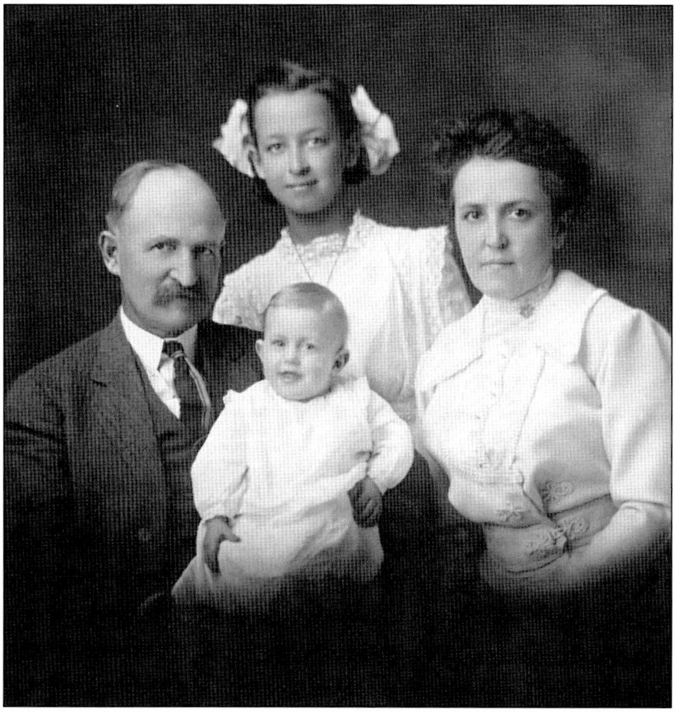

Dr. James L. Mitchell (1868–1945) was one of Pryor Creek's early doctors, arriving fresh out of medical school in 1893. His wife, Mary, or "Ma," ran a downtown coffee shop on Main Street. Probably the most famous guest to dine at Ma Mitchell's café was child actor Carl "Alfalfa" Switzer (of Little Rascals fame). He was traveling with his parents in September 1937. Shown here are Dr. and Mrs. Mitchell with children Josephine and John. (Courtesy of Nancy Mitchell Trundle.)

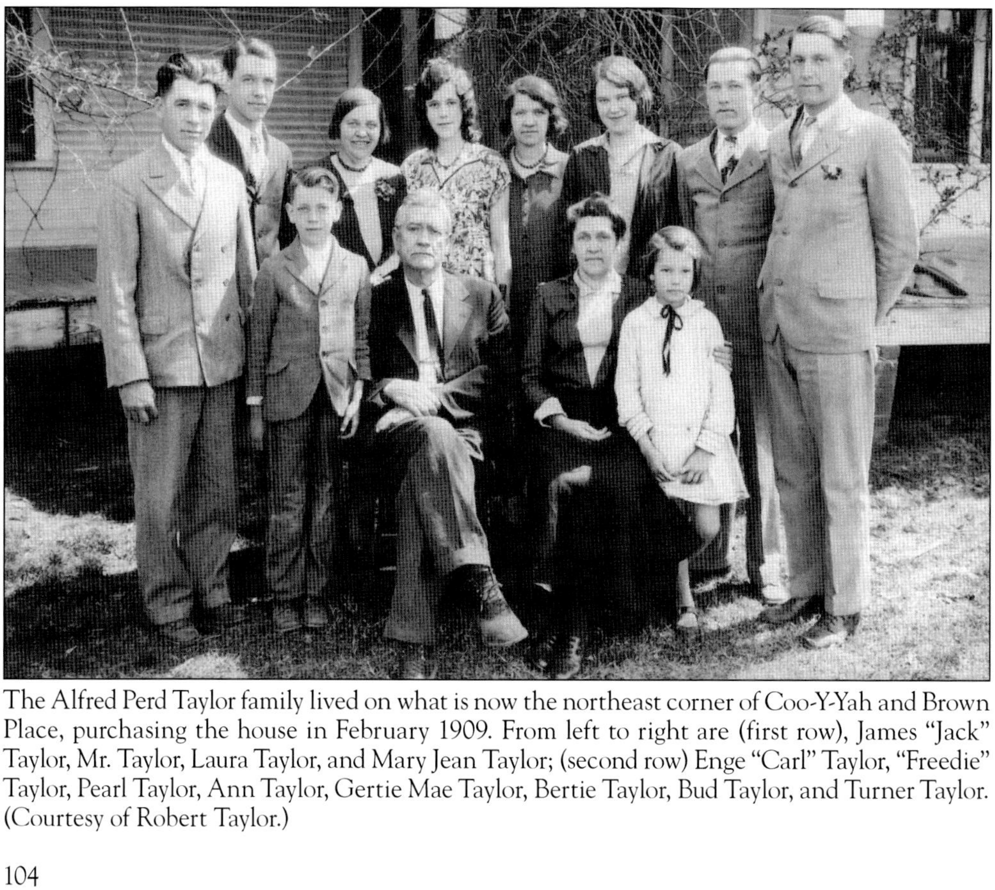

The Alfred Perd Taylor family lived on what is now the northeast corner of Coo-Y-Yah and Brown Place, purchasing the house in February 1909. From left to right are (first row), James "Jack" Taylor, Mr. Taylor, Laura Taylor, and Mary Jean Taylor; (second row) Enge "Carl" Taylor, "Freedie" Taylor, Pearl Taylor, Ann Taylor, Gertie Mae Taylor, Bertie Taylor, Bud Taylor, and Turner Taylor. (Courtesy of Robert Taylor.)

Burdette Green, son of Mr. and Mrs. E.A. Green, was the first Eagle Scout in the community, receiving the coveted award in 1914. A member of the troop sponsored by the Methodist Church, Green, 15, was at that time reported to have been the youngest Eagle Scout in America. He was the third Eagle Scout west of the Mississippi River.

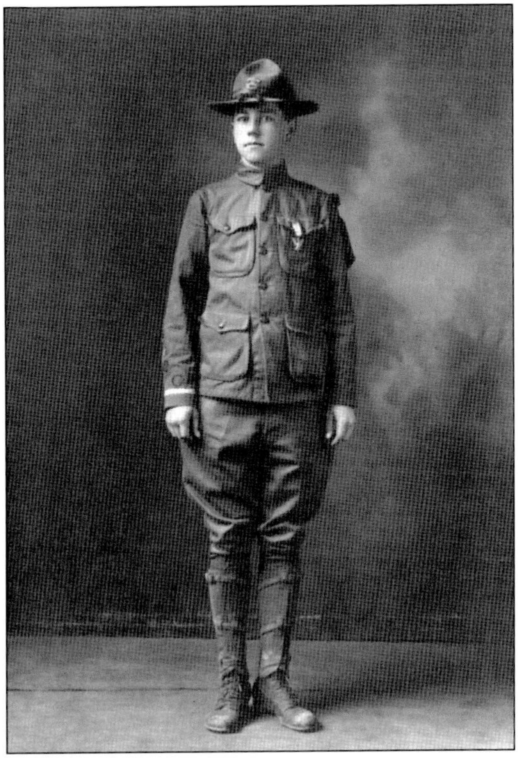

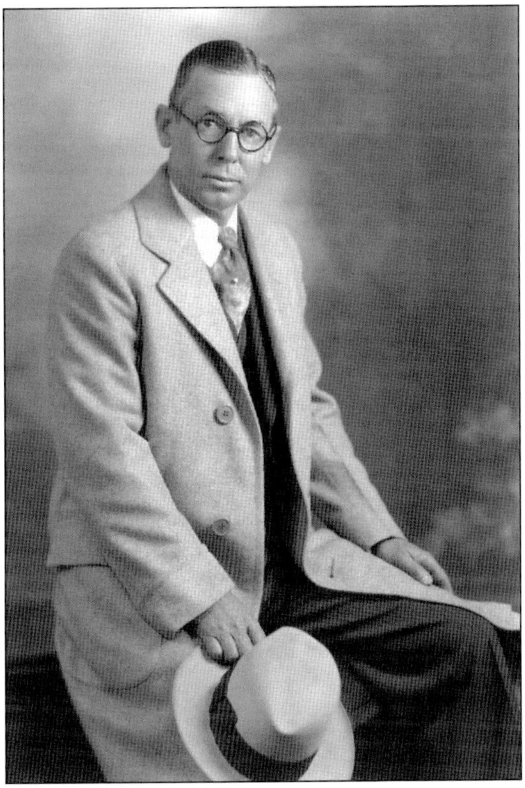

Thomas J. Harrison (1885–1963) was the mayor of Pryor Creek (1921–1931 and 1937–1943) and the town's foremost historian. He was an avid booster and sponsor of the Mayes County Fair and a member of the board of directors of the Oklahoma State Historical Society from 1941 until his death. He had a vast rare Bible collection, which was donated at the time of his death to the Bidwell Library at Southern Methodist University in Dallas, Texas. In his will, a trust was established that benefited the Bidwell and Pryor Public Libraries, Rotary Club, his local Methodist church, Children's Medical Center in Tulsa, Red Cross, and Boy Scouts. Founding the Pryor Public Library in 1939 was one of Harrison's greatest achievements.

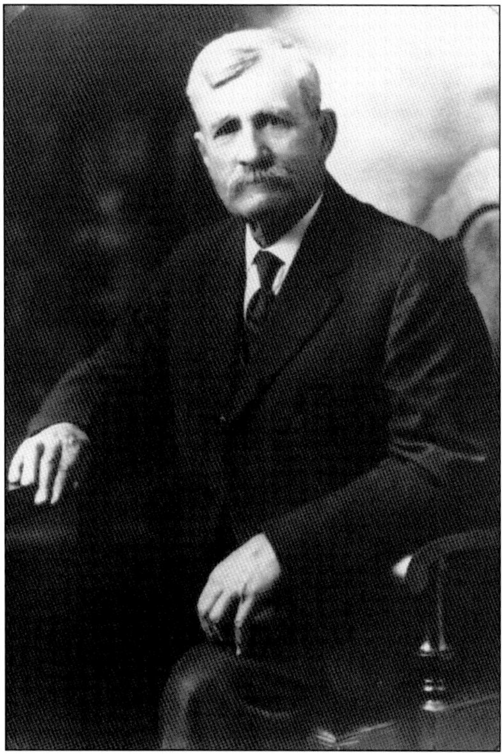

John C. Hogan (1847–1930) was an early-day cattle rancher, businessman, and civic leader who came to the Indian Territory from Georgia in 1870. He was responsible for building the first school in Pryor Creek and, along with W.T. Whitaker, worked to procure a federal courthouse in 1902.

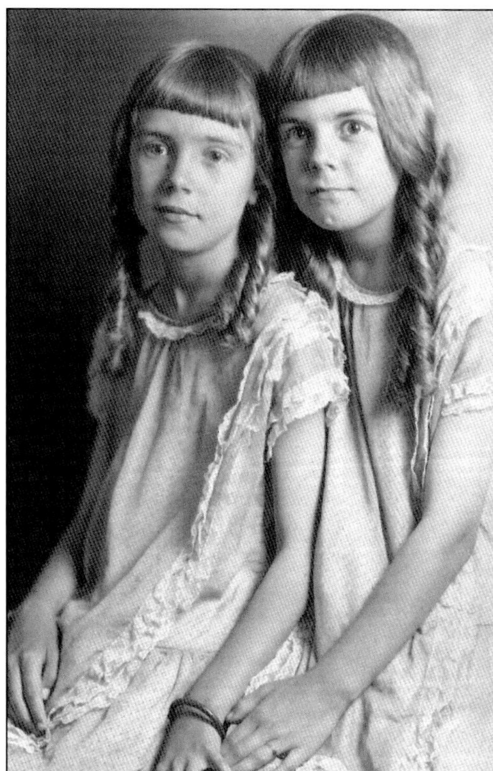

Sisters Kathryn "Kay" and Betina Hampton were the daughters of Mr. and Mrs. DeWitt Hampton. Both young ladies graduated from Pryor High School, married, and had families, one of which worked in the funeral business, the other in the state welfare department.

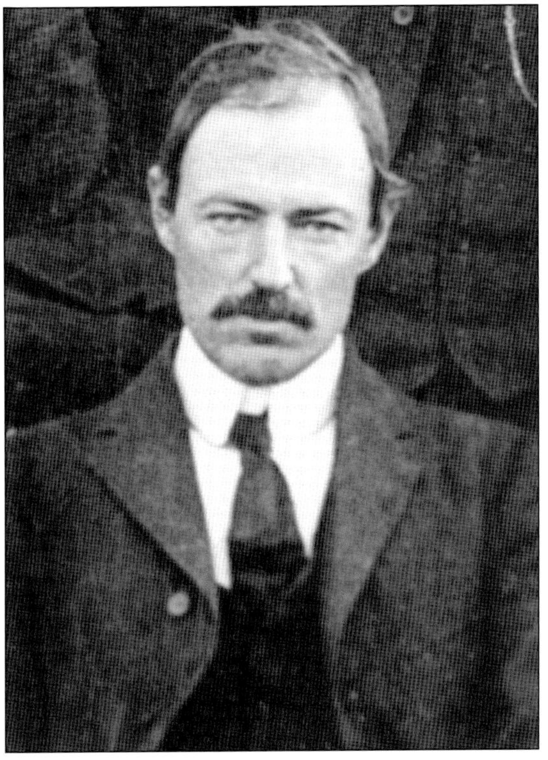

Dr. J.E. Bristow came to Pryor Creek in 1893, right out of medical school in Arkansas. He was elected mayor in 1902, county treasurer in 1907, county attorney in 1911, and county judge in 1913. Bristow (1870–1934) eventually left Pryor Creek and entered into the oil business at Ardmore, Oklahoma and San Angelo, Texas. In 1930, while gold mining in Mexico, Bristow was kidnapped by Mexican bandits and held for ransom. His son Gordon Bristow went to Mexico, paid the ransom, and secured J.E. Bristow's release. The bandits were then tracked down and killed by Mexican army troops.

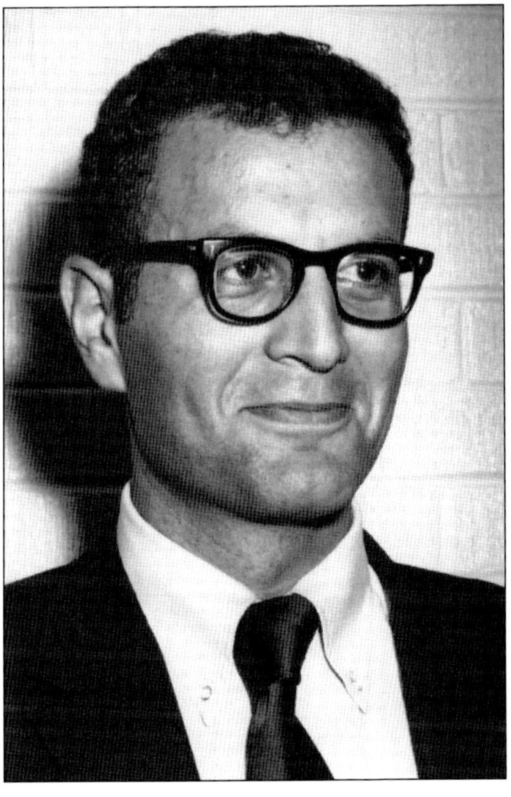

Practicing medicine in Pryor for over 45 years is Dr. Peter Sarfatis. A native of Greece, he attended medical school in Geneva, Switzerland, interned at Hillcrest Hospital in Tulsa, and did a surgery residency in Chicago. Dr. Sarfatis has been a skilled surgeon in the community and a physician who is very caring about his patients. He still maintains a general practice and is respected by his patients and their families.

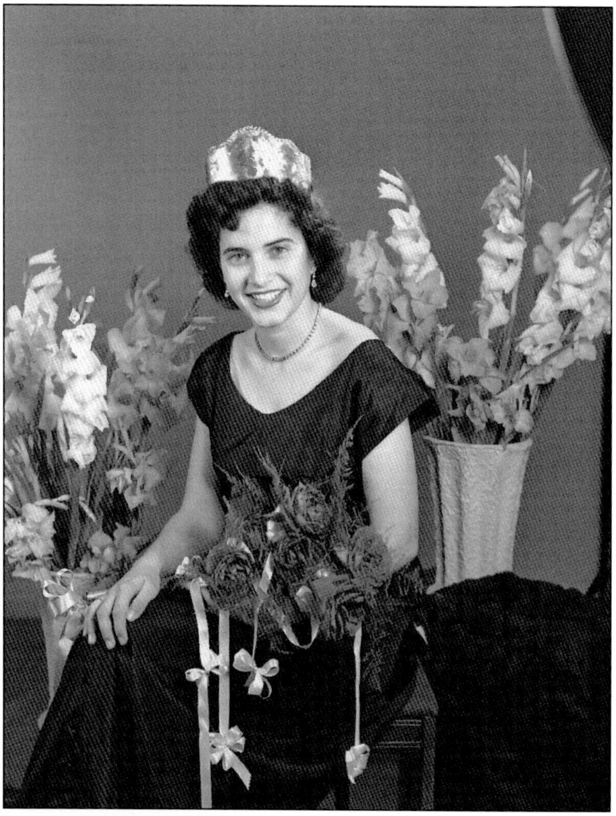

The first Miss Pryor was LaQuita Streeter (left). Below, she is seen being crowned in 1950 by Milt Lundquist, secretary-manager of the Pryor Chamber of Commerce. Posing with her are, from left to right, runners-up Carol Cunningham, Helen Van Dalsem, Mary Poplin, and Mary Littlefield. Streeter was selected by three judges from a field of 48 contestants.

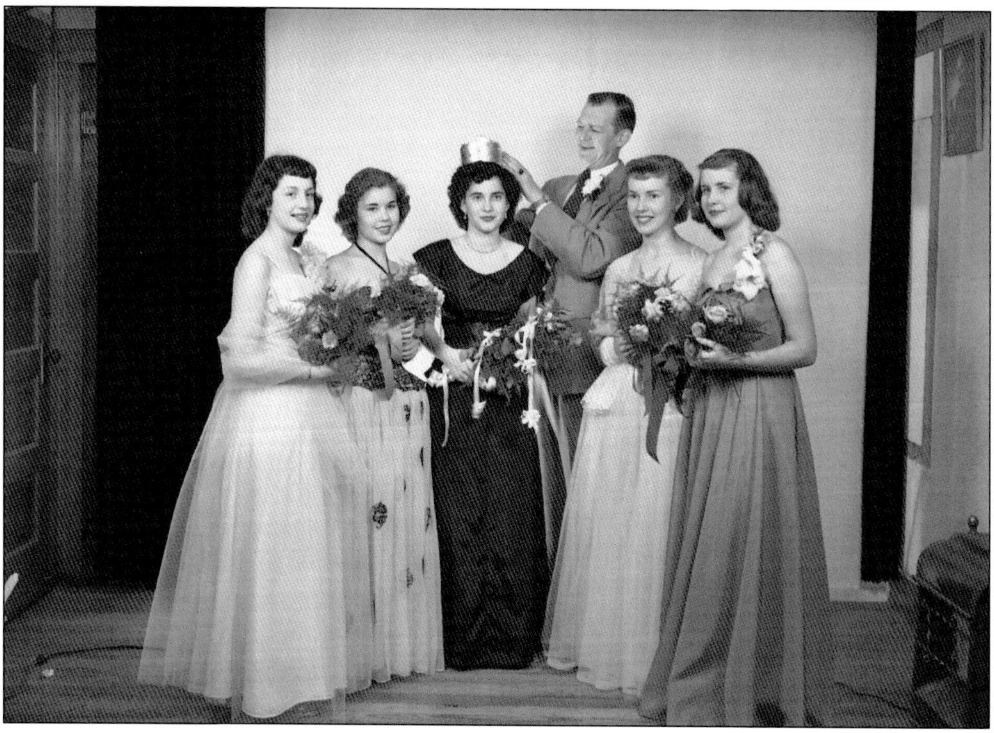

Bonnee Mallory Pierson was the 1962 Miss Pryor. She retired as an office clerk with the Municipal Utility Board.

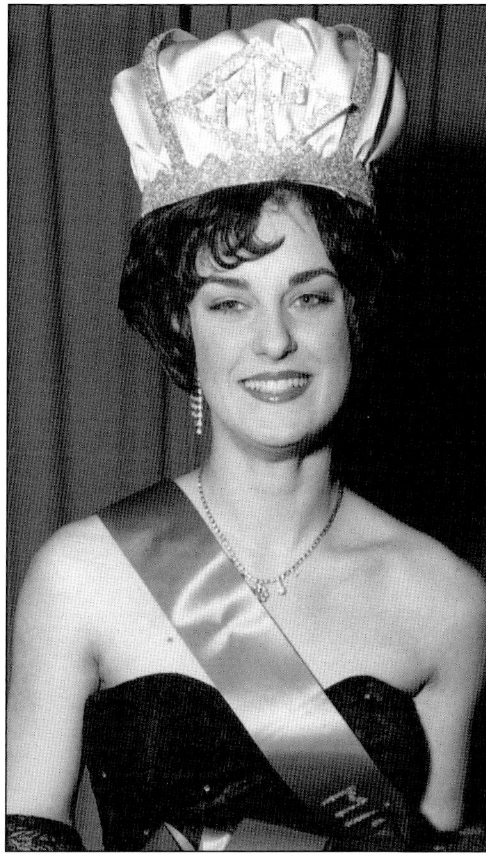

Miss Pryor 1979, René Kendrick Bell, is shown seated with, from left to right, runners-up Angela Southern Clement, Melanie Gipson, Paula Treas Mibb, and Jeroi Bowles Rott.

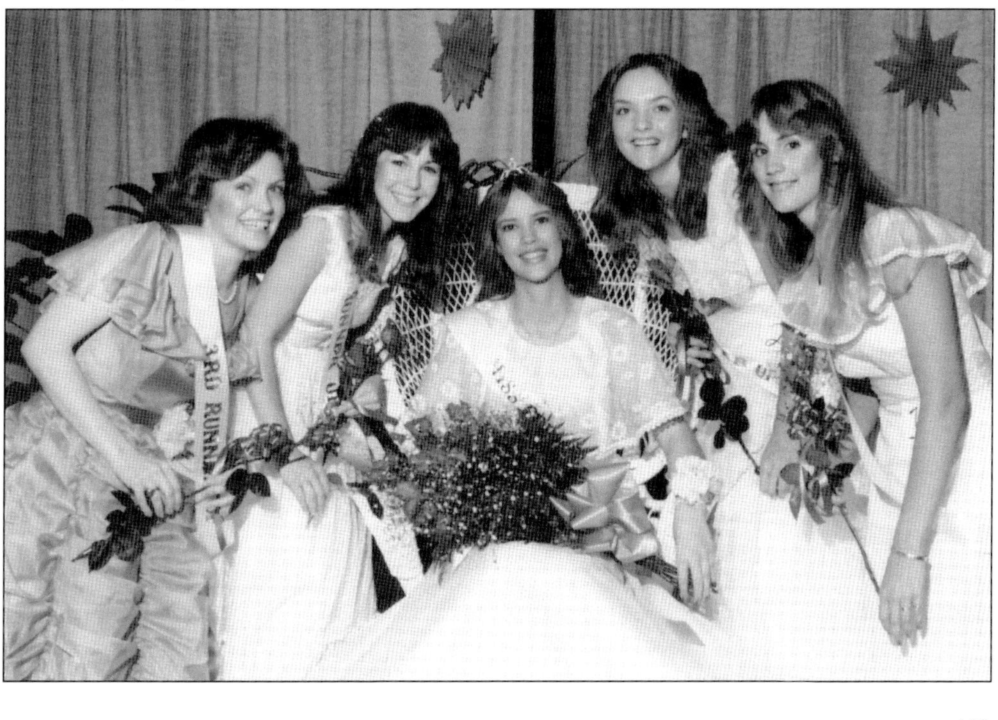

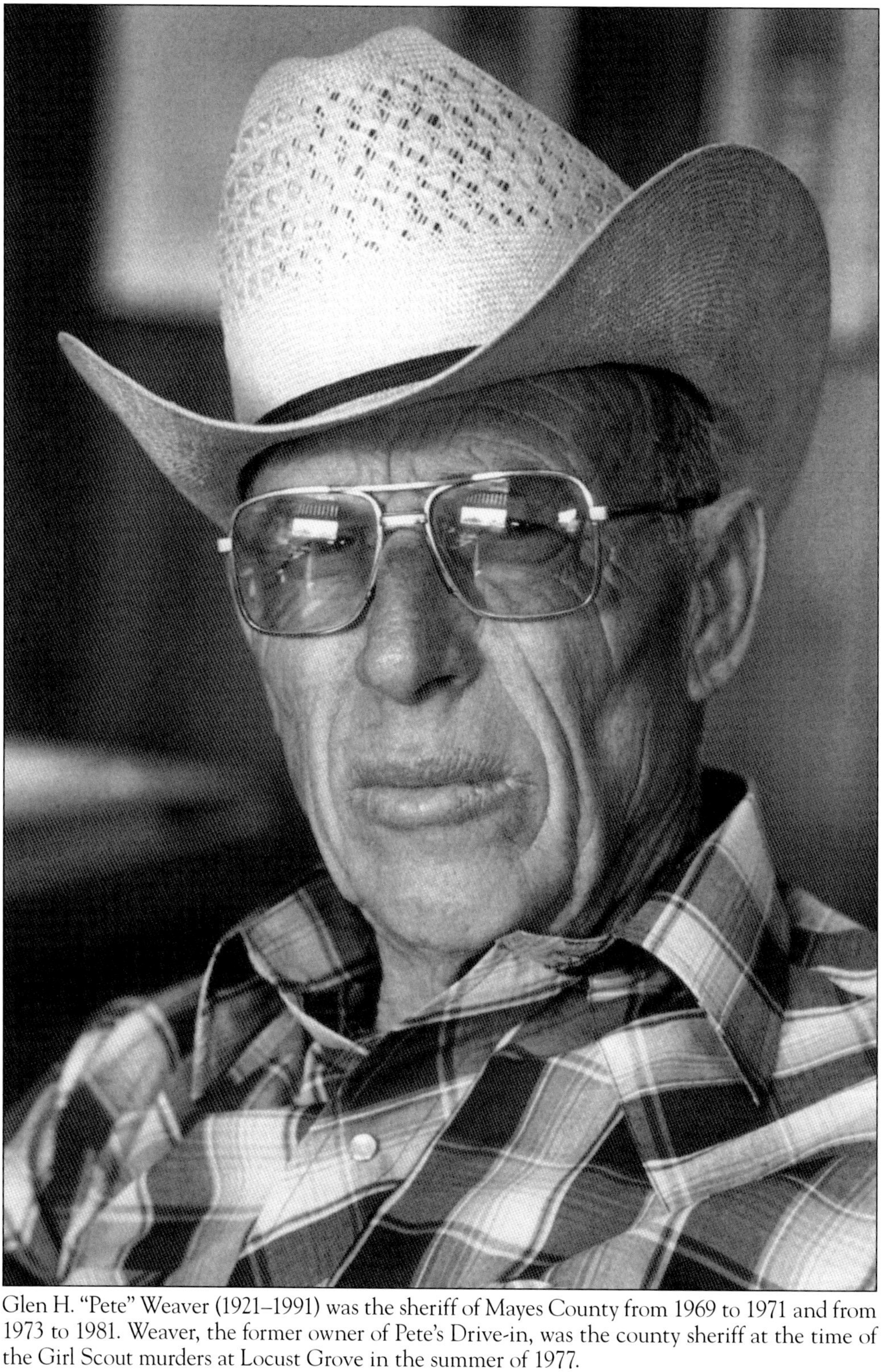

Glen H. "Pete" Weaver (1921–1991) was the sheriff of Mayes County from 1969 to 1971 and from 1973 to 1981. Weaver, the former owner of Pete's Drive-in, was the county sheriff at the time of the Girl Scout murders at Locust Grove in the summer of 1977.

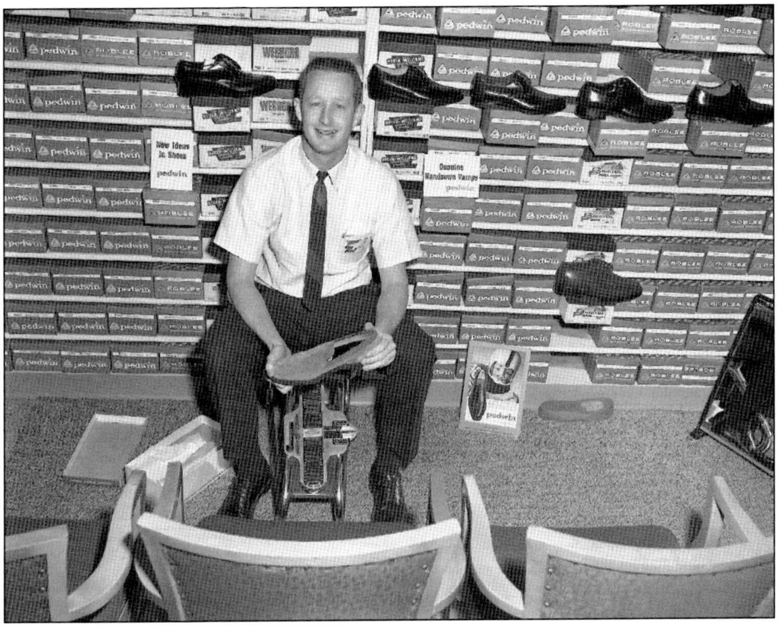

One of the most respected and well-liked businessmen was Don Stover. With his wife, Jackie, he established the Don Stover Shoe Store, located on Graham Avenue, in 1963.

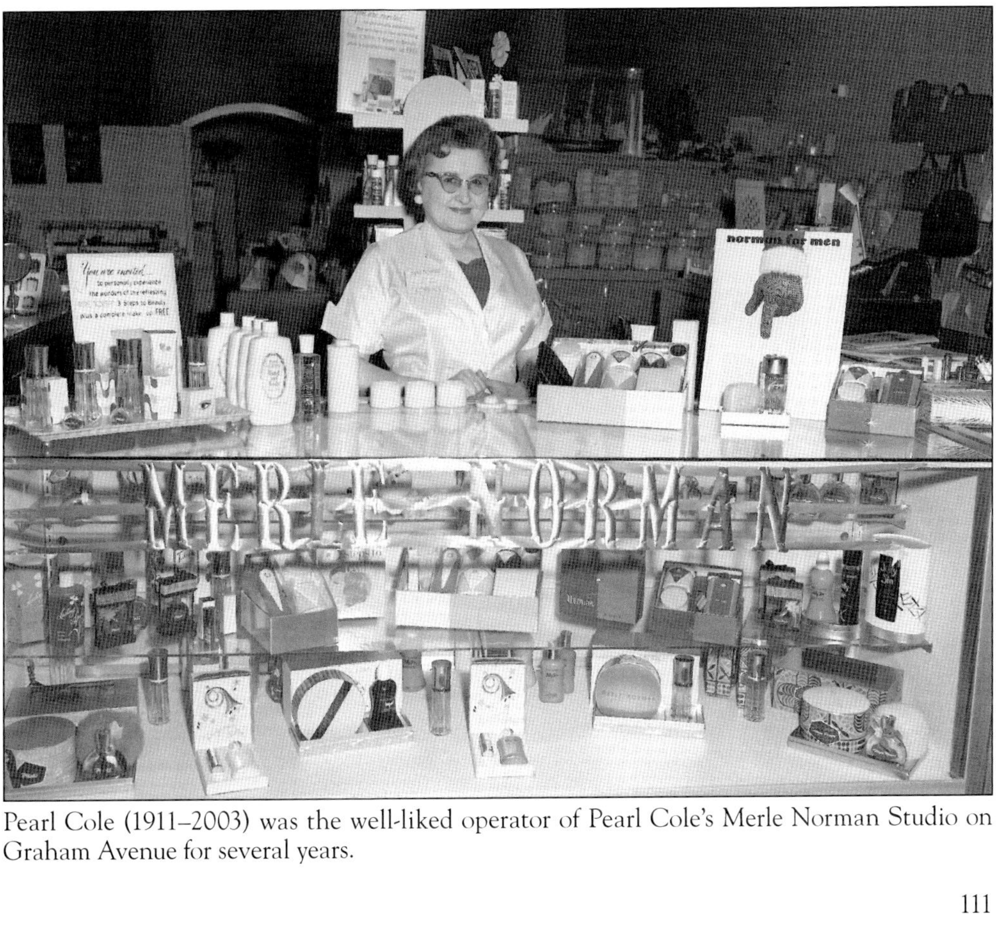

Pearl Cole (1911–2003) was the well-liked operator of Pearl Cole's Merle Norman Studio on Graham Avenue for several years.

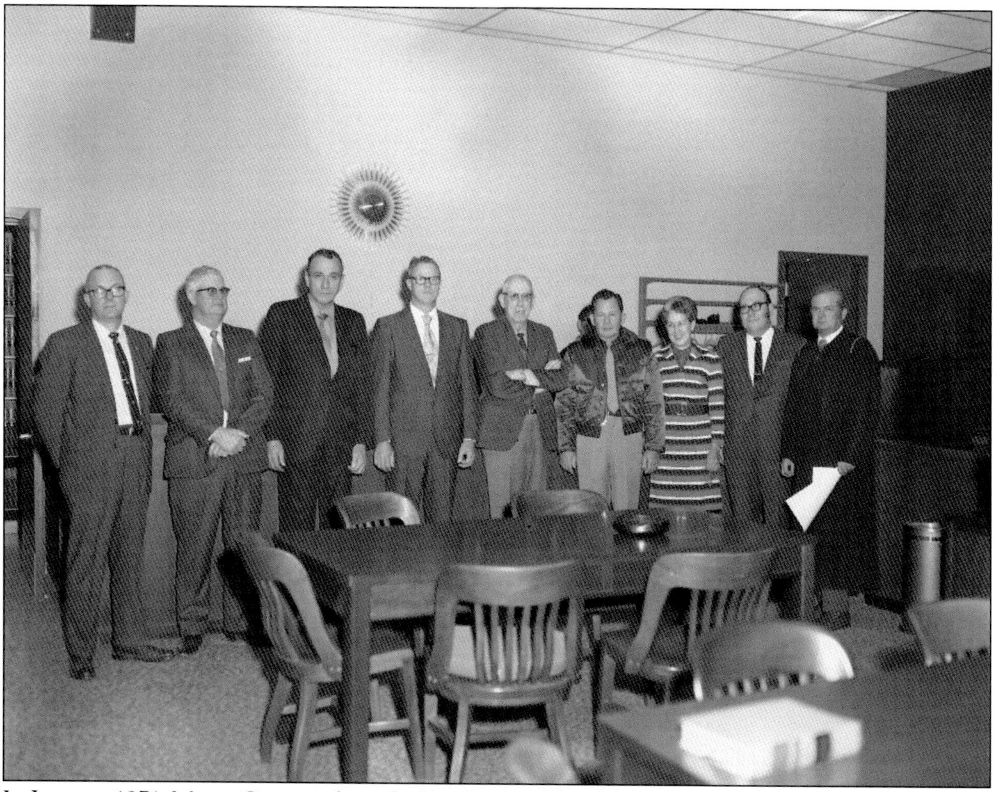

In January 1971, Mayes County elected officials posed for this photograph after being sworn in by Judge J.Q. Adams. From left to right are County Clerk Jack Porter, Commissioner Clete Hampton, Commissioner Henry Campbell, Commissioner Bo West, Assessor Chanie Bell, Sheriff Hokie Forman, Court Clerk Eloise Gist, Associate Judge Edwin Moore, and Judge Adams.

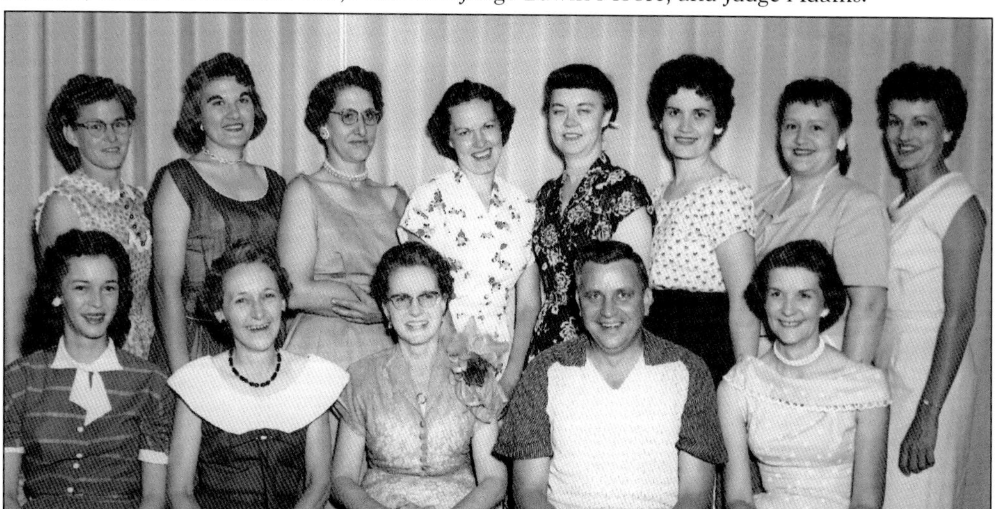

Pryor telephone operators in July 1956 are, from left to right, (first row) Ann Hesler, Maco Panter, Mirtie Boswell, Paul Riggs, and Betty Beemer; (second row) Sylvia Wheeler, Joan Littlefield, Ethlene Boston, Thomasine Ward, Lucy Belle Schultz, Dorothy Putman, Francis McNair, and Betty Christian.

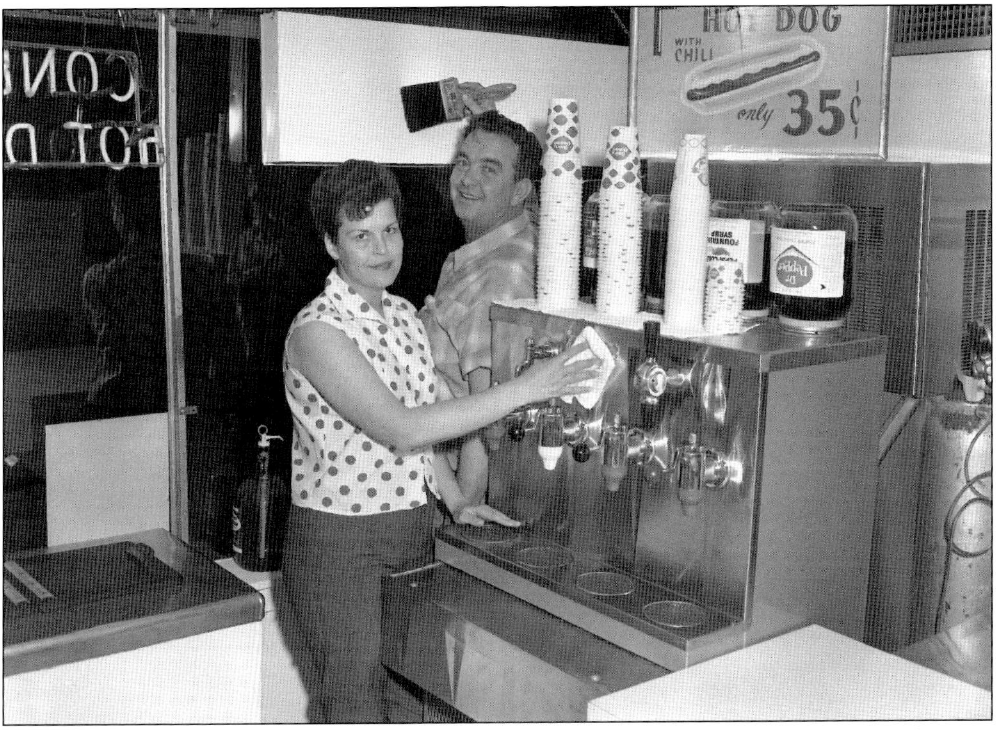

Longtime operators of the local Dairy Queen, Oma Lee and Leroy Stephens, are shown cleaning the store at closing time in February 1965.

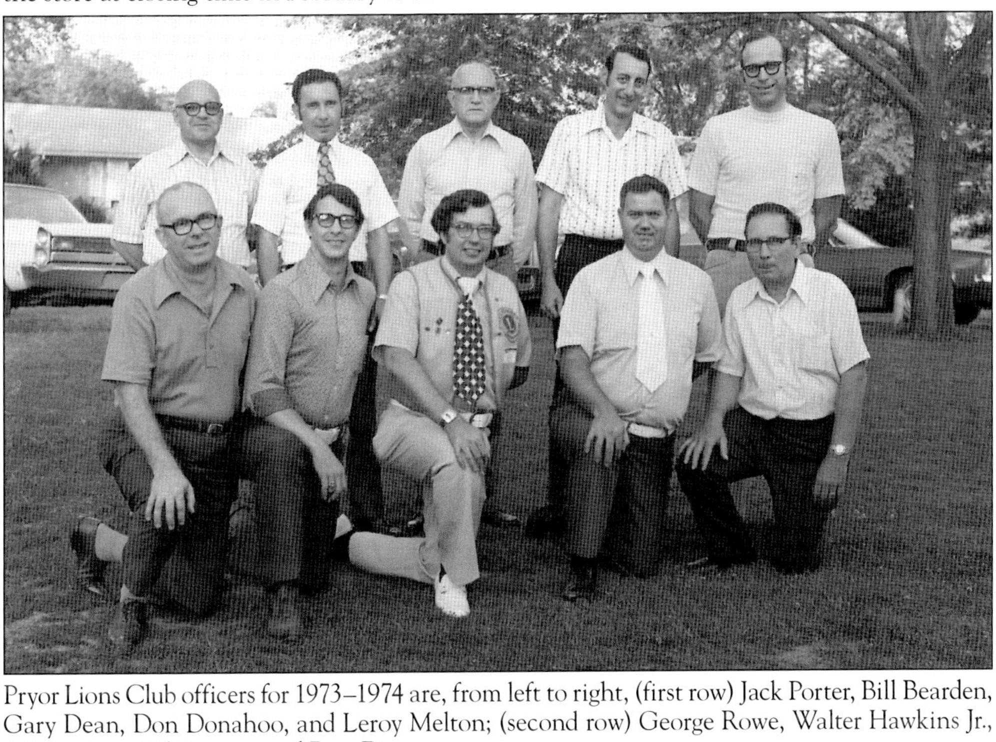

Pryor Lions Club officers for 1973–1974 are, from left to right, (first row) Jack Porter, Bill Bearden, Gary Dean, Don Donahoo, and Leroy Melton; (second row) George Rowe, Walter Hawkins Jr., Albert Fryer, Ed Sexton, and Ron Dossman.

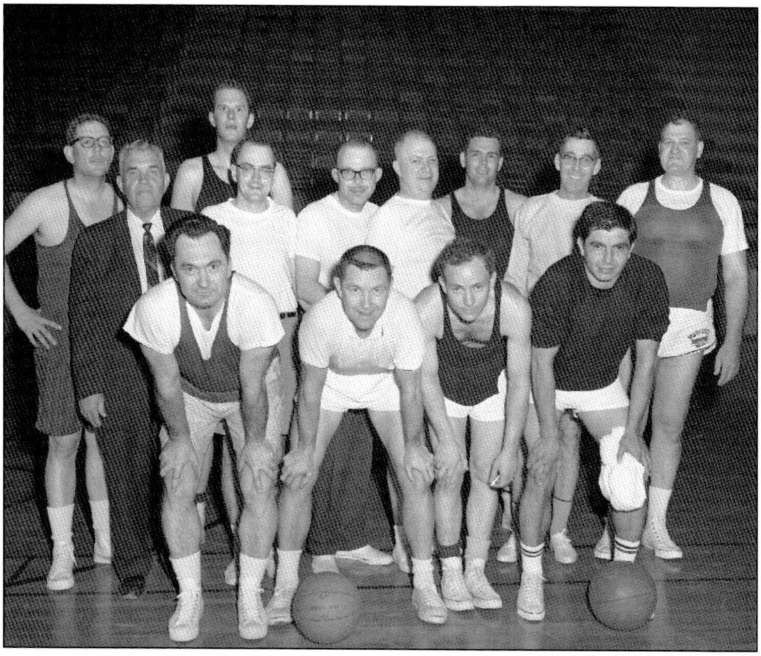

The Rotary Club "Gay Blades" basketball team poses for a photograph. From left to right are (first row) Glen Winters, Dr. Dwight Strawhun, Ray Dareing, and Jack Chaney; (second row) Clarence Mayberry, coach Howard Hunsaker, Ed Scruggs. Haskell Lee Gaither, Ernest Brown, Tom Stewart, Ernest Young, Bill Settle, and Mutt McArtor.

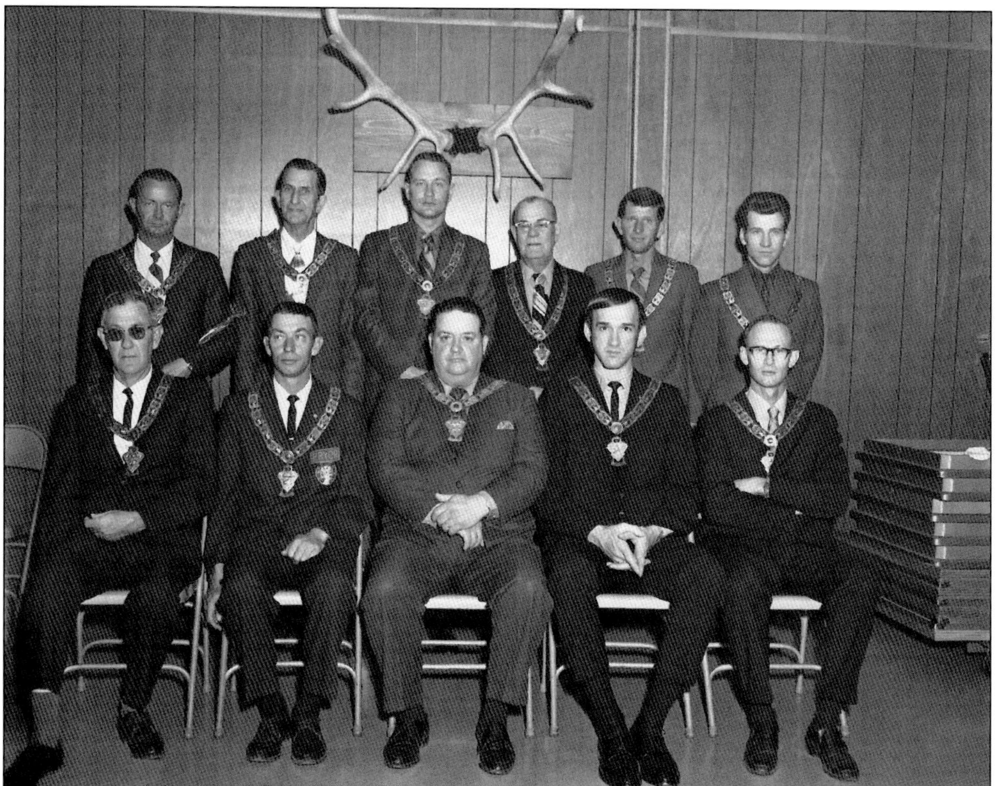

Pryor Elk's Lodge officers for 1971–1972 included, from left to right, (first row) V.O. Lamar, Matt Garner, Merwin "Poodle" Rush, Don Burford, and Welton York; (second row) Brice Wallis, Andy King, Bob Pierson, Gene Cole, Don King, and Brooks Ledbetter.

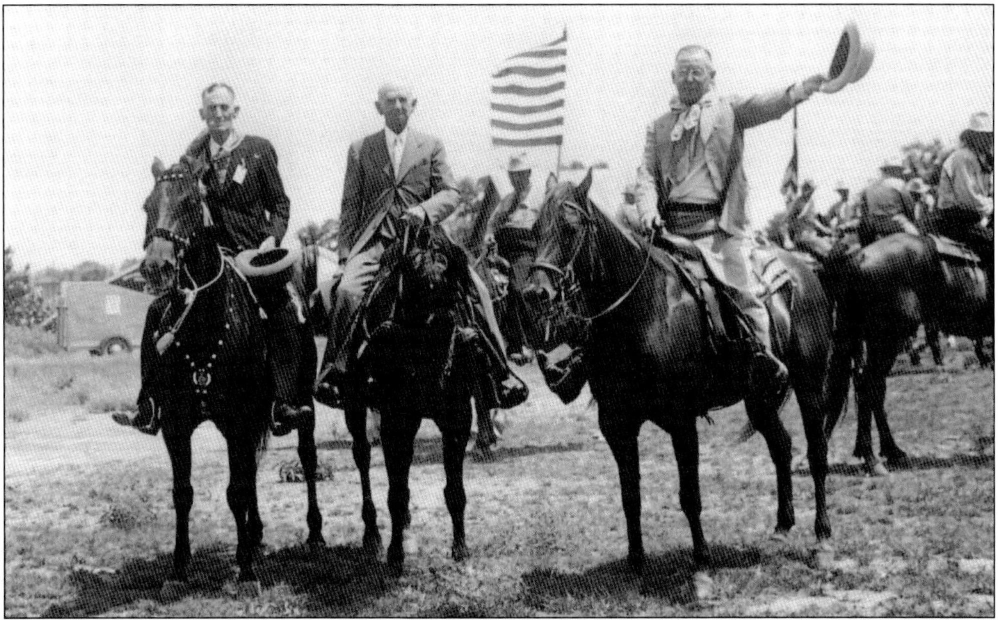

From left to right, Pryor Creek pioneers Coke Blake, W.A. Graham, and Tom Harrison participated in a 1940 rodeo parade. Blake was a well-known quarter horse breeder who was inducted into the Quarter Horse Hall of Fame in 1986. Graham was a banker, merchant, and philanthropist. Harrison was a longtime mayor, abstractor, community historian, and agriculture booster.

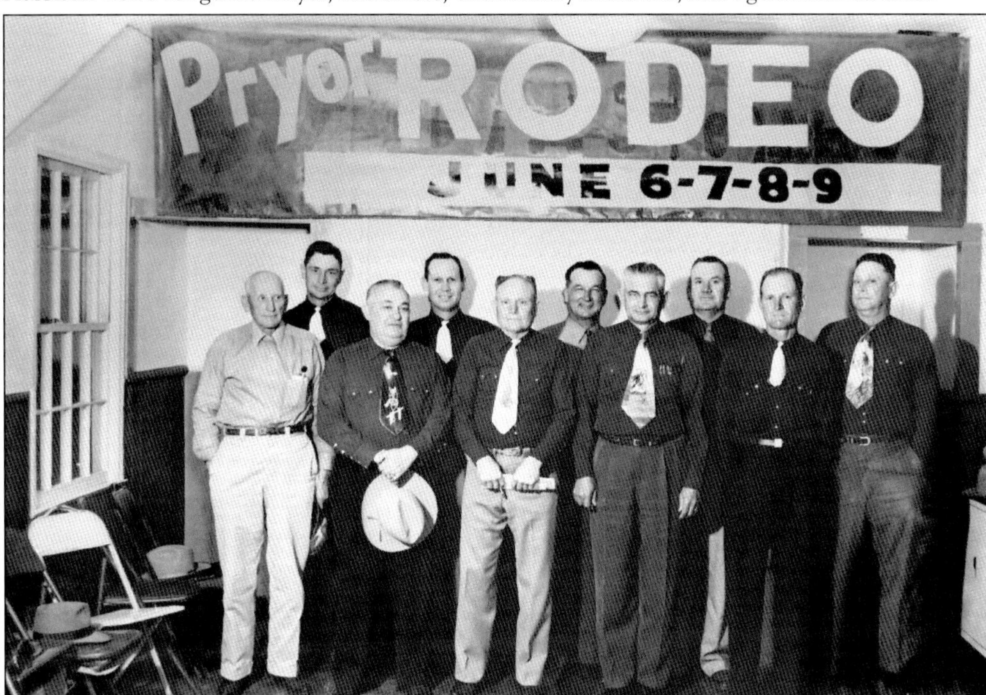

Pryor Rodeo Club officers promote a rodeo in May 1951. From left to right are (first row) John Barnes, Norvelle Green, Elmer Haddan, Steve Martin, and Ross Sievers; (second row) Herb Hammer, C.A. "Dutch" Atchison, Bill Odom, Jay Martin, and Jess Higgs.

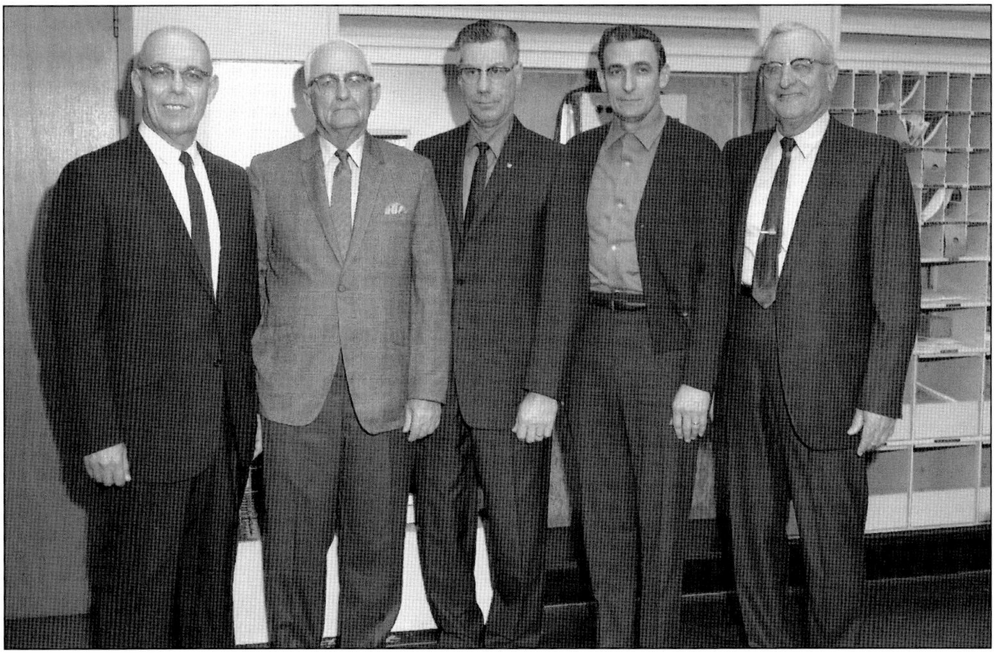

Pryor Post Office employees pose for a photograph about 1969. They are, from left to right, Vincil Hardy, Ewing Boatman, Bill Fiser, Carl Curry, and postmaster Jack Butler.

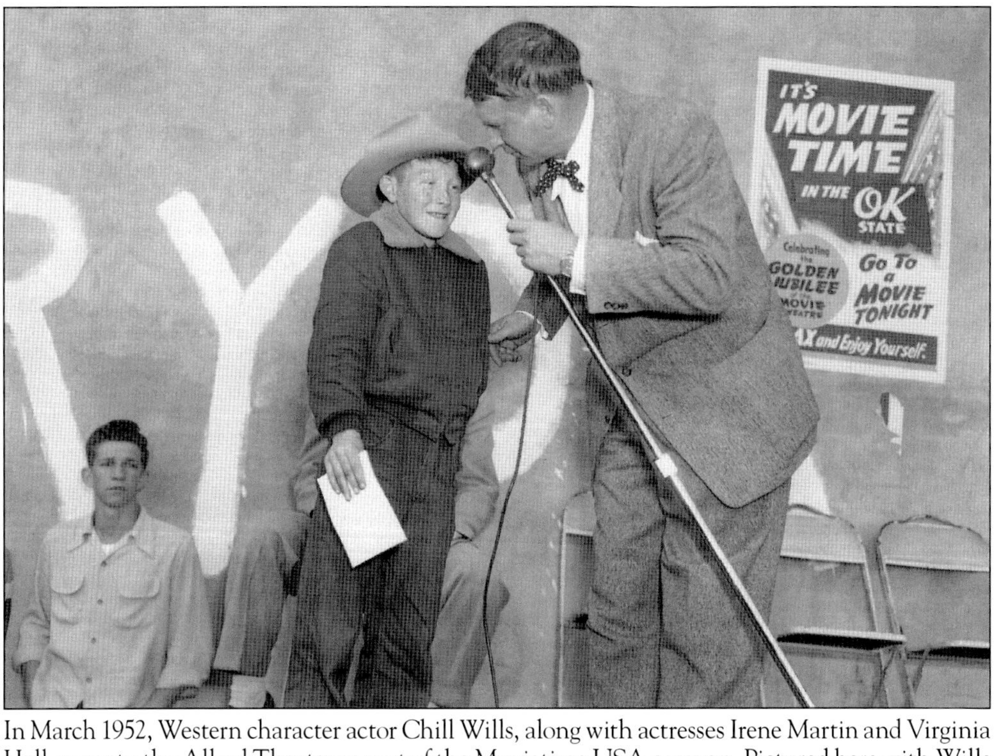

In March 1952, Western character actor Chill Wills, along with actresses Irene Martin and Virginia Hall, came to the Allred Theater as part of the Movietime USA caravan. Pictured here with Wills is 10-year-old Walter "Freck" Holler Jr. A 1959 graduate of Pryor High School, Holler worked for many years at a local grocery store. He retired from National Gypsum paper plant.

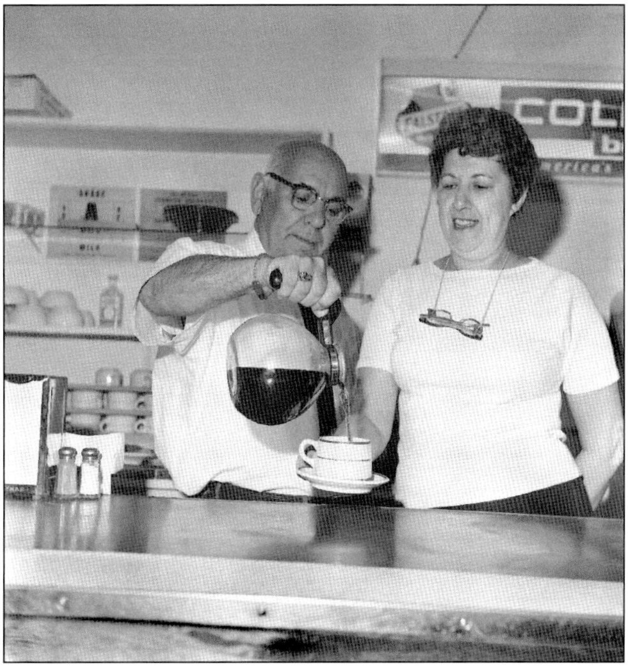

Iggy's Café, owned by Iggy and Rose Palumbo, was a downtown staple for good food from about 1953 to 1970. Iggy Palumbo, an Italian immigrant, was a longtime civic leader and county fair booster. The Palumbos sold their business to Mr. and Mrs. Roy Nabors, original owners of El Royal Mexican Restaurant. They transformed the café into the second home of El Royal.

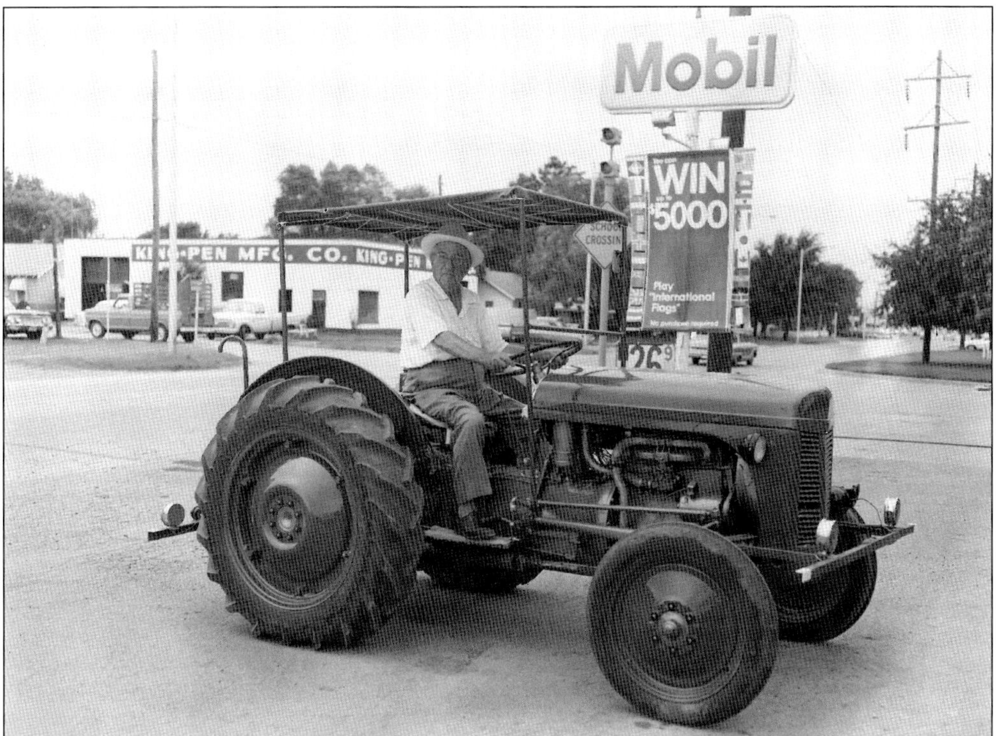

Floyd Shrum (1887–1982) drives his tractor into a gas station on West Graham Avenue for a fill-up. Shrum had his driver's license taken away because of failing eyesight. He then found out that he could drive a tractor without a license and putted around town for errands and appointments. He had retired from his job as the farm and business manager for the late W.A. Graham.

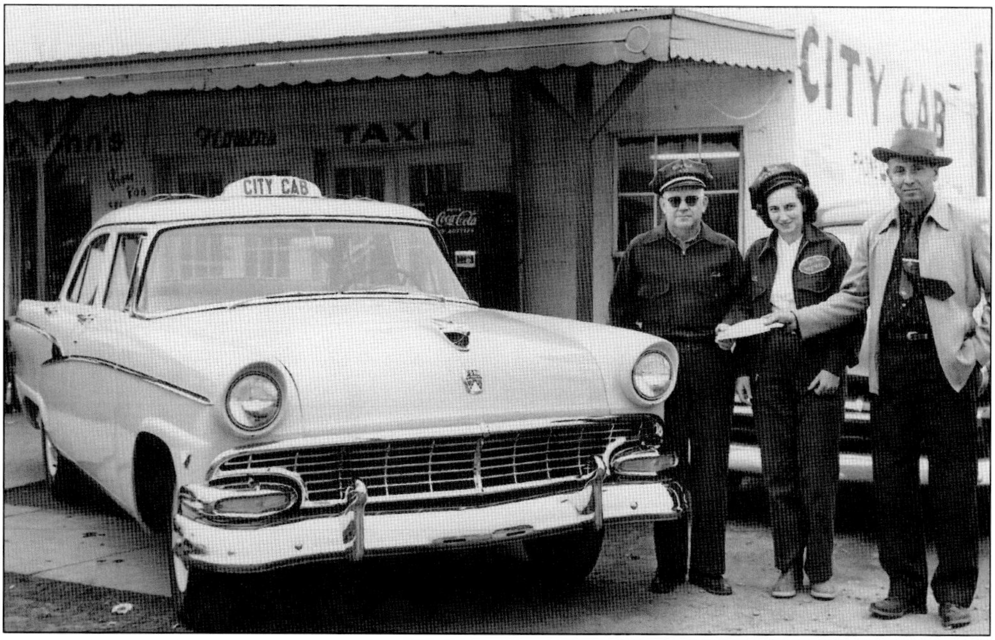

Earl and Violet Shearer, owners of a local taxi service, receive delivery of a new 1956 Ford taxicab from Merle Colvert (right) of Mayes County Ford.

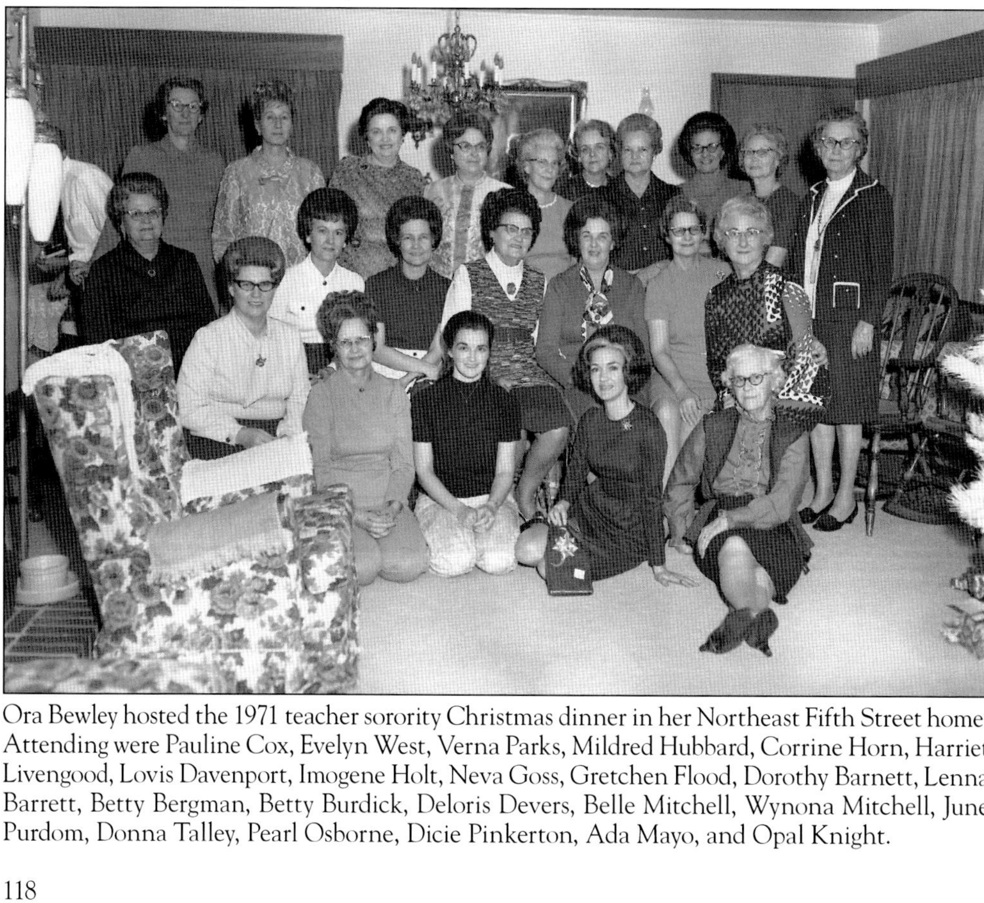

Ora Bewley hosted the 1971 teacher sorority Christmas dinner in her Northeast Fifth Street home. Attending were Pauline Cox, Evelyn West, Verna Parks, Mildred Hubbard, Corrine Horn, Harriet Livengood, Lovis Davenport, Imogene Holt, Neva Goss, Gretchen Flood, Dorothy Barnett, Lenna Barrett, Betty Bergman, Betty Burdick, Deloris Devers, Belle Mitchell, Wynona Mitchell, June Purdom, Donna Talley, Pearl Osborne, Dicie Pinkerton, Ada Mayo, and Opal Knight.

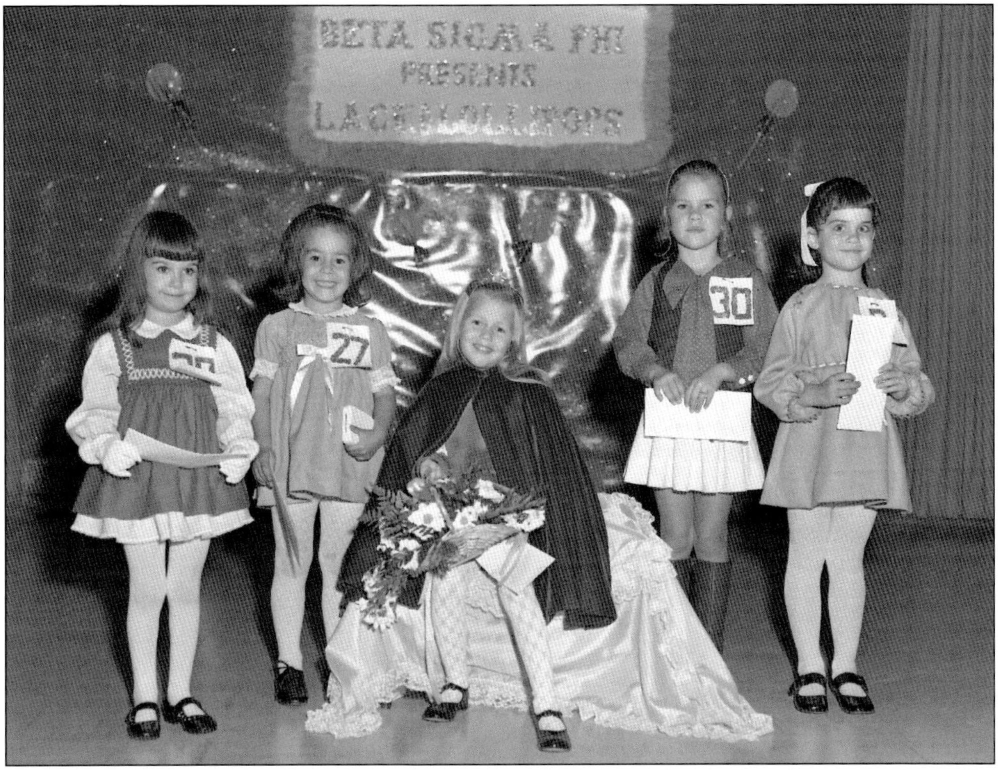

Jamie Carson (seated) was the first Little Miss Pryor, crowned in December 1971. She is the daughter of Mr. and Mrs. Doug Carson. Runners-up were, from left to right, Stephanie Wyse (third runner-up), Julia Graves (first runner-up), Julie Moore (second runner-up), and Ashley Kehl (fourth runner-up). The winner received a $25 savings bond, a crown, and a basket of flowers. The contest was sponsored by the Delta Beta chapter of the Beta Sigma Phi sorority.

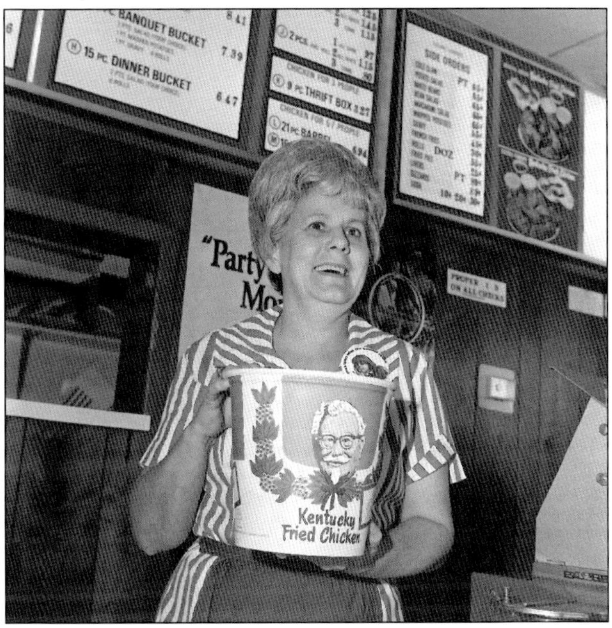

Wanda Head (1928–2000), shown here in December 1973, was the longtime manager at the local Kentucky Fried Chicken. Opened in July 1972, the restaurant is located on the northwest corner of Graham Avenue and Mill Street.

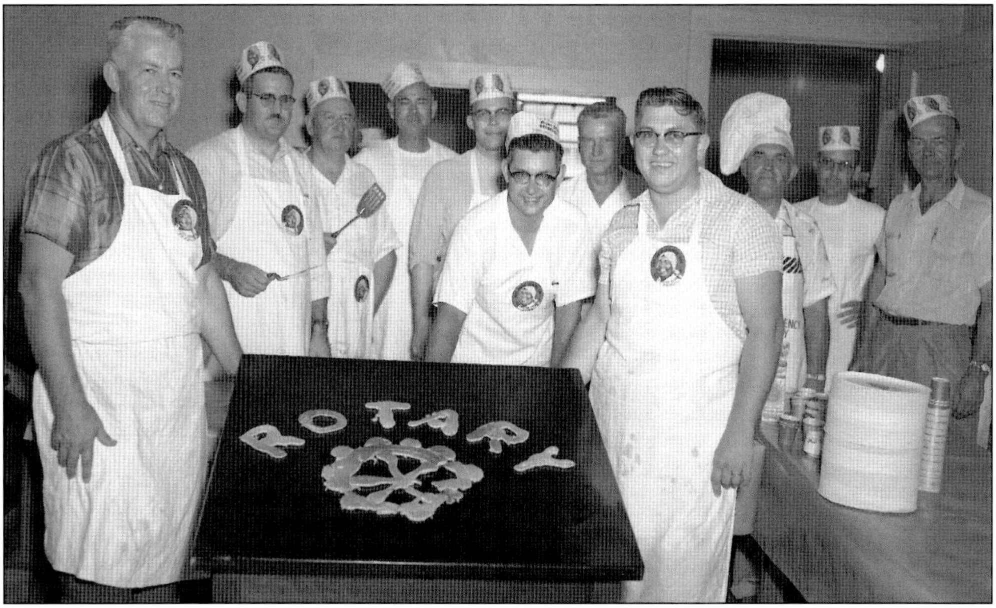

One of the favorite events of the year is the annual Rotary Club pancake breakfast, now held in the spring in the Graham Community Building. Here, Rotary pancake chefs promote the 1957 event. They are, from left to right, Hal Buchanan, Elwyn Thurston, Bob Sibley, Lon Kirk, Ernest Brown, Jim Hart, Howard Roy, Harold Weddle, Howard Hunsaker, Bob Harris, and Fred Fleak.

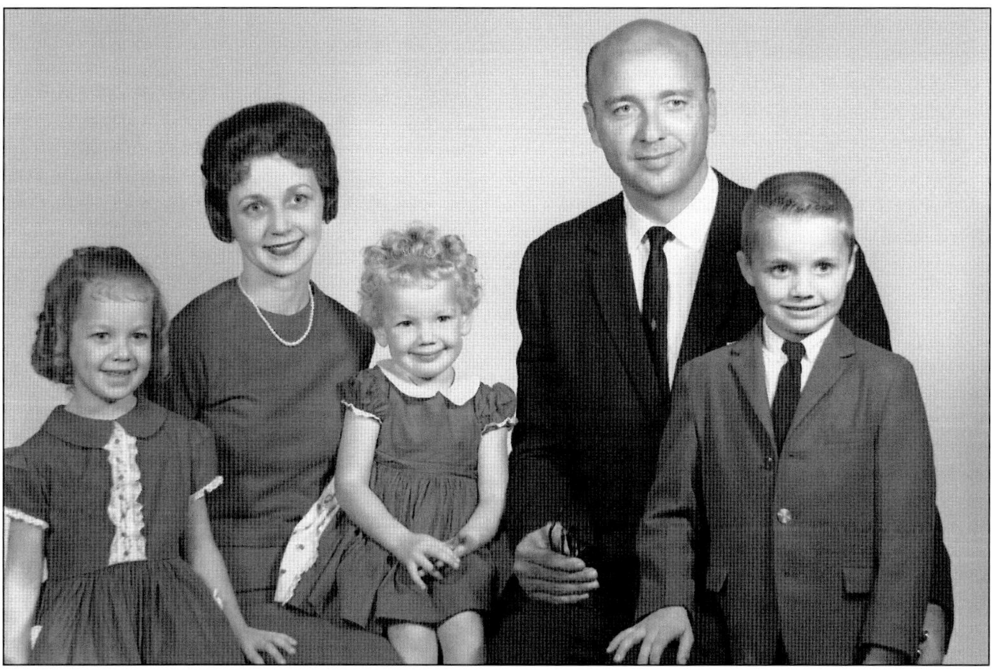

State senator John C. Wilkerson Jr. poses with his wife, Naomi, and children Nina (left), Julie (center), and John III in the fall of 1963. John Wilkerson was the last Mayes County resident to serve from this district in the senate. Wilkerson, along with his father, co-owned a real-estate and insurance business, which is one of the oldest continually operating firms in the city. Naomi Wilkerson was a music and English teacher at Rogers State College.

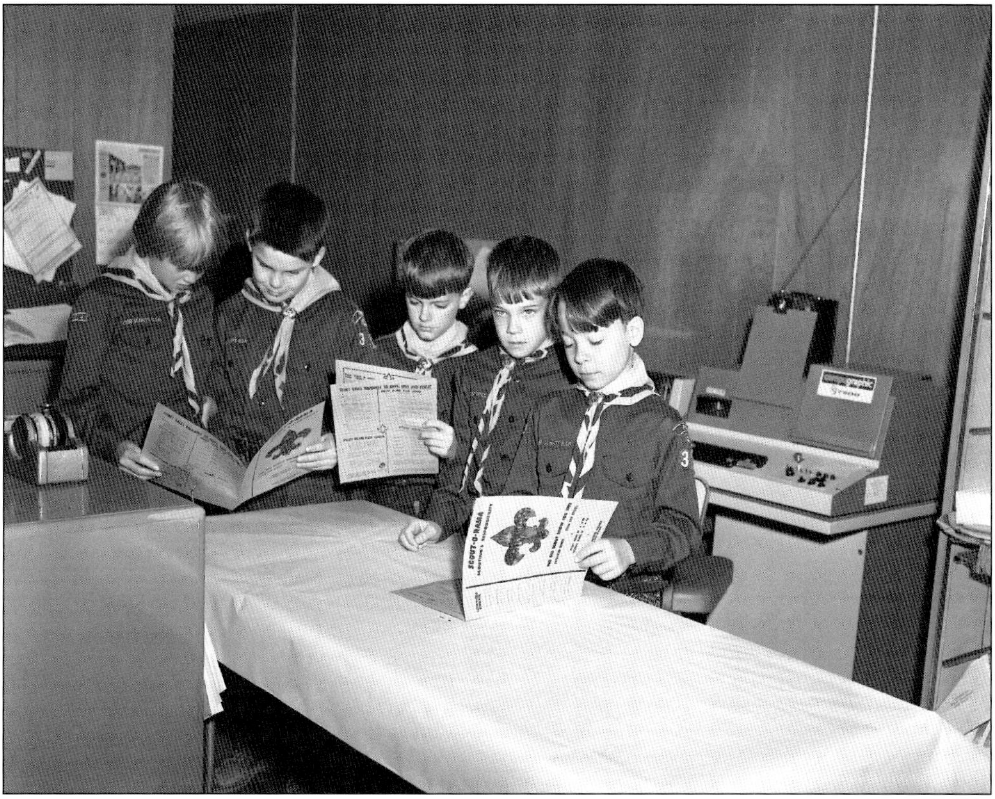

Cub Scouts read up on how to sell Scout-a-Rama tickets in February 1972. They are, from left to right, Steve Jarvis, Larry Brown, Kort Seigal, Mark Bowling, and Bryan Shelton. These energetic scouts were students at Lincoln Elementary School.

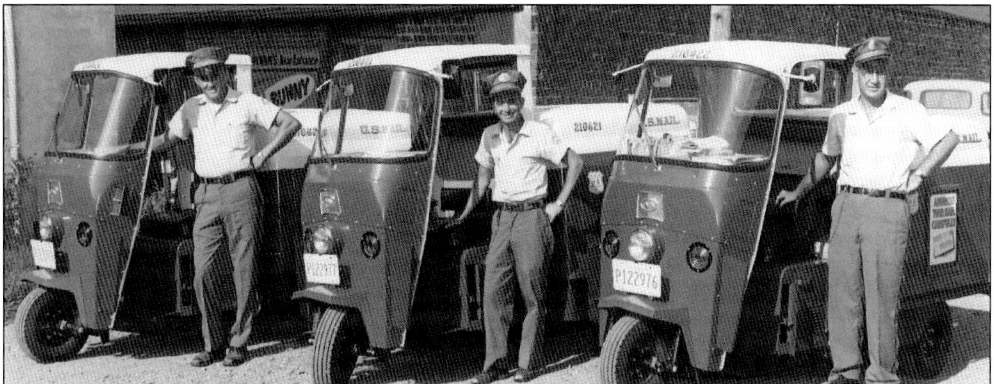

From left to right, Pryor postal carriers James Booth, Jerry Parsons, and Roy Nabors pose with their new quarter-ton Mailster carts in August 1962.

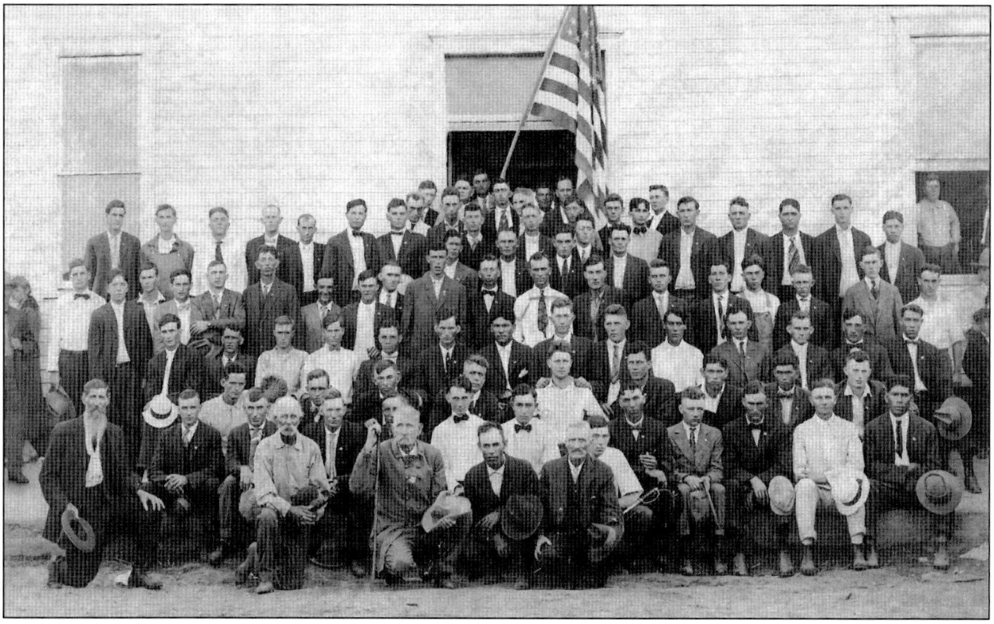

A handful of Civil War veterans meet at the courthouse to send the first round of World War I draftees off to fight a war "over there." The first Mayes County native to be drafted, in September 1917, was Charles Reed of Locust Grove. Grover Sullivan, a 25-year-old farm boy from rural Pryor, was the first Mayes County soldier to be killed in action. The Pryor American Legion Post was later co-named Sullivan-Lewis Post No. 182 in his honor.

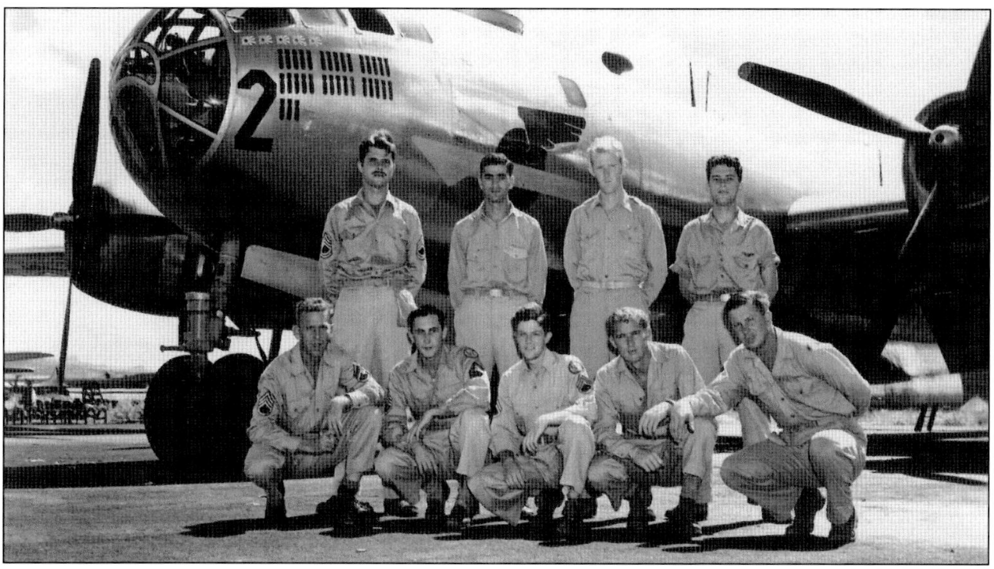

Carl Sandusky (1914–1988) was a B-29 tail gunner during World War II, flying 35 missions over Japan. He was shot down twice. Sandusky was awarded the Distinguished Flying Cross and the Air Medal with four oak leaf clusters for operations over Japan. He is pictured here, in the first row at far left, with his crew on June 25, 1945. Note the symbols on the side of the bomber, showing a record of their bombing missions. After the war, he returned to work in his family produce market and musical-instrument business, Sandusky's Market, on South Adair Street. (Courtesy of Leslie Sandusky.)

Capt. Martin Tull was the first Mayes County serviceman killed in action in the Vietnam War. A 1955 graduate of Pryor High School, he graduated from the US Naval Academy at Annapolis and was commissioned in the Marine Corps. He died on May 19, 1967, when his unit came under heavy mortar fire. He is buried in Arlington National Cemetery.

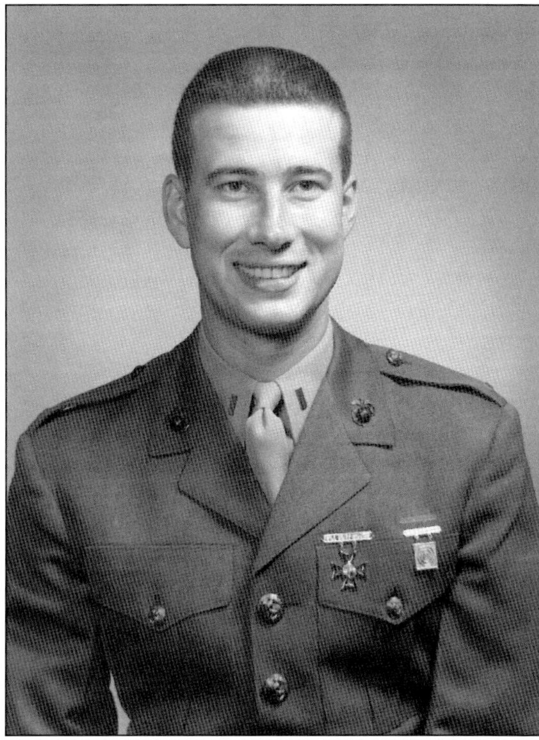

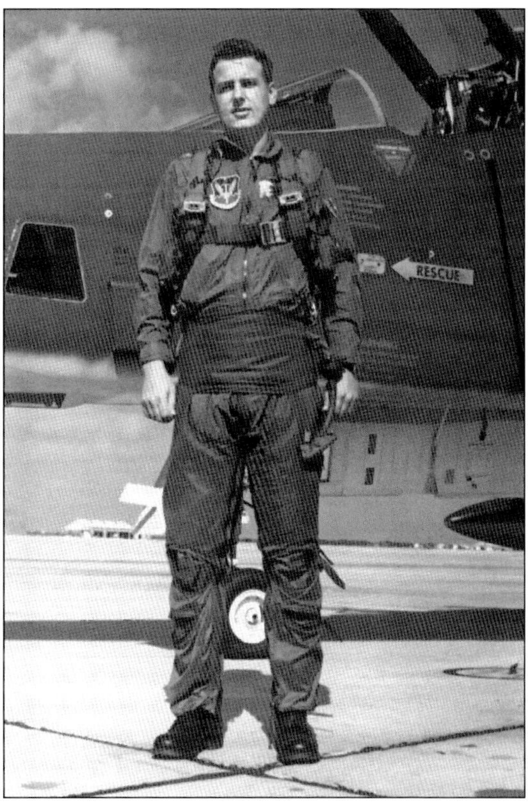

Air Force captain Tom Gist is Pryor's only Vietnam veteran listed as Missing in Action. As the backseater in an RF-4C, his plane was shot down on May 18, 1968. The 1957 graduate of Pryor High School and 1961 graduate of Oklahoma State University received his commission in the Air Force and was a bomber navigator before becoming a weapons-system operator on the F-4. His plane took a direct hit in the rear cockpit where he was sitting while on a daytime reconnaissance mission near Donghoi, North Vietnam. The pilot ejected and spent several years as a prisoner of war. After six years as MIA, Gist was promoted to major and reclassified as deceased on May 30, 1974. His remains have never been recovered. A street in south Pryor was named in his honor in 1991.

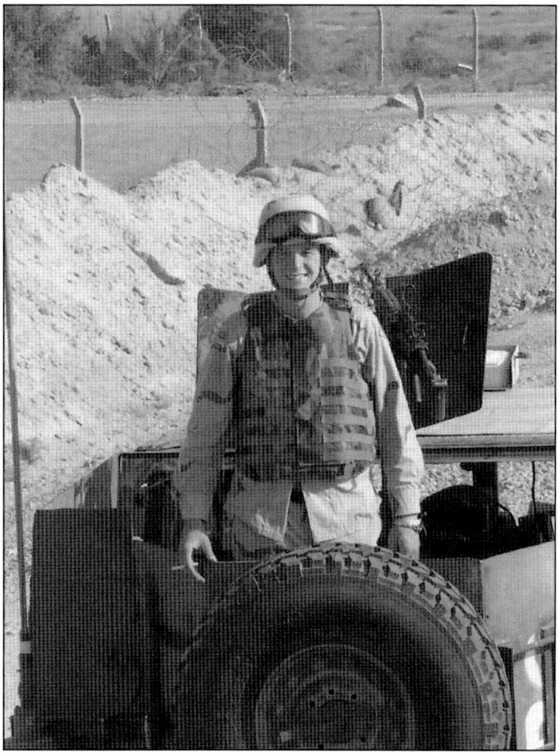

Oklahoma Army National Guard specialist Kyle Brinlee (1983–2004) was killed in action on May 11, 2004, near Al-Asad, Iraq. Brinlee was manning the gunner position while on a six-vehicle resupply convoy mission when the convoy came under an attack from improvised explosive devices. A 2001 graduate of Pryor High School and a member of the 120th Engineer Battalion, he had been in Iraq for about three months when he was fatally wounded. Specialist Brinlee was the first Oklahoma National Guardsman killed in combat since the Korean conflict. About 1,200 mourners, including Oklahoma governor Brad Henry, attended his funeral, which was held in the Pryor High School auditorium. Posthumously promoted to sergeant and awarded the Bronze Star and Purple Heart, Brinlee was laid to rest in Graham Memorial Cemetery. (Courtesy of John "David" Jordan.)

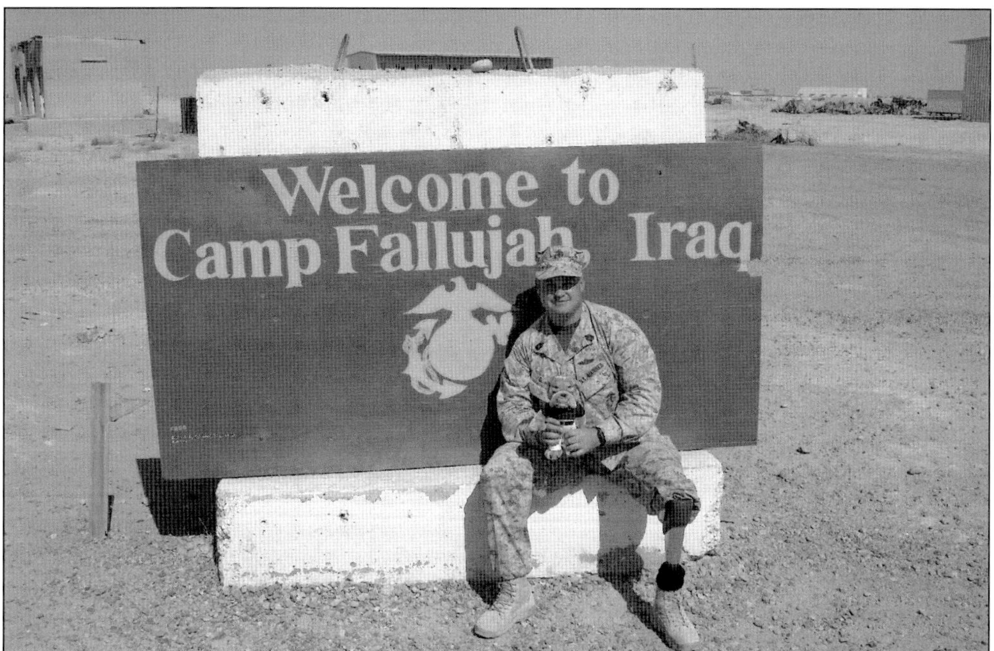

Now retired, USMC master sergeant William "Spanky" Gibson is the first above-the-knee amputee since the Civil War to return to combat. In 2006, while conducting house-to-house searches in Ramadi, Iraq, he was shot in the knee by a sniper's bullet. A 1989 graduate of Pryor High School, he is now a wounded veterans advocate and spokesman. (Courtesy of Spanky Gibson.)

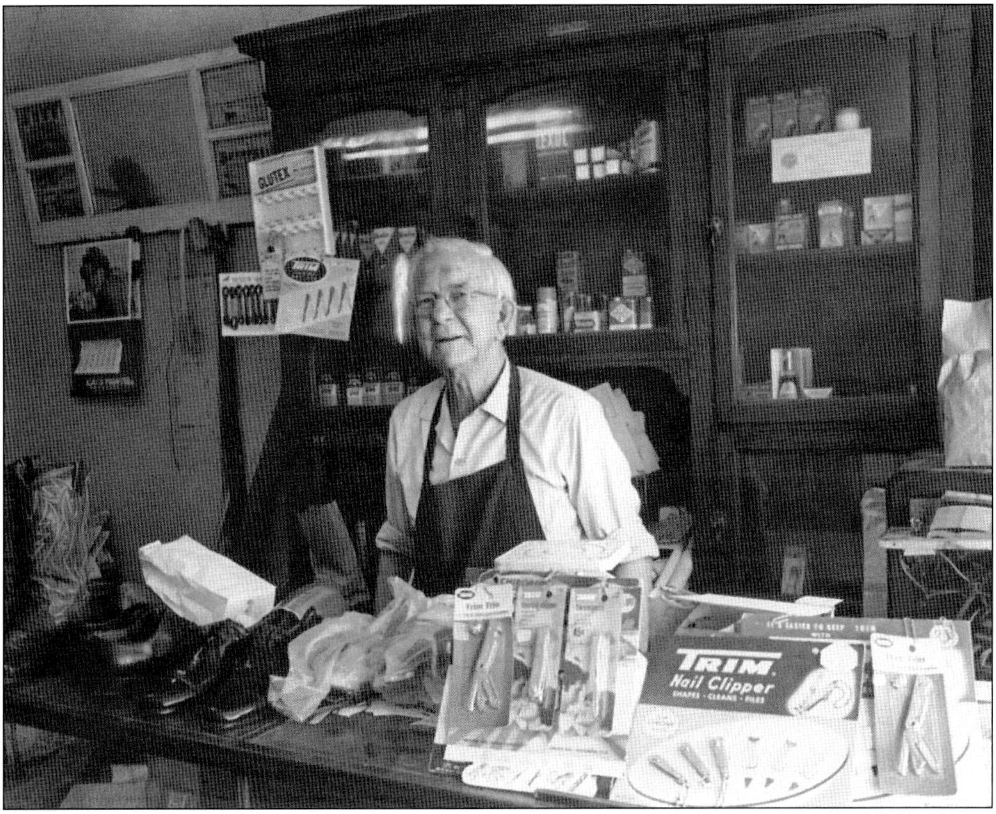

Jimmy Kitchens (1903–1991), Pryor's shoe-shine man for over 45 years, shows off behind the counter at his longtime parlor in the historic Hardy Building on North Adair Street. Customers could also enjoy hot roasted peanuts and a cold beverage from an old-fashioned pop box while waiting for a shine. Kitchens originally came to Pryor during World War II to work at the DuPont Powder Plant. He established his shine shop in the Hardy Building in January 1946. (Courtesy of Michael Wheat.)

The Hammer family, shown here around 1936, were prominent ranchers, rodeo and fair boosters, and stockyard operators. Seated are the parents, Marvin Hammer (1871–1959) and Mary Hammer (1869–1961). Standing in back are, from left to right, sons Clarence (1911–1979), Herb (1908–1998), Ellsworth (1906–2000), and Marvin (1904–1990).

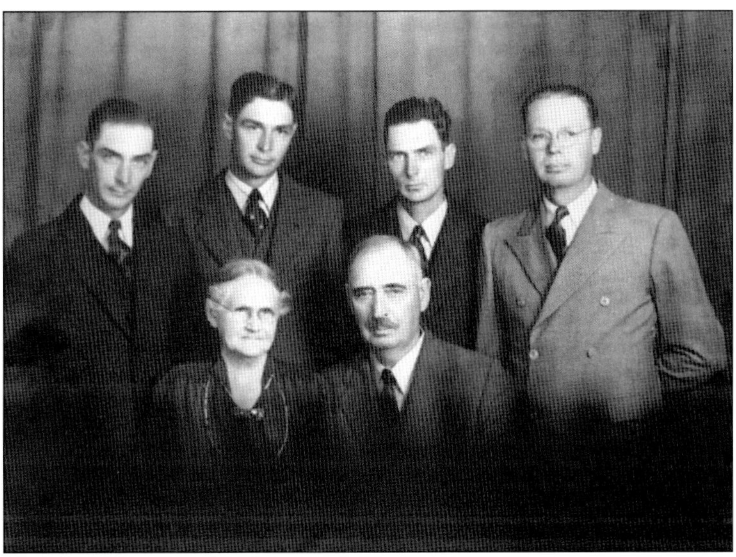

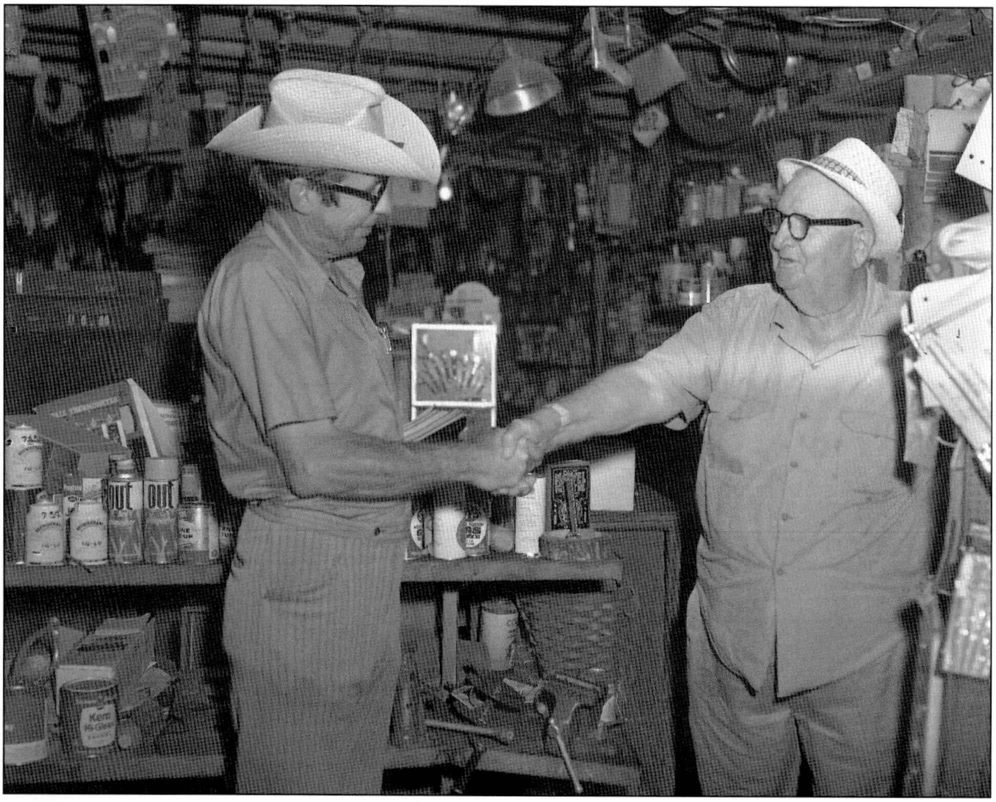

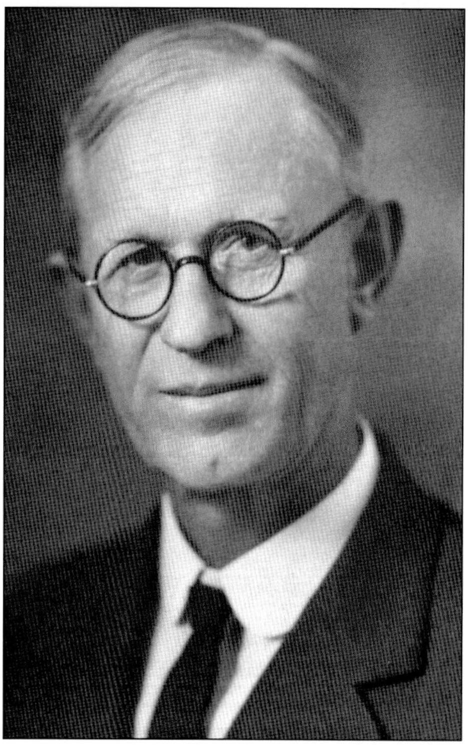

Jock Mayor (1898–1985), shown here at right in June 1972 selling his "House of a Million Parts" to John Campbell, was a self-made millionaire. Making his fortune in auto parts, land, and natural-resource drilling, Mayor left a $6 million estate. A trust, the O.D. Mayor Foundation, was formed. It benefits charitable groups and communities in Mayes County, Oklahoma, and Grayson County, Texas.

J. Howard Langley (1867–1935) was an early-day attorney who helped establish the Grand River Dam Authority. Prior to Oklahoma statehood, he was elected Pryor Creek's delegate to the Oklahoma Constitutional Convention. In 1930, Langley was elected to the Oklahoma Supreme Court. The town of Langley, in northeastern Mayes County, is named for him.

R.A. Wilkerson (1883–1967) was a colorful orator and criminal defense attorney. Courthouse legend has it that Wilkerson would cut up a raw onion and wrap it in his handkerchief and, at the right time during closing arguments in front of a jury, wipe his brow and face with that onion-soaked hankie. The effect of tears would often win over the sympathy of jury members. He also served as Pryor Creek's mayor, president of American National Bank, and principal of Pryor High School. At the time of his death, Wilkerson was an assistant district attorney.

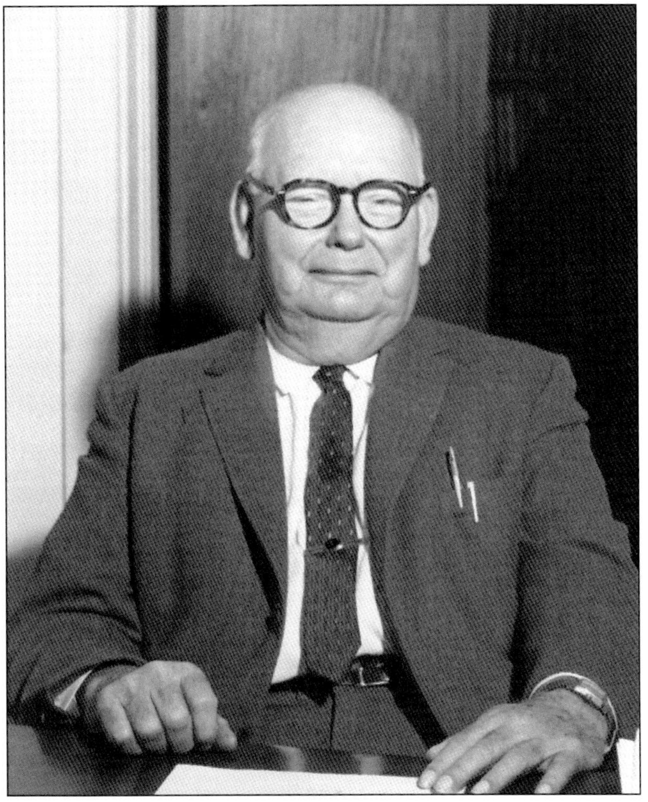

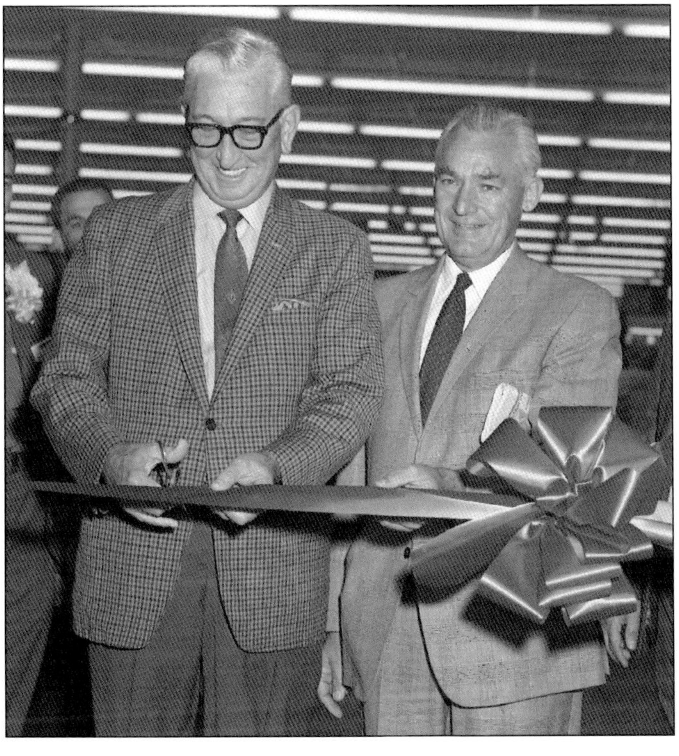

Mayor Carl Hogue (left) and Sam Walton cut the ribbon for the grand opening of the city's first Wal-Mart store in November 1970. The town's original Wal-Mart store was located near Fifth and South Mill Streets. Around 1989, it moved to Ninth and Mill Streets. Today, Wal-Mart has a store at 4901 South Mill. Hogue was the longtime operator of Hogue's Rexall City Drug, located at 303 East Graham Avenue. He served as Pryor Creek's mayor from 1969 to 1971.

Discover Thousands of Local History Books Featuring Millions of Vintage Images

Arcadia Publishing, the leading local history publisher in the United States, is committed to making history accessible and meaningful through publishing books that celebrate and preserve the heritage of America's people and places.

Find more books like this at
www.arcadiapublishing.com

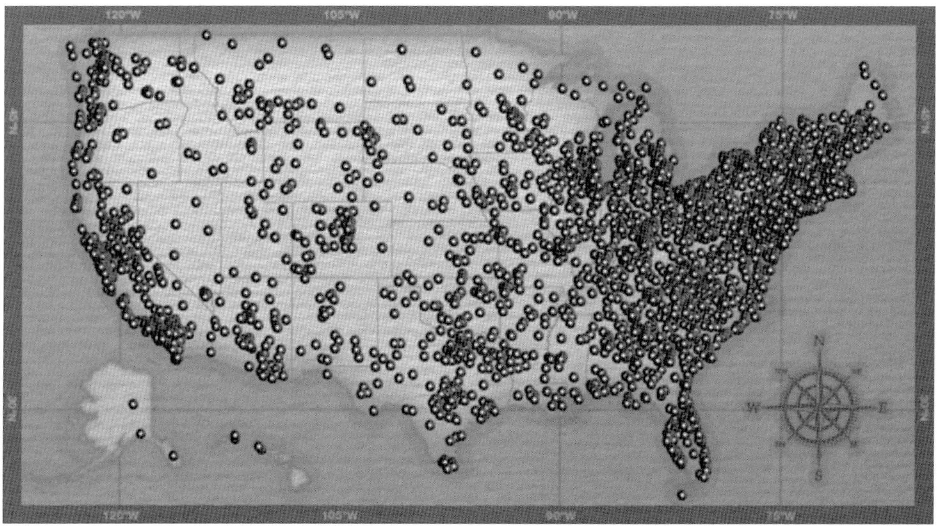

Search for your hometown history, your old stomping grounds, and even your favorite sports team.

Consistent with our mission to preserve history on a local level, this book was printed in South Carolina on American-made paper and manufactured entirely in the United States. Products carrying the accredited Forest Stewardship Council (FSC) label are printed on 100 percent FSC-certified paper.

MADE IN THE USA